THE ROUGH GUIDE TO

Horror Movies

ROUGH
GUIDES

www.roughguides.com

Credits

The Rough Guide to Horror Movies

Editor: Daniel Crewe
Layout: Link Hall and Dan May
Picture research: Michele Faram
Proofreading: Karen Parker
Production: Julia Bovis and Katherine Owers

Rough Guides Reference

Series editor: Mark Ellingham
Editors: Peter Buckley, Duncan Clark, Daniel Crewe, Matthew Milton, Joe Staines
Director: Andrew Lockett

Publishing Information

This first edition published September 2005 by
Rough Guides Ltd, 80 Strand, London WC2R 0RL
345 Hudson St, 4th Floor, New York 10014, USA
Email: mail@roughguides.com

Distributed by the Penguin Group:
Penguin Books Ltd, 80 Strand, London WC2R 0RL
Penguin Putnam, Inc., 375 Hudson Street, NY 10014, USA
Penguin Group (Australia), 250 Camberwell Road, Camberwell, Victoria 3124, Australia
Penguin Books Canada Ltd, 10 Alcorn Avenue, Toronto, Ontario, Canada M4V 1E4
Penguin Group (New Zealand), Cnr Rosedale and Airborne Roads, Albany, Auckland, New Zealand

Printed in Italy by LegoPrint S.p.A

Typeset in Bembo and Helvetica Neue to an original design by Henry Iles

A catalogue record for this book is available from the British Library

ISBN 10: 1-84353-521-1

ISBN 13: 978-1-84353-521-8

1 3 5 7 9 8 6 4 2

THE ROUGH GUIDE TO

Horror Movies

by
Alan Jones

Contents

The Icons:

The Global Picture:

The Information:

Foreword

If anyone is going to be your tour guide through the realm of horror movies, it has to be Alan Jones. I first read his name on many articles and reviews extolling the virtues (and failings!) of the dark side of movies, as an enthusiastic teenager already making my first tentative steps into film-making and eager to splash some blood and guts across the silver screen.

And I've two reasons to be eternally grateful to Alan. The second he's only too well aware of, and I'll get to later. The first came about many years before I made my first horror movie. Back in the early 1980s the only access I had to horror materials was Newcastle's sci-fi and horror shop, Timeslip, a cramped and dusty Aladdin's cave. Back then, movie memorabilia was sacred, and unavailable in the high street stores, and on Saturday afternoons I would rummage through the boxes hoping to find hidden gems, such as rare back issues of magazines like *Starburst*, *Fantastic Films* and *Fangoria*. It was through these that I began to read Alan's work and gain an appreciation and appetite for all things horror that has taken me to where I am now.

Twenty years later came the second reason I have to thank Alan. It was 2001 and I had just completed my first feature film, *Dog Soldiers*, which Alan helped to make successful. The film's producer had come to the conclusion that the title would be "Night Of The Werewolves", and no amount of persuasion would convince him otherwise. However, at the eleventh hour Alan heard of this development and intervened, telling him that *Dog Soldiers* was the best title for the film and always would be. What Alan had was clout – the producer listened, and *Dog Soldiers* won awards at film festivals on both sides of the Atlantic.

So thank you Alan, for many hours of quality reading and a film title I can be proud of. All of which brings me, in a roundabout way, to this book. Alan Jones and horror movies go hand in hand, and with the *Rough Guide to Horror Movies*, Alan takes you beyond the shadows, through the places you are afraid to go, and shows you horror in all its bloody glory. Enjoy.

Neil Marshall, director of *Dog Soldiers* (2002) and *The Descent* (2005)

Introduction

Horror has been a part of my life for as long as I can remember. Even as a child growing up in the late 50s, I was drawn to the lurid poster art gracing every release with the promise of forbidden terror. The first design to have a real impact on my consciousness was *Circus Of Horrors* (1960) – "He turned the greatest show on earth into a ... Circus of Horrors!" – which was complete with tumbling trapeze artists and knife-throwing gone wrong. I lost my horror virginity to that film as soon as I could pass for sixteen, as was necessary then to see an X-rated film then, and it was on a double bill with the equally classic *Horrors Of The Black Museum* (1959).

The moment the victim's eyes were gouged out in the latter by booby-trapped binoculars, everything I'd heard about the horror film was proven true. I was shocked rigid! And the next week, when I braved the steely stare at the box office to see the Italian movie *Blood And Black Lace* (1964), I knew I'd never be the same again. From that moment on I wrote diary reviews of everything I saw, a practice I kept up until I became a professional journalist specializing in the genre in 1977. I still go back to those reviews today for my gut reaction to seeing *Rosemary's Baby* (1968) or the countless Hammer horrors of the period for the first time. You will read many of those original observations in this Rough Guide.

My journalistic career began because of two men. Mike Childs is my best friend, and a producer at London's Capital Radio, who was asked to become the UK correspondent for the influential American fantasy magazine *Cinefantastique/CFQ*. He asked me to help him write the feature interviews and much of what we did together on *The Wicker Man* (1973), *Carrie* (1976) and *Star Wars* (1977) is still being reprinted in books and read by scholars today.

To go from being a starry-eyed rabid fan to interviewing *Carrie* director **Brian De Palma** for two hours in the back of his limo on the way to Heathrow airport was amazing and unforgettable. When Mike bowed out because of his workload, I took over as sole *CFQ* correspondent and editor Frederick S. Clarke let me do anything I wanted.

Thanks to him I've met all my film idols, have covered every major horror movie on location – the main body of quotes in this book coming from those interviews – and have banked a raft of memories; these range from becoming director **Dario Argento**'s official biographer and visiting Chernobyl for *Return Of The Living Dead: Necropolis* (2005) to being a jury member at every international horror film festival (and being given the original Lament Configuration box by **Clive Barker** for helping him on 1987's *Hellraiser*). Fred is so longer with us but there isn't a single day I don't mentally thank him for turning my obsession into my profession.

So what is horror?

This strong emotion, one of the oldest and deepest of humankind, is what we feel when anything frightens us or promotes fear or terror.

The urge to scare oneself witless might seem masochistic. But exploring the notion of fear is revealing. We can open ourselves up to being scared if we know that no harm will befall us. And it's the wave of relief once the fright is over that makes being scared so much fun.

Since the invention of cinema more than a century ago, this relief is what the horror movie has provided, while frequently dragging itself from the grave and reinventing itself. So it's no accident that the birth of the horror movie in Paris in 1896 coincided with the public acceptance of psychoanalytical theory (and especially the teachings of **Freud**), which for the first time openly discussed the ambivalence of human desire – horror is a direct conduit to unconscious fears and thoughts of love, pain and loss. And it's because it speaks of the unspeakable that it's so frequently attacked. Self-appointed moral guardians often don't like the questions that are asked.

But the roots of horror go back further. Safe inside the four walls of a darkened cinema, we are begging to be frightened in the same way that we were in previous centuries, when sitting by campfires listening to stories about mythical creatures and demonic villains. And countless horror movies relate to the Bible. Religions extol a divinely inspired division between Good and Evil and have rules to follow, and many horror films are about breaking those rules and the punishment that rains down from above for such arrogantly transgressive behaviour.

Even if elements of horror stories are universal, what scares us depends on the age we are and the age we live in, and even on our gender. As children it's the fear of abandonment or the death of a parent. In our teenage years it's rite-of-passage anxiety about our burgeoning sexuality that fuels the flames of fear. In middle age it's the possible death of a child or a loved one that haunts our daily life. And in our older years it's the fear of loneliness, isolation and death that remains uppermost in the mind.

As long as film exists as something that provokes the essential emotions of humanity, the horror film will continue to exist too. The technology behind films will change, as will the way that we view the finished product. But our vulnerability, our terror of the unknown and our nightmares won't disappear; those irrational forces of chaos will, however, always be defeated by a movie genre that is defined purely in terms of its intended emotional impact.

The Rough Guide to Horror Movies is designed to help you understand horror movies. You'll find out how horror developed from its literary origins. You'll discover how the genre developed, decade by decade, from the nineteenth century to the twenty-first. You'll meet the icons of horror, from the directors to the most famous characters. You'll encounter the themes of horror movies around the world. And then you can see where to head for more, depending on where your taste lies.

You'll also be given a tour of the 50 horror movies that are essential when getting to grips with the history of horror. The list will, of course be, controversial – that is inevitable, and no bad thing. But there are also dozens of shorter reviews of other horrors to satisfy your curiosity.

Alan Jones, 2005

Acknowledgements

Thanks to Keith Williams, Geoff Simm, Kjell Wirum, Frances Lynn, David Cox, Mark Kermode, Nigel Floyd, Rel Pinto, Fernando Dos Reis Prazeres, Mark Ashworth, Dez Skinn, Alan McKenzie, Stephen Payne, Jonathan Rutter, Anthony Timpone, Sharon Kent, Julia Wrigley, Stefan Jaworzyn, Tim Lucas, Sue Oates, Buddy Giovinazzo, Kim Newman, Damon Wise, Jamie Graham, Greg, Sofie and Tobias Day, John Fallon, Colin Pregent, Paul McEvoy, Ian Rattray, Billy Chainsaw, Sloan Freer, Rosemary Goodfriend, Debbie Turner, Sue Blackmore, Chris Paton, Jane Gibbs, Frederic Albert Levy, Angel Sala, Mario and Beatriz Dorminsky, Chiara Barbo, Nicole Gregory, Asia Argento, Guillermo del Toro, Don Mancini, Neil Marshall, Brian Yuzna, Christophe Gans, Chris Smith, Nicolas Winding-Refn and my tireless Rough Guides editor Daniel Crewe.

For Diego Hernan Cavallaro

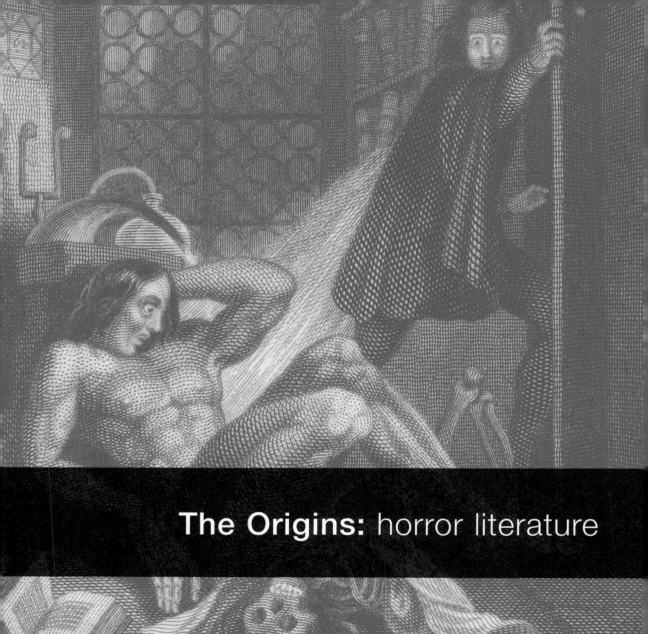

The Origins: horror literature

Frontispiece from an 1831 edition of Mary
Shelley's *Frankenstein*

The Origins:
horror literature

Fear of death and the unknown, and a sense of awe at the uncontrollable power of nature are common to almost all cultures. One of the functions of ancient religions and mythologies has been to explain the many violent – and seemingly arbitrary – events that shaped peoples' lives. It has mostly done so by creating an alternative world of gods and monsters beyond the realm of man. A supernatural world, where the forces of good and evil are forever locked in conflict, and with which mankind struggles to exist.

Man's heroic, and often horrific, interaction with forces larger than himself forms an integral part of the oldest surviving examples of literature, religious and otherwise. Both the Babylonian *Epic Of Gilgamesh* (c.2000 BC) and Homer's *Odyssey* (c.800 BC) involve adventurers battling against an array of malevolent monsters, sometimes helped and occasionally hindered by the gods. The Bible also contains an extraordinary collection of monsters and demons, from the sea-beast Leviathan to Satan (aka the Devil), the arch-enemy of God. Satan was developed by Christianity into the absolute embodiment of evil, and appears in the apocalyptic *Revelation of St John* – along

with other terrifying beasts – where, in the form of a dragon, he is eventually vanquished by the archangel Michael.

Man's essentially sinful nature (according to Christianity) led to an obsession with the fate of souls after death. This is reflected in Dante's elaborate poem of the after-life, *The Divine Comedy* (c.1310), as well as in the wealth of horrific depictions of the Last Judgement that appeared in the Middle Ages and the Renaissance – of which the nightmare visions of Bosch and Bruegel are simply the most famous examples. The Middle Ages also produced an early werewolf tale in Marie de France's *Bisclavaret (Lay Of The Werewolf)*, and the first mention of the legend of the man who mocked Jesus on his way to the cross, and who was thereby condemned to roam the earth until Judgement Day. Recorded in the chronicles of **Roger of Wendover** and **Matthew of Paris**, the man was only identified as the "Wandering Jew" in later versions of the tale.

One of the most compelling legends of the Renaissance period was that of Faust, an actual German necromancer whose exploits were embroidered after his death into the tale of a man who sells his soul to the Devil in exchange for all the knowledge in the world. Among the many writers to exploit the story were **Christopher Marlowe** in his play *The Tragicall History of Doctor Faustus* (c.1590) and **Goethe** in his two-part dramatic poem *Faust* (1808 & 1833).

The work of Marlowe's contemporary **William Shakespeare** also contains a good deal of horrific and supernatural elements – from the witches and ghosts in *Macbeth* (a supposedly jinxed play), through the blood-soaked shocker *Titus Andronicus* (which features rape, hand amputation and cannibalism), to *The Tempest,* set on an island where a banished magician rules over a motley assortment of spirits and monsters.

Ironically horror as a recognizably autonomous genre had its main origins in the eighteenth century, the so-called Age of Enlightenment when science and reason were meant to banish superstition and ignorance for ever. Perhaps as a reaction against this optimism, certain artists and writers produced work that explored the darker side of their own imaginations. One such was **Horace Walpole**, the dilettante aesthete and son of the prime minister, who produced the first British horror novel. *The Castle Of Otranto* (1764). Prompted by a nightmare (but claimed to be based on an Italian original), it's a tale of usurpation and skullduggery among the Italian aristocracy – complete with ghosts, prophecies and poisonings. The novel established a vogue for what became known as Gothic fiction and spawned a host of imitators.

Among the most successful was **Ann Radcliffe**, who took Walpole's approach even further in her five novels, and set out the parameters of the Gothic horror romance in the most popular

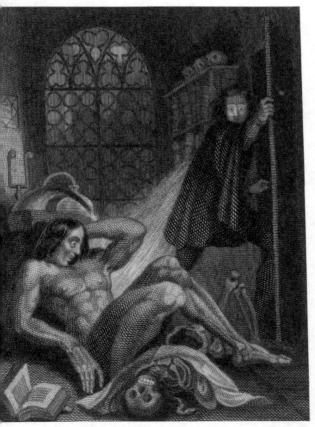

An early vision of the Frankenstein monster

Seasons griefings

Christmas became the traditional time to tell ghost stories in the middle of the nineteenth century, and **Charles Dickens** came up with one of the best, creating the quintessential image of the winter wonderland season, complete with puddings and parties, in the process. *A Christmas Carol* has been Muppeted, *Scrooged* (1988), animated and made into a musical, and the fable of the miser-turned-philanthropist, its plot based around Yuletide ghosts and dark miracles, rarely fails to move.

Christmas cheer as a backdrop to crisis remains one of horror cinema's most frequently used devices, from Deanna Durbin discovering husband **Gene Kelly** is a murderous psycho in *Christmas Holiday* (1944) to the trashed trappings of a traditional Noel in *Gremlins* (1984). If that wasn't bad enough, Father Christmas was attacked by demons in the Mexploitation *Santa Claus* (1959), abducted by aliens in *Santa Claus Conquers The Martians* (1964) and zombie-fied in *Trancers* (1986).

But Santa has struck back in the most prolific of all Christmas-themed horrors, the violent night psycho Santa slasher. The Amicus anthology *Tales From The Crypt* (1972) had **Joan Collins** bludgeoning her husband to death under the Christmas tree just as an escaped maniac dressed as Santa terrorizes the neighbourhood. *Silent Night, Bloody Night* (1973) and *Black Christmas* (1974) also link the holiday with escaped lunatics and in *You Better Watch Out* (1980) Santa steals from the toy company rich and gives to the handicapped poor while gouging out eyes with tin soldiers. The film that became the pariah of parent-teacher associations in America, *Silent Night, Deadly Night* (1984) had nude sleaze queen **Linnea Quigley** impaled on reindeer antlers; the free publicity made it a hit and four sequels followed in rapid succession.

---

one, *The Mysteries Of Udolpho* (1794). With her crumbling castles, misty landscapes, monstrous crimes, and rationalized supernatural happenings, Radcliffe laid the foundation for the entire genre, and in *The Italian* (1797) created the seminal dark and sexy hero. Her novels nearly always include a beautiful, virtuous heroine and a male tyrant, with a powerful tension between the two.

More sensational still is *The Monk* (1795) by **M.G. Lewis**, which tells of a charismatic and devout preacher who becomes a slave to lust and sexual depravity. The novel is set in Catholic Spain which, like Radcliffe and Walpole's Italy, is an exotic fantasy world where barbarism and civilization are only thinly separated. Lewis's emphasis on the extreme psychological struggles of his protagonist is even more marked in **Charles Maturin**'s *Melmoth The Wanderer* (1820), which

concerns a man's bargain with Satan to extend his life, and its terrible consequences.

Gothic fiction was brilliantly mocked in 1818 by **Jane Austen** in her clear-headed parody of the genre, *Northanger Abbey*, but the same year saw the publication of one of the greatest works of literary horror: **Mary Shelley**'s *Frankenstein; Or, The Modern Prometheus*. Begun as a ghost story, the finished work is a powerful tale of corrupted scientific ambition and nature's terrible revenge. Some critics have interpreted it as expressing an underlying social anxiety at the speed of technological change brought about by the Industrial Revolution.

Mary Shelley was part of the Romantic movement which, with its emphasis on subjectivity and opposition to the idea that the universe could be understood in purely rational terms, was ideally attuned to exploring supernatural themes. It was also very much a pan-European phenomenon, existing against the backdrop of the Napoleonic wars that were convulsing the continent in the early nineteenth century. In Germany **Heinrich von Kleist** wrote a series of deeply pessimistic short novels in which arbitrary and irrational acts of violence seem to govern people's lives. **E.T.A.** **Hoffmann**'s work is even stranger: his first weird tale, *Ritter Gluck* (1809), tells of a musician convinced he is the famous composer Gluck, but his most familiar tale is probably *The Sandman* (1816), a story of a young man who cannot free himself of the memory of a traumatic childhood incident which blights his existence. *The Sandman* reads like a Freudian case history, and indeed Freud made the story the centre of an influential essay in which he defined the uncanny as deriving its terror "...not from something externally alien or unknown but – on the contrary – from something strangely familiar which defeats our efforts to separate ourselves from it." The early nineteenth century also saw an increasing awareness of indigenous folk literature, with writers like the brothers Grimm rekindling an interest in folk tales and fairy tales.

The weaving of the bizarre into the real world by Hoffmann had an enormous influence on the grotesque humour of **Nikolai Gogol**'s Russian stories (such as *Diary Of A Madman*, 1835), as well as on the Americans Washington Irving, Nathaniel Hawthorne and Edgar Allan Poe. **Irving**'s most famous work, *The Sketch Book Of Geoffrey Crayon* (1819), includes the short stories *The Legend Of Sleepy Hollow* and *Rip Van Winkle*; while **Nathaniel Hawthorne** wrote several successful horror stories, collected in *Twice Told Tales* (1837). Even more significant for the genre was **Edgar Allan Poe**, one of the originators of the detective mystery story with *The Murders In The Rue Morgue* (1841). Poe brought a new psychological depth to tales of terror, for example in *The Tell-Tale Heart* (1843) in which a man develops a neurotic obsession with the diseased eye of the old man with whom he boards. In the era of modern cinema Poe became the most adapted of American authors.

As the nineteenth century was transformed by the Industrial Revolution, economic growth led to an increasing appetite for reading material, which was satisfied through the relative cheapness of mechanized printing; and so the "penny dreadful" was born. From the 1830s crudely printed and illustrated forerunners of the comic book, such as *The Terrific Register*, *Leisure Hour* and *Family Herald*, began pandering to prurient and bloodthirsty tastes; horror tales published included **Frederick Marryat**'s *The Phantom Ship* (1839), based on the *Flying Dutchman* legend, and **Lady Esther Hope**'s *The Blue Dwarf* (1861). The most famous was *Varney The Vampire, Or The Feast Of Blood* (1845), one of the earliest vampires and the first to sport fangs, whose authorship was attributed to **J.M. Rymer**, though it may be the work of **Thomas Preskett Prest**. It was Prest who wrote the famous penny dreadful based on a French murderer of fourteenth-century legend that led to several versions of *Sweeney Todd, The Demon Barber Of Fleet Street*. The period also saw something of a craze for sensational theatrical melodramas, the most famous being *Maria Martin or Murder In The Red Barn* (1840), based on the famous murder case of 1827.

Often the penny dreadful stories were adapted from the pages of contemporary newspapers, with the facts so distorted in their breathless retelling that they became tangled up with reality. This was the case with the story of "Spring-Heeled Jack", a bogeyman of uncertain origin who assaulted women indiscriminately and

Johnny Depp and Marc Pickering in *Sleepy Hollow* (1999), which was based on the timeless tale by Washington Irving

escaped from crime scenes by taking giant leaps on supposedly spring-loaded boots; the image of him with pointy ears and nose, red glowing eyes and ability to emit flame from his mouth are only embellishments to a figure who terrorized London, starting in the 1830s. Headlines were also made by Scottish body-snatchers **Burke and Hare** in the late 1820s – the influence for Robert Louis Stevenson's *The Body Snatcher* (1885).

Real life crime stories and the conventions of the Gothic novel were fused in the work of the now largely forgotten **William Harrison Ainsworth**, whose 1834 novel *Rookwood* – a highly romanticized account of the highwayman Dick Turpin – catapaulted him to success. Crime stories (so-called "Newgate novels") were taken up by other novelists, including the young **Charles Dickens** (*Oliver Twist*, 1838) and **Edward Bulwer Lytton** (*Eugene Aram*, 1832), although compared to Ainsworth their agenda was more social than sensational. The only Ainsworth novel to remain in print is *The Lancashire Witches* (1849), about a monk who sells his soul to Satan and brings forth a whole progeny of witches. The rather more talented Charles Dickens was responsible for the appearance of the first detective in British fiction (Inspector Bucket in *Bleak House*, 1853) and for some of the finest ghost stories ever, including *A Christmas Carol* (1843) and *The Signal-Man* (1866).

Dickens's friend **Wilkie Collins** was the key exponent of a literary sub-genre, the "sensation" novel, which reached the height of its popularity in the 1860s. Credited by Henry James with introducing into fiction "those most mysterious of mysteries, the mysteries which are at our own doors", Collins wrote *The Woman In White* in 1860 – a brilliantly plotted thriller that is equally strong on atmosphere and suspense. By the time of *The Moonstone* (1868), which involves the

fallout from the theft of a gemstone sacred to Hindus, Collins was pretty well burned out as a novelist.

Meanwhile, in the same decade Irish writer **J. Sheridan Le Fanu** was producing his own contribution to horror literature: a series of supernatural tales which emphasised the mysterious and the inexplicable. His novel *Uncle Silas* (1864) and his most famous story, the vampire tale *Carmilla* (1871), have both been filmed – the latter several times.

By the 1880 and 90s the supernatural had become so respectable a literary subject, that many highly regarded authors tried their hand at it. In France the cult of Poe (fuelled by **Baudelaire**'s translations) fed into the decadent sensibilities of the Symbolists to produce a number of darkly morbid works such as the *Contes Cruels* (1883) of **Villiers de l'Isle-Adam** and **J-K. Huysmans**'s Satanist novel *La-bas* (1891).

Huysmans was an important influence on **Oscar Wilde** whose *The Picture Of Dorian Gray* (1890) provides a modern take on the Faustian pact. Four years earlier **Robert Louis Stevenson** penned his famous tale of a hubristic scientist in *The Strange Case Of Dr Jekyll And Mr Hyde* (1886), a story which offers an intriguing look at the idea of a divided or repressed personality. Stevenson's friend **Henry James** also wrote a number of ghostly tales, of which the most disturbing is the deeply ambiguous *The Turn Of The Screw* (1898), with its hints of child abuse and its unreliable narrative voice.

The same period also produced a classic vampire novel in **Bram Stoker**'s *Dracula* (1897) and saw the appearance of **Arthur Conan Doyle**'s great detective Sherlock Holmes, a character with an almost uncanny ability to unravel difficult, and often gory, cases. One real-life case that Holmes might well have struggled with was that of **Jack**

the Ripper, who between August 1888 and July 1889 committed a series of horrifyingly brutal murders of women in London's Whitechapel area that remain unsolved to this day. Fictionalized accounts of the murders appeared almost immediately, but the best-known early novel based on the case is *The Lodger* (1913) by **Mrs Belloc Lowndes**, filmed by Hitchcock in 1926.

As the cinema era dawned, filmmakers appropriated the bestsellers of the day to ensure a guaranteed audience. So despite the diversity of their themes, authors such as Poe, Conan Doyle, Shelley, Stevenson, Stoker, **H.G. Wells** (*The Island Of Dr Moreau*, 1896), **Gaston Leroux** (*The Phantom Of The Opera*, 1911) and **Gustav Meyrink** (*The Golem*, 1915) were all lumped together as horror writers, simply because their material was voraciously drawn upon by the founders of the genre. Also placed in this group was the German writer **Hanns Heinz Ewers**. A friend of occultist Aleister Crowley, Ewers popularized the *Schauerromans* ("shudder novels") of the early twentieth century with his short stories, *Der Zauberlehrling* (*The Sorcerer's Apprentice*, 1907), *Alraune* (1911) and *Vampir* (1921). One of Ewers' translators in America was Guy Endore, who went on to write *The Werewolf Of Paris* (1933).

In England the scary ghost story was practically re-invented by **M.R. James**'s *Oh Whistle And I'll Come To You, My Lad* (1904) and *Casting The Runes* (1911). His stories emphasized the hair-raisingly intangible to such a degree that they are rarely filmed; the same is true for those of the American writer responsible for creating a wave of abnormally warped Gothic horror, **H.P. Lovecraft**. His work was directly inspired by his nightmares, and it is this insight into the symbolic subconscious that resonates with latter-day filmmakers, as seen, for example, in Stuart Gordon's *Re-Animator* (1985, see Canon), based on the

story from 1922. Heavily influenced by Poe, the dreamy settings of Lord Dunsany and the mystical writings of Arthur Machen, Lovecraft had a limited readership during his short lifetime, but his works in turn had a crucial impact on horror writers including **Ramsey Campbell, Clive Barker** and **Stephen King**.

Two further Lovecraft disciples were responsible for reshaping the horror genre in modern times. By attempting to get inside the mind of a psychopath – in novels like *The Will To Kill*

An engraving, published in *Illustrated Police News* in 1889, imagines Jack the Ripper being caught

(1954) and *Psycho* (1959) – **Robert Bloch** succeeded in blurring the distinction between crime and horror fiction. More recently **Anne Rice**, in her *Vampire Chronicles* series, breathed new life into what had become the most cliché-ridden of horror sub-genres. *Interview With The Vampire* (1976), the first and most celebrated of the series, is remarkable for the way it creates a fully-realized world, one in which the vampires possess a wide range of recognizable feelings and emotions.

Sweeney Todd: The Demon Barber Of Fleet Street
dir George King, 1936, US, 76m, b/w

Until Stephen Sondheim's musical, George King's creaky and campy "quota quickie" was the most famous account of the barber with the trapdoor under his chair providing fillings for Mrs Lovett's pie shop. As played by the appropriately named Tod Slaughter, Sweeney Todd is a cackling villain of the hammiest order whose corpulence can be attributed to the steady supply of pastries.

The Flesh And The Fiends
dir John Gilling, 1959, UK, 97m, b/w

Of the numerous films based on the exploits of body-snatchers William Burke and William Hare, only director John Gilling's Hammer-influenced chiller creates an atmosphere that is both morbid and bleak. Peter Cushing stands out as effete pioneer surgeon Dr Knox, who strikes a fatal bargain with the venal grave robbers (played by George Rose and Donald Pleasence) for corpses on which to experiment.

Le moine (The Monk)
dir Ado Kyrou, 1972, Fr/It/WGer, 92m

This adaptation of M.G. Lewis's trend-setting Gothic novel, without the book's supernatural excesses and shocking finale, has depraved Father Ambrosio (Franco Nero) making a pact with the Devil to escape investigation by the Spanish Inquisition for imprisoning and raping virginal nun Antonia (Eliana De Santis). Scripted by Luis Buñuel, who had always wanted to film it, the uninspired direction makes for jumbled, academic sexploitation.

Phantom Of The Paradise
dir Brian De Palma, 1972, US, 91m

Brian De Palma's highly entertaining take on the Faust myth features the first rock'n'roll Faust. That's diabolical impresario Swan (Paul Williams), who buys the soul of naïve composer Winslow Leach (William Finley) in return for stardom for his ingénue, Phoenix (Jessica Harper). A savvy satire on the music industry, it delivers glam rock camp, fun chills and a witty send-up of the *Psycho* shower scene.

Interview With The Vampire
dir Neil Jordan, 1994, US, 122m

Anne Rice's chic and influential page-turner got short shrift in Neil Jordan's lacklustre, lightweight adaptation. Plantation owner Louis (Brad Pitt) is the reluctant bloodsucker who tells journalist Malloy (Christian Slater) the story of how his life changed two centuries earlier when he met master vampire Lestat (Tom Cruise). Only Antonio Banderas (as the bisexual Armand) exudes any sense of the sinister/sexy charisma of the book.

Sleepy Hollow
dir Tim Burton, 1999, US/Ger, 105m

Washington Irving's legend of the Headless Horseman had been ill-served until Tim Burton magisterially combined alchemic adventure, splendid visuals, sly humour and dreamy bloodthirstiness. A perfect cast – Johnny Depp, Christina Ricci, Miranda Richardson and Michael Gambon – milk every nuance of menace and mirth from Irving's timeless tale while creating a supernatural Gothic whodunit.

From Hell
dir Albert Hughes & Allen Hughes, 2001, US/Cz, 123m

By far the most enthralling and visceral stab at putting across the squalid horror of the Jack the Ripper story, the Hughes brothers' adaptation of the cult graphic novel by Alan Moore and Eddie Campbell is wonderfully textured and surreal. Fred Abberline of Scotland Yard is played by a superb Johnny Depp in a blood-soaked ripping yarn poised brilliantly between the stylization of Hammer and the atmospherics of Dickens.

The History:
over a hundred years of horror

Drew Barrymore in the self-reflexive
Scream (1996), Wes Craven's post-
modern *Halloween* homage

The History:
over a hundred years of horror

There are certain themes that have recurred during the history of horror – vampires, ghosts, zombies – all of which have been chosen to frighten the willing audience. But in the past hundred years the films in which they have appeared have changed, influenced by social, political and technological developments, and the genre that exists today is also the result of the interaction between Hollywood and the film industries outside America, who will be the focus of chapter five.

The early years

A large bat flies into a medieval castle. Circling slowly, it flaps its monstrous wings and suddenly changes into Mephistopheles. Conjuring up a cauldron, the demon then produces skeletons, ghosts and witches from its bubbling contents before one of the summoned underworld cavaliers holds up a crucifix and Satan vanishes in a puff of smoke. With this two-minute short, *Le manoir du diable* (*The Haunted Castle*), on **Christmas Eve, 1896**, at the Théâtre Robert-Houdin, 8 boulevard des Italiens, Paris, the horror film was born.

On the night in 1895 that cinema was unveiled to the world by **Louis and Auguste Lumière**, through the everyday image captured in *The Arrival Of A Train At La Ciotat*, women had screamed while men tried to hold on to their reserve. But the shriek of fearful surprise, when the locomotive seemed to be coming at them, became a laugh of relief. And that night this timeless combination, the cornerstone of the horror film to the present day, was famously noted by the renowned stage illusionist **Georges Méliès**.

Fired by the possibilities opened up by the new medium of the Kinetoscope, developed in the laboratory of Thomas Edison, Méliès bought a camera to show moving pictures of magic tricks between the vaudeville and conjuring acts that he showcased each night. Realizing at the turn of the century that the only way that cinema could have a future was if the boring travelogues and historical reconstructions were replaced by engaging dramas, he built the world's first movie studio in the Paris suburb of **Montreuil** and devised the first special effects. By simply stopping and restarting the camera, he made people disappear; by replacing someone with a skeleton he simulated a supernatural transformation.

Such tricks reached their apotheosis in his film *Cinderella* (1899) and in his classic achievement of the first decade of film, *Le voyage dans la lune* (*A Trip To The Moon*, 1902). Meanwhile, in

Méliès (bald, with moustache) directing at the end of the nineteenth century

England **George Albert Smith** had invented "spirit photography" – double exposure – for ghostly apparitions in *The Corsican Brothers* (1898); and although it was patented in Britain, Méliès stole it wholesale for *The Cave Of The Demons* (1898).

Such trickery meant that the fresh medium of cinema was giving a new visual form to nightmares. But it was only when filmmakers went beyond the short sharp sudden jolt into longer pieces that horror really took a hold; adult audiences started paying attention to the circus sideshow elements of early cinema only when the wealth of horror literature and the often more lurid and melodramatic stage adaptations started making their way onto the screen via the studios – worldwide dream factories.

The freak shows that horror films in many respects resembled became more sophisticated when Victor Hugo's *Notre-Dame de Paris* (1831) became *Esmeralda* (1906), featuring Quasimodo the hunchback. Directed by a woman, **Alice Guy**, the pantomime plot was successfully pirated around the world – in America it led to *The Hunchback* (1909) and in Britain *The Love Of A Hunchback* (1910) – and Quasimodo soon became the first monster in a full-length horror film, in the French triptych *Notre-Dame de Paris* (1911).

Before that the Danish director **Viggo Larsen** had put Sherlock Holmes in the ghostly *The Grey Lady* (1909) and Sir Arthur Conan Doyle's famous detective then appeared in three German versions of *The Hound Of The Baskervilles* (one in 1914, two in 1915). But for those with a more macabre palette, in 1908 there was *Dr Jekyll And Mr Hyde*, which used the atmosphere and faster pace of the theatrical adaptation upon which it was based to appeal to broader, cinematically inclined audiences. It was the first of many versions of Robert Louis Stevenson's doppelganger classic – five were released in the silent era alone.

Stevenson's good-against-evil staple reflected the direction in which horror cinema was moving. The monsters, myths and topics that endured all appeared from the very beginning because of their prior success in other media. *Frankenstein* (1910), directed and written by **J. Searle Dawley**, was the first attempt to capitalize on the popularity of the many stage versions of Mary Shelley's monster; the second feature-length attempt was Joseph W. Smiley's *Life Without Soul* (1916). Filmmakers grabbed bestselling books and theatrical triumphs, as adaptations of work by Edgar Allan Poe demonstrated: *The System Of Doctor Tarr And Professor Feather* became Maurice Tourneur's *The Lunatics* (1912); *The Tell-Tale Heart* provided technique pioneer **D.W. Griffith** with the basis for his first horror hit, *The Avenging Conscience* (1914); and *The Masque Of The Red Death* became Fritz Lang's *The Plague In Florence* (1919).

Other traditional themes appeared in films such as *The Werewolf* (1913) and adaptations of Oscar Wilde's Faustian *The Picture Of Dorian Gray*. Meanwhile *The Monkey Man* (1908) and *Island Of Terror* (1913), a thinly veiled version of H. G. Wells's *The Island Of Dr Moreau*, foreshadowed gruesome transplant movies. *The Vengeance Of Egypt* (1912) was the first feature to be sold on the strength of its Mummy terrors; *Balaoo* (1913), based on a newspaper serial by Gaston Leroux, featured as its title character horror's first rampaging ape-man; and *The Miser's Conversion* (1914), from man to ape, contained the first screen transformation to use primitive make-up dissolves rather than a single jump cut.

But the country most open to the imaginative possibilities of the fledgling fear industry was Germany. If Americans cared more about keep-

The Cabinet Of Dr Caligari (1919), a classic work of German Expressionism

ing audiences interested with pace and action, the Germans, who dominated the Expressionist art movement, accented the weird and wonderful. *The Student Of Prague* (1913) borrowed from Poe's *William Wilson* and E. T. A Hoffmann's *The Sandman*; it starred and was directed by **Paul Wegener**, who while filming in Prague came across the legend of the Golem, just before the publication of Gustav Meyrink's novel focusing on the man of seventeenth-century Jewish folklore moulded from clay to protect the ghetto from persecution. Wegener went on to play the milestone German Frankenstein three times and directed the two later manifestations (1917, 1920) himself.

While the most fashionable German horror of the Great War era was the six-hour epic *Homunculus* (1916), about a laboratory-created superman turning malevolent, and the popular *Schauerroman* ("shudder novel") oeuvre produced the first version of *Alraune* (1918) and its mad scientist, it wasn't until *The Cabinet Of Dr Caligari* (1919, see Canon) that horror lost its pulp image and took its rightful place as an artistic cinematic genre to be taken seriously.

Dr Jekyll And Mr Hyde
dir William Selig, 1908, US, 16m, b/w

The first American horror movie stuck closely to the 1897 stage version by Luella Forepaugh and George F. Fish, which starred Richard Mansfield, and it compressed the novel into four acts, with a curtain rising and falling at each start and finish. The three-character piece – Jekyll, the vicar and his daughter Alice, all played by actors who were not credited – accented the sensational transformation that resulted in the vicar's death.

Frankenstein
dir J. Searle Dawley, 1910, US, 16m, b/w

"Many repulsive situations have been eliminated", stated the official press release for J. Searle Dawley's short version of Mary Shelley's classic. It was hardly selling the product, but was symptomatic of horror cinema's beginnings. Starring as the Monster, made like Shelley's in "a cauldron of blazing chemicals" rather than through the electrical birth of later versions, Charles Ogle created his own make-up for the role of the untidily misshapen man who eventually looks in the mirror and flees in shock.

The Avenging Conscience
dir D. W. Griffith, 1914, US, 78m, b/w

Widely regarded as horror cinema's first masterpiece, this adaptation of Edgar Allan Poe's *The Tell-Tale Heart* (also with sections from his *Annabel Lee*) finds Henry B. Walthall justifying the murder of his sweetheart's tyrannical uncle among potent religious visions and spider-web images. Effective editing of clock-ticking, shoe-tapping and bird-calling establishes the dead man's heartbeat before the nightmarish conscience attacks.

Alraune
dir Mihály Kertész, 1918, Hu, 80m, b/w

Because of its popularity, two versions were filmed in 1918 of Hanns Heinz Ewers' *Schauerroman* about a mad scientist artificially inseminating a prostitute with a hanged murderer's seed to produce the demonic beauty Alraune. The German version, directed by Eugen Illés and Joseph Klein, was not as good as the effort by Hungarian director Mihály Kertész – who changed his name to Michael Curtiz for *Doctor X* (1932) – which had the prostitute copulating with a mandrake root.

The Twenties

The Twenties started with the expressionism of films led by *The Cabinet Of Dr Caligari* showing what could be achieved. Germany proffered one menace masterpiece after another. **F. W. Murnau** ripped off *Dr Jekyll And Mr Hyde* for *Der Januskopf* (1920) before feeding on Bram Stoker for *Nosferatu – eine Symphonie des Grauens* (1921, see Canon) and minting an enduring vampire classic. Paul Wegener's *The Golem* (1920), an elaborately expanded version of the novel, superbly lit by cinematographer Karl Freund, was a classic of the legend, and **Paul Leni** directed the remarkable omnibus *Waxworks* (1924). **Fritz Lang's** *Between Two Worlds* (1921), in which Death recounts three tragic tales, so impressed **Alfred Hitchcock** (see Icons), then an inter-title designer, producing dialogue frames, that it confirmed his desire to become a director and greatly influenced his killer chiller *The Lodger* (1926).

All these foreign names would be lured to America to help shape the Hollywood horrors that the rest of the world would rush to imitate. Sweden's **Victor Sjöström** followed the émigré talent after his skilled direction and starring role in *The Phantom Carriage* (1920), which outlined the story that anyone dying at the stroke of midnight on New Year's Eve is condemned to drive a death coach for the next twelve months. The Danish director **Benjamin Christensen**, who had made *Witchcraft Through The Ages* (1922), also went to America, where he switched to a similar if less threatening parade of witches, dwarfs, madmen and crazed gorillas in *Seven Footprints For Satan* (1929). Italian directors stayed put, even though Eugenio Testa's *The Monster Of Frankenstein* (1920) was the last horror film in the country for nearly forty years because of hugely restrictive censorship.

The contrast between European and American horror movies was stark. Whereas European studios went for dark artistry and inner meaning, in America studios were interested solely in cheap thrills and marquee exploitation. *Dr Jekyll And Mr Hyde* (1920) was the prime example: **John Barrymore**, the prince of Broadway's royal family, played handsome Henry Jekyll, who under close scrutiny contorted himself into an expression of ancient evil; only after inserting a shot of fingers dissolving into bony talons did director **John S. Robertson** cut back to show Mr Hyde's abnormal pointed head and his face in grease-painted glory. A theatrical tour de force of character dislocation, associated with the prestigious name of Barrymore, it led many film critics to proclaim that horror was, in effect, the new black.

The true make-up genius of the era was the startling **Lon Chaney** (see Icons), who starred in *The Hunchback Of Notre Dame* (1923) and *The Phantom Of The Opera* (1925, see Canon). He was also the first horror artist to understand genuinely that no amount of facial distortion, skin putty or false hair could itself create a believable character; he realized that however warped his monstrosities were in body and soul, unless his characters retained their humanity they wouldn't reach out to the audience.

But it was the combination of Chaney and director **Tod Browning** (see Icons) that gave the silent screen its most chilling moments and

John Barrymore (standing), whose name contributed to the success of *Dr Jekyll And Mr Hyde*

grotesque villains. Exercises in disturbing and masochistic self-loathing hit home because people had become used to the scarring and amputation of World War I: the victims of barbarity were visible on street corners begging for charity, and newsreel footage had often been seen unedited, so Chaney and Browning had to crank up their images to make an impact.

Meanwhile D. W. Griffith's *One Exciting Night* (1922) profited from the trend of jokey haunted house mysteries that peaked with **Paul Leni**'s *The Cat And The Canary* (1927, see Canon). And as was also visible in the Benjamin Christensen films *The Haunted House* (1927) and *The House Of Horror* (1929), and Browning's Chaney vehicle *London After Midnight* (1927), these horrors rationalized their denouements, underlining the American practice of debunking real fears with laughter and deception. This vogue for tiresome spoof shockers would smother the gentle flowering of a darker and broader-based horror genre until the start of the Thirties.

The movies that took their subjects more seriously included two Faustian tales. Frank Tuttle's *Puritan Passions* (1923), an adaptation of Nathaniel Hawthorne's *Feathertop*, borrowed German imagery for its depiction of a witches' Sabbath and a mirror of truth where sinners see themselves for whom they really are. D. W. Griffith's *The Sorrows Of Satan* (1925), based on Marie Corelli's Victorian bestseller, laid down the first guidelines for future psychological horrors. By giving the hero's reaction to Lucifer, who was visible as giant bat-wing shadows, Griffith established the precept of never showing too much on screen.

After the first tearful sobs of Al Jolson in *The Jazz Singer* (1928) shook silent Hollywood to the

Laura La Plante with company in the haunted house mystery *The Cat And The Canary* (1927)

core, the second all-talking motion picture from Warner Bros, **Roy Del Ruth**'s *The Terror* (1928) – the first was *The Lights Of New York* (1927) – tested the waters of sound for the growing horror industry. An adaptation of a play by Edgar Wallace that had become an enormous West End success, it was essentially just another haunted house affair, and owed debts to both *The Phantom Of The Opera* and *The Cat And The Canary*. It featured a homicidal asylum escapee hiding in an old country mansion and terrorizing the guests with his organ playing and his habit of creeping around in a hangman's hood and cloak. The credits were spoken and scenes set by Conrad Nagel and the effects of the Vitaphone sound–on–disc process meant that for the first time every door–creak, wind–howl and flash of lightning could be heard, as well as eerie organ music. *The Terror* was hopelessly stagy and acted stiffly – everyone was too self-conscious about being in the range of a microphone – and received poor reviews, but what it showed about the contribution that sound could make to a horror story did not go unnoticed.

It was also clear that sound could be used for effects that were marvellously macabre. For when Lon Chaney, dressed as a woman in the remake *The Unholy Three* (1930), gave away his identity on the witness stand by accidentally letting his voice assume its normal masculine sound, audiences realized how powerful the fusion of images and sound could be.

Witchcraft Through The Ages
dir Benjamin Christensen, 1922, Swe, 87m, b/w

Christensen, a former opera singer, found his surreal silent shockumentary banned in many countries because of its nudity, stomach-turning fiction and sacrilegious imagery. Tracing the history of diabolism from the witchcraft trials of the fifteenth century to modern-day possession, this grotesque terror inspired by Bosch and Goya attempts "to reconstruct those wretched aberrations of an age when Satanism disturbed many souls" and is still powerful and unique. Christensen plays the Devil as well as the psychiatrist who explains the strange happenings.

The Hunchback Of Notre Dame
dir Wallace Worsley, 1923, US, 108m, b/w

This silent version of Victor Hugo's classic novel impresses with its epic sets and showcasing of Lon Chaney's inimitability as a pantomime artist and make-up genius; here he wears a plaster hump for his performance. As Quasimodo, infatuated with gypsy dancer Esmeralda (Patsy Ruth Miller), and outraged at the social injustice she faces, Chaney reveals one of horror cinema's purest hearts – one willing to risk ridicule in order to be loved.

Waxworks
dir Paul Leni, 1924, Ger, 65m, b/w

Designed with swirling Expressionistic flair and using light and shadow to perfection, director Paul Leni's classic anthology, about a writer furnishing the proprietor of a wax museum with stories of various chamber of horrors exhibits, artfully unleashes the full stylistic potential of silent horror. Caliph Harun al-Rashid, Ivan the Terrible and Jack the Ripper are the three historical figures seen respectively in opulent palaces, nightmarish torture chambers and London's East End in a slice of fanciful fear that looks fabulous.

The Lodger
dir Alfred Hitchcock, 1926, UK, 96m, b/w

A policeman's sexual jealousy compels him to accuse a mysterious stranger of being the strangler terrorizing London in Hitchcock's third film, subtitled *A Story Of The London Fog*. It was the first of his works to show the influence of German Expressionism and introduces many of his favourite plot devices (false accusations, moral ambiguity) as well as many images that he would later develop brilliantly (staircases, psychological symbols).

The Thirties

There were two forces behind the true start of cinematic horror – a description that can be used in only the loosest of ways to describe the genre during Hollywood's formative years. First, as the movie industry experimented with the possibilities of sound, many silent crowd–pleasers were made into talkies, the results including Lon Chaney's swansong *The Unholy Three* (1930) and **Rupert Julian**'s *The Cat Creeps* (1930), a remake of *The Cat And The Canary*. Second, the world desperately needed diversions after the Wall Street Crash in 1929 ushered in the Depression, and through horror films audiences could draw slight comfort in fates worse than their own.

Only when Universal found that the medium-budget *Dracula* was building into their biggest cash cow did the studio declare in the trade press their intention of making "*another* horror film". It was the first time the term had been used, and so the Stoker saga became the inaugural horror film in retrospect. But the floodgates soon opened, with Universal unleashing their iconic catalogue of monsters and mayhem: *Frankenstein* (1931, see Canon), *The Mummy*, *Murders In The Rue Morgue* (both 1932), *The Old Dark House* (1932, see Canon), *The Black Cat* (1934), *The Raven* (1935), *Werewolf Of London* (1935), and son, daughter and bride sequels to their most famous franchises.

The innocent pathos of *Frankenstein* turned in *The Bride Of Frankenstein* (1935, see Canon) to cynical wit, because **James Whale** (see Icons) so resented being forced to direct it, and *Son Of Frankenstein* (1939) was pure exploitation; and this cycle of peaks and troughs was repeated by other studios, producers and actors tied to the genre. The careers of **Bela Lugosi** and **Boris Karloff** (see Canon in both cases) echoed the trend and served as a sobering thought to anyone who saw one of these typecast individuals and thought about following their footsteps.

Other studios saw the huge grosses that were being earned and eagerly hopped onto the horror bandwagon. *Dr Jekyll And Mr Hyde* (1931) featured **Fredric March** in the first Oscar-winning horror performance, as well as groundbreaking transformation effects achieved with clever lighting techniques. *Doctor X* (1932) was the first horror to be shot in two-strip Technicolor, which presented an oddly ethereal atmosphere to the few people who saw it, and the second *Mystery Of The Wax Museum* (1933) was the first film using the same process to be distributed on a wide scale; the latter also launched the combination of chills and laborious comedy

A key moment from *The Black Cat (1934),* starring Bela Lugosi, a classic Universal horror from the Thirties

But new stories were needed for this new-found voracious mass audience. **Universal** had made a name for themselves in the silent horror tradition with groundbreakers such as *The Hunchback Of Notre Dame* and *The Phantom Of The Opera*, so business sense, particularly in tough economic times, led them to similar frights from literature and legend. Yet only with the success of Tod Browning's *Dracula* (1931, see Canon) did the recognizable world of movie monsters take shape – the claustrophobic universe of fog-bound forests, imposing castles, torch-bearing peasants and gothic melodrama firmly placed in a mythic Mitteleuropa.

Fay Wray (1907-2004)

Horror cinema's first "scream queen" was the Canadian-born actress best remembered as the leather-lunged heroine Ann Darrow who fascinated the giant ape in *King Kong* (1933). Born Vina Fay Wray, she made her horror debut in the human-hunting shocker *The Most Dangerous Game* (1932), which she followed with *Doctor X* (1932), *Mystery Of The Wax Museum* and *The Vampire Bat* (both 1933), before nestling in Kong's paw. Her career then went into decline and at the start of the Forties she retired for ten years. Her autobiography, *On the Other Hand: A Life Story*, was published in 1989, and just before her death in 2004 she turned down an offer from director Peter Jackson of a cameo appearance in his *King Kong* remake.

Peter Lorre (1904-1964)

Twelve lines of dialogue in Fritz Lang's *M* (1931) made Peter Lorre a star. As the psychopathic child-killer who screams that he can't help his compulsion, the pop-eyed, squat Hungarian, born Laszlo Lowenstein, made the most of his whining accent, and it became his signature. Although best known for *The Maltese Falcon* (1941) and *Casablanca* (1943), horror was Lorre's forte, as he proved in films such as *Mad Love* (1935), *The Face Behind The Mask* (1941) and *Arsenic And Old Lace* (1944), and then in the early Sixties in two Poe films with Roger Corman, *Tales Of Terror* (1962) and *The Raven* (1963), and Jacques Tourneur's *The Comedy Of Terrors* (1964). He was known for his wicked sense of humour, quipping to Vincent Price on seeing Bela Lugosi's body at his funeral: "Do you think we should drive a stake through his heart just in case?"

Lorre in the film that established him, *M* (1931)

that became more pronounced as the decade wore on. Meanwhile *White Zombie* (1933) was the debut for a sub-genre that was soon to be far grislier and **Peter Lorre** astounded in his first American role in *Mad Love* (1935), the best version of Maurice Renard's terror staple *The Hands of Orlac*. And in the "Beauty and the Beast" fable *King Kong* (1933), starring **Fay Wray**, Willis

O'Brien's stop-motion model created the world's most famous ape, thanks to skilful mixing of exotic adventure and horror-tinged fantasy by Ernest B. Schoedsack and Merian C. Cooper.

In the rest of the world, horror movies almost failed to develop at all, with other countries' film industries affected by civil wars, political turmoil and stricter censorship. But from Germany came

Vampyr (1931). Based on J. Sheridan Le Fanu's *Carmilla*, **Carl Theodor Dreyer**'s pale and hazy impressionism – initially the result of a lighting fault but then adopted throughout – formed one of horror's most powerful evocations of a nightmare world that was logically skewed. It was the first horror to find cryptic chills in the recesses of the unconscious mind, but like Arthur Robison's remake *Der student von Prag* (*The Student Of Prague*, 1935), it barely found an international audience because it was not recreated and refashioned by Hollywood.

The only country where there was no downswing during this period was Mexico. Thanks to interest in the Spanish version of *Dracula*, shot on Tod Browning's sets during the night by **George Melford** and starring **Carlos Villarías**, the native horror tradition flourished. *La llorona* (*The Crying Woman*, 1933) was the first Mexican horror to feature the legendary wailing ghost mourning her dead child that would last into the Sixties; it was scripted by **Fernando de Fuentes**, who directed the country's best-known horror of the period, *El fantasma del convento* (*The Phantom Of The Convent*, 1934), about a mummified monk haunting an eerie monastery. Its writer, **Juan Bustillo Oro**, also became a director, making the Caligariesque *Two Monks* (1934), and *Nostradamus* (1936). Two variations on *Frankenstein*, *The Macabre Trunk* (1936) and *The Macabre Legacy* (1939), continued the Mexican wave.

The decade ended with three landmarks in 1939 – Bob Hope's comedy horror vehicle *The Cat And The Canary*, Tod Slaughter's *The Face At The Window* and Sidney Lanfield's *The Hound Of The Baskervilles*, the first appearance by **Basil Rathbone** as Sherlock Holmes – but it was apparent that the genre was deteriorating, often turning into plodding pastiche. The innovation

of the horror movie had been diluted by studio complacency, as was clearest when Bela Lugosi met the three Ritz Brothers in *The Gorilla* (1939), and what had at first been treated as a serious genre with great potential was downgraded to popcorn material.

Vampyr
dir Carl Dreyer, 1931, Ger/Fr, 83m, b/w

Although not a great success when released, and despite mainly featuring non-professionals, this revered genre pioneer's evocation of a nightmare world, based on J. Sheridan Le Fanu's *Carmilla*, later became widely acclaimed. Baron Nicolas de Gunzberg financed the project and plays the hero, David Gray, who is given a vampire combat book by an apparition. In the most celebrated sequence Gray is buried alive in a glass-windowed coffin.

Dr Jekyll And Mr Hyde
dir Rouben Mamoulian, 1931, US, 96m, b/w

"Put yourself in her place! The dreaded night when her lover became a madman!" ran the tagline to a classic, enduring adaptation of Robert Louis Stevenson's oft-abused text, in which the timeless theme is given a powerful and shocking adult treatment. Fredric March supplies the first of his two Oscar-winning performances, and particularly impressive is the one-take metamorphosis using Wally Westmore's celebrated make-up and special lighting filters.

Island Of Lost Souls
dir Erle C. Kenton, 1932, US, 72m, b/w

This is the definitive adaptation of *The Island Of Dr Moreau*, though it was loathed by H. G. Wells and banned in Britain until 1958. It features fabulous photography, an atmosphere that is morbidly perverse, and one of Charles Laughton's best performances, as the crazed doctor transforming wild beasts into hideous manimals. The grim finale, in which Moreau is dragged to the House of Pain for surgical torture, is a suitable climax to a gripping, uncompromising and mature vivisectionist nightmare.

The Most Dangerous Game (aka The Hounds Of Zaroff)
dir Ernest B. Schoedsack, 1932, US, 63m, b/w

Produced by the same creative team as *King Kong*, and at the same time, this Sadeian shocker concerns decadent connoisseur of forbidden pleasures Count Zaroff (Leslie Banks), who hunts shipwrecked humans (including Fay Wray) for fun. Its top-notch art direction, and Banks's style and restraint as the twisted hedonist, produce a tightly constructed terror zinging with nastiness that in its time was hard-hitting and explicit – not least in the dark eroticism implied in the post-chase revels.

The Forties

By 1940 Hollywood film production and distribution was highly organized and stratified. The double feature was the norm, resulting in a division between A- and B-movies; the latter got lower budgets and lower billing, and became the home for horror because the saturated market for products of the genre had resulted in audiences declining significantly.

Horror directors, including Tod Browning and James Whale, had been weeded out of the system by the studios, though there were exceptions, such as **Erle C. Kenton** (*Ghost Of Frankenstein*, 1942) and **Robert Florey** (*The Beast With Five Fingers*, 1946). Films in the declining genre were aimed increasingly at younger audiences, and the quirkiness of auteurs such as Whale didn't sit well with such superficial thrill-seekers. In any case, adults were far more preoccupied with the very real terrors of World War II. In Britain, horror movies were effectively suppressed at this time; there was no actual ban but films that already had the H certificate, introduced in 1937, were withdrawn by studios and distributors and between 1940 and 1945 only four made it to the screen.

Hurd Hatfield, forever young in *The Picture Of Dorian Gray* (1945), which won an Oscar for its photography

A few horror productions with big stars, lush settings and soft shocks rather than hard ones made inroads into the collective consciousness: the lavish *The Phantom Of The Opera* (1943), starring **Claude Rains**; *The Climax* (1944), an attempt at a sequel in which Boris Karloff makes his debut in colour; the elegant *The Uninvited* (1944, see Canon) with Ray Milland; the stately *The Picture Of Dorian Gray* (1945), for which **Angela Lansbury** was nominated for an Oscar and the magnificent photography won one; and the respectable, if ponderous, Spencer Tracy remake of *Dr Jekyll And Mr Hyde* (1941).

At the other end of the spectrum were a host of cheaper horrors, with either Bela Lugosi or the still commanding Boris Karloff (or both), or lower-ranked wannabes such as **Lon Chaney Jr** and **John Carradine**. There was the occasional innovative idea, such as the mummifying gas in *The Mad Ghoul* (1943) or **Erich von Stroheim** as a sleazy magician in *The Mask Of Diijon* (1946). But most of these potboilers had make-do production values, and usually they were bottom-of-the-barrel fillers, like *The Ape* (1940), *The Devil Bat* (1941) and *The Mad Monster* (1942), made by bargain-basement outfits such as Monogram and PRC who established themselves as efficient if threadbare fear factories.

Only RKO producer **Val Lewton** (see Icons) cut through the dross, with his eleven evocative horrors that started with *Cat People* (1942, see Canon). Another highly influential movie was **Robert Siodmak**'s *The Spiral Staircase* (1946), which concerned a homicidal maniac whose dedication to preserving beauty compels him to rid the world of maimed or disfigured imperfect women. Alfred Hitchcock and Dario Argento would dramatically embellish Siodmak's startling use of a murderer's point-of-view.

Lon Chaney Jr (1906-1973)

Always to remain in the shadow of his iconic father, the actor born Creighton Chaney first found fame when he played the simple-minded Lennie in Lewis Milestone's adaptation of John Steinbeck's *Of Mice And Men* (1939). Using the same brand of pathos, *The Wolf Man* (1941) made him a star, and he became the only actor to play all four classic movie monsters: The Wolf Man, the Frankenstein monster, Kharis (the Mummy) and Count Dracula. But personal problems, including alcoholism, gradually pushed him towards horrors that were cheaper and trashier, including *Man Made Monster* (1941), *Face Of The Screaming Werewolf* (1959) and *The Alligator People* (1959), and among his later credits only *Spider Baby, Or The Maddest Story Ever Told* (1968), for which he sang the theme song, has any real cult merit. *Dracula Vs Frankenstein* (1971), his last film, is his worst.

John Carradine (1906-1988)

"I've made some of the greatest films ever made – and a lot of crap too," said the actor born Richmond Reed Carradine of a career that took in more than 250 movies. The good ones include *Stagecoach* (1939), *The Grapes Of Wrath* (1940) and *The Ten Commandments* (1956); the bad mostly include his horror output, examples being *Revenge Of The Zombies* (1943), *Billy The Kid Vs Dracula* (1966) and *Satan's Cheerleaders* (1977). His association with Universal began with *The Black Cat* (1934) and included the role of Dracula in *House Of Frankenstein* (1944) and *House Of Dracula* (1945), and later notable horrors included *The Boogey Man* (1980) and *House Of The Long Shadows* (1983), the only film to star Carradine, Christopher Lee, Peter Cushing and Vincent Price. But in his declining years he was mainly locked into cheap exploitation, such as *Vampire Hookers* (1978) and the disco horror *Nocturna* (1979). Three of his sons became actors.

When the first wave of horror had receded, **Universal** had stayed afloat thanks to the modest musicals starring Deanna Durbin; but when all the horror classics were re-released and made just as much money second time around the studio found itself back in the fright business. But no real care or protective handling was taken when the favourite old monsters returned in ever more routine and desperate sequels: *The Mummy's Hand* (1940), *The Mummy's Tomb* (1942), *The Ghost of Frankenstein* (1942) – the first without Karloff – and *Son Of Dracula* (1943) were all racked by sloppy storytelling and continuity errors. (In *The Mummy's Hand*, Wallace Ford's character is Babe Jenson, but in *The Mummy's Tomb* he returns as a member of the original expedition with the name Babe Hanson.) Telling the stories for sheer dramatic effect, Universal never worried if an ending precluded the possibility of a character returning; when a profit-making sequel was required, any inconveniences were simply ignored.

But Universal did create a classic monster character in *The Wolf Man* (1941), through the addition of fake folklore to the werewolf myth and Lon Chaney Jr's sympathetic central performance. And it was Universal who had the idea of adding monsters to successive features: *Frankenstein Meets The Wolf Man* (1943) led to the rallies *House Of Frankenstein* (1944) and *House Of Dracula* (1945), both of which feature the Frankenstein monster, Dracula and the Wolf Man. The conclusion of these creature features was the first of the virtually laughter-free scare spoofs, *Abbott And Costello Meet Frankenstein* (1948).

Around the world horror movie production had virtually evaporated, but there were again decent efforts from the Spanish-speaking territories. Mexican filmmakers made monster combos like Universal did, such as **Adolfo Fernández Bustamante**'s *The Revolt Of The Ghosts* (1949), in which the phantoms of Chopin, Paganini, Caruso, Tutankhamun, Don Quixote, The Crying Woman and The Wandering Jew join forces to stop a house being demolished. There were also three notable Mexican movies directed by **René Cardona** starring English illusionist David T. Bamberg, appearing under his stage name **Fu Manchu**: *El espectro de la novia* (*Spectre Of The Bride*, 1943), *El as negro* (*The Black Ace*, 1944) and *La mujer sin cabeza* (*The Headless Woman*, 1944). In Japan the *kaidan eiga* ("ghost story"), which had been seen as irrational and suspicious in the war years, regained its footing; the foundations were laid when **Keisuke Kinoshita** made Nanboku Tsuruya's mythic kabuki play of 1825 into *Shinshaku Yotsuya kaidan* (*The Ghost Of Yotsuya – New Version*, 1949).

The first horror film to be made in Britain after the wartime smothering adopted Val Lewton's philosophy of suggestion. Ealing Studios' *Dead Of Night* (1945), an omnibus with parts directed by Alberto Cavalcanti, Charles Crichton, Basil Dearden and Robert Hamer, starred **Michael Redgrave** as the host at a country cottage that one guest recognizes as a place from his worst nightmares, triggering an exchange of frightening stories; and a vicious circle of terror is formed by the self-contained tales, including Hamer's *The Haunted Mirror* and Cavalcanti's *The Ventriloquist's Dummy*, in which Redgrave surrenders his will to his living puppet. Acclaimed as a supernatural masterpiece, it tentatively began the British horror revival that would explode in the mid-Fifties thanks to the efforts of **Hammer**, and also foreshadowed the frequent use of the anthology format by another British studio, **Amicus** – Hammer's biggest rival.

Creature feature meets scare spoof: *Abbott And Costello Meet Frankenstein* (1948)

The Ghost Breakers
dir George Marshall, 1940, US, 82m, b/w

This horror comedy remake of Paul Dickey and Charles W. Goddard's play from 1909 is definitely Bob Hope's best movie vehicle. Hiding from the Mob, radio personality Larry Lawrence (Hope) and his manservant (Willie Best) go to Cuba, where Mary Carter (Paulette Goddard) has inherited a haunted castle. Cue the beloved Hope quips – when they arrive during a thunderstorm: "Basil Rathbone must be throwing a party" – and well-orchestrated frights from zombies, coffins and poltergeists.

The Picture Of Dorian Gray
dir Albert Lewin, 1945, US, 110m

The classic, award-winning version of Oscar Wilde's novel stars Hurd Hatfield as the Victorian London rake staying young while his portrait ages because of his decadent lifestyle. As the cynical friend Lord Henry Wotton who puts evil thoughts into Dorian's impressionable mind, George Sanders shines, playing Wilde in all but name, spouting pithy one-liners ("Faithfulness is merely laziness"). Meanwhile the dark depravity builds up to the climactic revelation – in colour!

The Beast With Five Fingers
dir Robert Florey, 1946, US, 88m, b/w

In the last decent American horror movie for nearly a decade, Peter Lorre is superb as the occult scholar who is driven to murder the famed pianist (Victor Francen) for money and is then psychologically terrorized by his victim's severed hand. Brilliantly directed by Robert Florey for maximum eeriness, scenes of the disembodied hand crawling like a spider, poised like a cobra while playing Bach, getting impaled by a letter spike and strangling Lorre contain awe-inspiring special effects.

Shinshaku Yotsuya kaidan (The Ghost Of Yotsuya – New Version)
dir Keisuke Kinoshita, 1949, Jap, 85m, b/w

Radically altering the plot of Nanboku Tsuruya's kabuki staple from 1825 for the spirit of the post-Hiroshima era, Keisuke Kinoshita energized the moribund *kaidan eiga* genre with his poetic, subtle and seductive tale of an unemployed samurai who is haunted by the ghost of the wife whom he killed in order to marry a rich heiress. The accepted definitive version of this classic tale, however, came from Nobuo Nakagawa in 1959.

The Fifties

It's no wonder that the science fiction genre was created at the beginning of the Fifties: humankind was on the threshold of space travel and paranoia reigned as the development of nuclear weapons during **the Cold War** hinted at the extinction of the species. But the sci-fi genre, after starting with thoughtful, hopeful space opera parables such as *Destination Moon* and *The Day The Earth Stood Still* (both 1951), gradually moved on. By taking rules and characteristics of the horror film – such as the adoption of the classic horror creature the spider, in *Tarantula* (1955) – it became a far more frightening hybrid and before long cinema audiences were being terrorized by *Them!* (1954) and *Invasion Of The Body Snatchers* (1955).

Horror suffered initially as a result of the subtle drift of science fiction, but before long there was a major revival for the genre. The studio system, in which organizations such as **MGM** kept stars on salaries and had their own cinemas, had collapsed, and with many stars freelancing to boost their salaries, it was attention-grabbing, sensational plots rather than individuals that had to become the selling points; and this was also the case at a time when fewer but more lavish films were made to challenge the rising medium of television.

The film industry had to find ways of luring back patrons with anything that marked out the cinema as different. One was to increase screen dimensions, with use being made of Cinemascope and Cinerama away from large expositions and

Vincent Price hovering over a victim in *House Of Wax* (1953), the first major feature in 3-D

theme parks; stereophonic sound also helped; and so did a range of **gimmicks**. Stereoscopic **3-D**, a process that had been around since the Thirties, came into its own, with a series of "in your face" effects arriving in the wake of *House Of Wax* (1953), the film that made **Vincent Price** (see Icons) a star.

Television also played a key role in fuelling the flames of the fear renaissance. In 1957 Universal sold many of their monster movie

William Castle (1914-1977)

A producer, director and master showman, William Castle was the undisputed king of the **gimmicks** in an era when every means necessary was employed to attract crowds. For *Macabre* (1958) he issued insurance policies covering death by fright; *The House On Haunted Hill* (1959) featured a process called "Emergo", in which a skeleton was cranked across the cinema ceiling when Vincent Price mirrored the action on screen; for *The Tingler* (1959) "Percepto" buzzers under seats administered mild shocks when the monster was let loose; *Homicidal* (1961) had a "fright break" so that scaredy-cats could leave before the surprise revelation; and *Mr Sardonicus* (1961) supposedly allowed the audience to choose the fate of its villain. (Castle often boasted he never had to use the "happy" ending, so his gamble worked.) After directing the Hammer disaster remake *The Old Dark House* (1962), Castle marked time before producing *Rosemary's Baby* (1968), and his final production was *Bug* (1975), for which he sought unsuccessfully to fit fake cockroaches to cinema seats. Affectionate homage was paid in *Popcorn* (1991) and *Matinee* (1992) to Castle's brand of eccentric showmanship and desire for communal participation that captured imaginations.

An ad block for *Homicidal* (1961), for cinemas to use in local papers

Gimmick gimmick gimmick

It wasn't only William Castle's famous audience lures or the 3-D glasses that tried to part audiences and their cash. If Castle's insurance policies, electric jolts or animated skeletons weren't enough, there were other fun means of heightening the terror in a movie experience, with numerous films being marketed through gimmicks that were unique and memorably titled.

• **"Duo-Vision"**. "See the hunter, see the hunted – both at the same time," boasted the tagline for Richard L. Bare's *Wicked, Wicked* (1973). The method was the split screen, used throughout the entire feature; the idea was that all the action, revolving around a seaside hotel handyman in a monster mask killing and dismembering women with blonde hair, could be viewed from more than one angle.

• **"Psychorama"**. Also known as "The Precon Process", this use of subliminal imagery, with information flashing on screen so quickly that it was picked up only subconsciously, was used for an axe murderer movie directed by Harold Daniels, *My World Dies Screaming* (1958); fear was instilled through graphics of a Devil face and messages like "Get ready to scream". The process was banned because of its moral implications, but the success of *The Exorcist* was supposedly due to a revival of this technique.

• **"Hallucinogenic Hypnovision"**. "Monsters come real! Crash out of screen! Invade audience! Abduct girls from their seats! Not 3-D! Don't miss it!" This wonderfully lifelike gimmick was devised by director Ray Dennis Steckler for *The Incredibly Strange Creatures Who Stopped Living And Became Mixed-Up Zombies!!?* (1964). When at the start of the film a hypnotist called The Great Ormond appeared on screen to warn that the story's three homicidal mental patients would soon be on the loose in the theatre, usherettes and cleaners employed by the cinema ran through the audience wearing phosphorescent masks to terrorize planted stooges.

• **"The Fear Flasher" & "The Horror Horn"**. Whenever a gory scene was about to begin in Hy Averback's *Chamber Of Horrors* (1966), about the exploits of the owners of Baltimore Wax Museum, the screen flashed red and a siren sounded so that those of a nervous disposition could look away. A similar audible ploy was used for Ivan Reitman's *Cannibal Girls* (1972) – "The picture with the warning bell. When it rings … close your eyes if you're squeamish!"

• **"The Final Warning Station"**. "The first motion picture to require a face-to-face warning," cautioned the posters for the American release of Mario Bava's *Twitch Of The Death Nerve* (1971). This meant the cinema manager stood in front of grouped patrons advising them that the body-count movie they were about to see had "thirteen periods of intense shock".

• **"The D-13 Test"**. Before seeing Francis Ford Coppola's *Dementia 13* (1963), producer Roger Corman's attempt to copy *Psycho*, you had to fill out a questionnaire to see if you were psychologically sound enough to take the shock content: "Are you afraid of death by drowning? … Have you ever attempted suicide? … Have you ever thought of committing murder?" Accompanying the yes/no queries was the statement: "If you fail the test … you will be asked to leave the theatre."

• **"Hypno Vista"**. American audiences had *Horrors Of The Black Museum* (1959) extended by 13 minutes thanks to a prologue preparing them for the autosuggestion shock contained in the Grand Guignol spectacle. Emile Franchel, "registered psychiatrist in the State of California, speciality hypnotism", invited the audience to take part in a series of simple tests and, accompanied by an Archimedean spiral graphic, he guaranteed that once the "truly frightening" motion picture commenced they would experience "the damp chill of the tomb" and "the panic of fear".

classics to American networks in a package that had the series title *Shock Theater*, which reached a massive audience that was suddenly hungry for more. And that audience was mainly drawn from an entirely new section of the population, newly dubbed "teenagers". Before the chart-topping arrival of *Rock Around the Clock* by **Bill Haley & His Comets** in 1955, children went straight from adolescence to adulthood; but rock'n'roll changed all that: it created a new youth market eager to

spend money on anything that was seen as a rebellion against staid adult values, and along with Elvis Presley, "race music" and beatniks, horror movies fit the bill. Heavy petting went in tandem with screaming at drive-in screenings of *I Was A Teenage Werewolf* (1958) and its ilk, where budding sex drives were equated with monster-hood, and from this point on teenagers were added to the list of horror protagonists; they played increasingly active roles as the decades rolled on.

The screaming to radical reinventions of horror themes had started in Italy in 1956, with Riccardo Freda's *I Vampiri* (*Lust For A Vampire*, aka *The Devil's Commandment*). But the film's worldwide release in 1957 tied it irrevocably to the **Hammer** juggernaut that was breaking global box-office records with the epoch-making *The Curse Of Frankenstein* (1957, see Canon). Hammer had seen their audiences increasing every time they raised the shock bar – *The Quatermass Xperiment* (1955) was the first movie to exploit the new "adults only" certificate

Michael Landon in *I Was A Teenage Werewolf* (1958), which drew teenagers in to the genre by using the letter of the rating in the title – and although critics hated the sexed-up, bloodied-up, colour reinterpretation of Mary Shelley's myth by **Terence Fisher** (see Icons), audiences flocked to it. They liked *Dracula* (aka *Horror Of Dracula*, 1958, see Canon) even more, and made the tiny British company who accidentally established the modern horror film the leading brand name to this very day.

Hammer even had the temerity to turn the recent past into powerful horror. One sensation, advertised with the tagline "Jap War Crimes Exposed", was *The Camp On Blood Island* (1958), which tapped into the raw nerve of xenophobia that remained from the war years, with borderline offensive taste. Val Guest's brutal depiction of POWs preventing their sadistic captors from discovering that World War II has ended in case of cruel reprisal may have been made with honourable intentions, but its orgy of atrocities played to the gladiatorial bloodlust of spectators who had unforgiving memories. The squalid prequel *The Secret Of Blood Island* (1965) jettisoned all serious intent for an audience-pleasing parade of abominations.

Hammer's success soon had an impact on film industries around the world. Barely thirty horror movies were made outside the US and UK in the first half of the decade, but in the second half the figure quadrupled. As usual, Mexico stumbled on indefatigably, and *The Vampire* and *The Curse Of The Aztec Mummy* (both 1957) were the first Mexican horrors to be sold internationally. The French films *Diabolique* (1955, see Canon) and *Eyes Without A Face* (1959, see Canon) had an influence on America's mainstream and **Kenji Mizoguchi** introduced Western audiences to Japanese cinema with *Ugetsu monogatari* (*Tale Of The Pale And Mysterious Moon After The Rain*, 1953), which adopted an elegant neo-realist

Edith Scob during her perfect performance in the influential French film *Eyes Without A Face* (1959)

approach to seduce audiences into the unfolding mystery; it was veteran director **Nobuo Nakagawa,** though, who set off the new wave of *kaidan eiga* horrors, first with *Kaidan Kasanegafuchi* (*The Kasane Swamp*, 1957), based on a nineteenth-century vampire tale, and later with *Tōkaido Yotsuya kaidan* (*The Ghost Of Yotsuya*, 1959), the definitive version of the famous kabuki play.

This period also saw the launch in 1958 of *Famous Monsters Of Filmland*, the first magazine aimed specifically at those who rushed to see any horror movie, no matter how bad the reviews were; this resilient breed, with low expectations and high tolerance, stood in line in the hope of something never seen before, as promised by the hype on the sensational posters. Despite the childish puns of the editor, memorabilia collector **Forrest J. Ackerman** (columns included "Ghoulden Days of Horrorwood", "You Axed for It" and "Fang Mail"), his informed enthusiasm for all matters monster led to a rapid increase in the number of horror movie buffs.

This flew in the face of the 1953 controversies involving **EC Comics** and the excessive violence and gore in the company's titles *Haunt Of Fear*, *Vault Of Horror* and *Tales From The Crypt*. It would take nearly twenty years before a compendium of those nasty stories would make it to the screen, in *Tales From The Crypt* (1972); and in 1989 there was a TV series in the United States. By then the horror genre had faced uninformed attacks from self-appointed moral guardians for a long time.

I Was A Teenage Werewolf
dir Gene Fowler Jr, 1958, US, 76m, b/w

The trendsetting, youth-focused horror had rock'n'roll, teen angst and campus fistfights. Michael Landon, playing in the style of James Dean, is Tony Rivers, the troubled student turned into a murderous hairy monster by mad Dr Brandon (Whit Bissell). Hypnotism causes him to undergo an animalistic makeover whenever he's startled – as he is in the classic moment when the school bell rings while he's watching a girl hanging upside down from the parallel bars.

Horrors Of The Black Museum
dir Arthur Crabtree, 1958, UK, 81m

After one of the most vicious shocks of the era – a girl unwraps a gift of binoculars, looks through them and has two spring-loaded metal spikes gouge her eyes out – a crime book author commits horrendous murders to give him details that will satisfy his reader's demands. With

Circus Of Horrors (1959) and *Peeping Tom* (1960), this sensational shocker forms a trilogy of charnel-house terror made by the British company Anglo-Amalgamated.

A Bucket Of Blood
dir Roger Corman, 1959, US, 66m, b/w

House Of Wax meets the Beat Generation in this $50,000 cult comedy horror. There are guffaws and there's gore as beatnik beret-wearing busboy Walter Paisley (Dick Miller) kills a cat accidentally, covers it in clay and displays it as modern art. Hailed a genius sculptor, he murders a nosy cop and a nude model for further exhibits before he becomes his last masterpiece. Charles Griffith's hip script, Miller's performance and Corman's unpretentious direction make for a cool classic.

The Sixties

The Fifties saw a revival of horror cinema, but when the Swinging Sixties began the genre flourished like never before, and went to unthinkable places. The main appeal was simple: although British kitchen-sink dramas discussed sex frankly, the horror film remained the only place to see passionate encounters between the two sexes. And if the grappling wasn't sexual, it could certainly be deadly: it was possible to show an erotic high-angle shot of a lingerie-clad blonde prostitute in bed having her head severed by a guillotine (in *Horrors Of The Black Museum*, 1958), though the censor would never have allowed the same shot of a girl having sex with her boyfriend no matter how innocent their lovemaking was.

Much horror film imagery was based on the similarity of the sexual embrace to the homicidal one and the overtly phallic thrust of knives, and medical horror movies became the vogue for similar reasons; this was evident in the surgical debasement shown in **Riccardo Freda**'s *The Terror Of Dr Hichcock* (1962), spelt without the T so that Hitchcock wouldn't be offended, and in the soon-to-be ubiquitous **Jess Franco**'s *The Awful Dr Orloff* (1962).

But many of the more restrictive countries did not see the overt imagery and brief nudity that was getting into many productions in continental Europe where competition was stiff. In Britain, horror films were forbidden for those under the age of sixteen, and salacious and shocking material was censored; the spiked mask opening of the landmark movie from **Mario Bava** (see Icons), *Black Sunday* (1960, see Canon) was still cut when released after a seven-year ban. In America the core audience for horror movies has always been the adolescent, and most of the genre was censored for a PG (parental guidance) rating, though

children could still see the stronger R (restricted) movies if accompanied by an adult.

It was because Hammer geared their products to specific countries, and because they continued with their traditional monsters, that they still dominated the global market. Stronger scenes were filmed for release in continental Europe and the strongest ones for Japan. *The Curse Of The Werewolf* (1961) is the most famous example of a Hammer horror being more heavily censored in its country of origin than anywhere else. Cuts to the contentious scene in which a servant girl is raped and the three killings made the British version three minutes shorter than the export.

Terence Fisher's haunting classic bore the brunt of British censor wrath because of timing. Just

Viva las divas

After fading, feuding divas **Bette Davis** and **Joan Crawford** gritted their teeth and co-starred as washed up Hollywood has-beens in Robert Aldrich's *Whatever Happened To Baby Jane?* (1962), every ageing femme fatale followed their lead and gave the horror genre a stab. The spectacle of previously glamorous leading ladies indulging in psychological torture and grotesque punishments proved massively successful, and in Aldrich's companion pieces *Hush ... Hush Sweet Charlotte* (1963) and *Whatever Happened To Aunt Alice?* (1969) Olivia de Havilland, Agnes Moorehead, Geraldine Page and Ruth Gordon added pensioner power. Curtis Harrington's *What's The Matter With Helen?* (1971), starring Debbie Reynolds, and *Whoever Slew Auntie Roo?* (1971), with Shelley Winters, were similarly popular "trash yourself terrors". Joan Crawford hilariously parlayed her bravura turn into mature love-interest roles in *Straight-Jacket* (1964), *I Saw What You Did* (1965) and *Trog* (1970).

Whatever happened to Bette and Joan?

Roman Polanski in front of the camera in the Hammer tribute *Dance Of The Vampires* (1967)

before its release *Psycho* (1960, see Canon) and, to an even greater extent, **Michael Powell**'s *Peeping Tom* (1960, see Canon) had focused yet more unwanted attention on the genre, with pressure groups, including religious authorities and tabloids, insisting on a total ban. Although Hitchcock's sly shocker prompted Hammer to produce a series of suspense thrillers that were high on screams and low on logic – *Maniac* and *Paranoiac* (both 1963), *Nightmare* and *Hysteria* (both 1964), *Crescendo* (1970) – and influenced the genre more in the long run, Powell's stand-alone masterpiece remains the definitive discourse on voyeuristic terror.

Other films pointed to the future too. *Night Of The Living Dead* (1968, see Canon), directed by **George A. Romero** (see Icons), introduced the flesh-eating zombie to the glossary of horror. **Herschell Gordon Lewis** was responsible for the forerunner of the splatter genre, *Blood Feast* (1963), which updated Grand Guignol gore trickery with its mutilation shots. It was a huge grind house drive-in smash and soon became part of a hastily assembled gore trilogy alongside *2000 Maniacs* (1964) and *Color Me Blood Red* (1965). But it was **Roman Polanski** (see Icons) who covered every significant Sixties trend with his distinguished terror-filled trio – the distaff *Psycho* equivalent *Repulsion* (1965, see Canon), the elegant Hammer tribute *Dance Of The Vampires* (1967) and the biblical witchcraft fable *Rosemary's Baby* (1968, see Canon).

Meanwhile, after years of working in B-movie Hollywood, director **Roger Corman** (see Icons) finally convinced his main employer, American International Pictures, to follow Hammer's lead and produce colourful costume horror with a distinctly New World flavour, and beginning with *The Fall Of The House Of Usher* (1960), Corman brought numerous Edgar Allan Poe stories to the screen with great box–office and critical success. Films such as *The Pit And The Pendulum* (1961, see Canon), *Tales Of Terror* (1962) and *The Masque Of The Red Death* (1964) created a marketing device whereby Poe was quickly attached to any dubious investment; one of his poems was the source of the seemingly arbitrary title that **Michael Reeves**'s *Witchfinder General* (1968, see Canon) went by in America, *The Conqueror Worm*.

As the Hammer formula, and that of its closest rival **Amicus**, which borrowed the House of Horror's stable of stars, got cloned internationally, many sub-genres started to percolate in different cultures. **Paul Naschy** became the Hispanic Christopher Lee and embarked on a long career as the werewolf Count Waldemar Daninsky in *La marco del hombre lobo* (*Frankenstein's Bloody Terror*, 1968). The South American actor turned director **Narciso Ibáñez Serrador** circumvented General Franco's stringent censorship by making a film about repression as a horror, the nightmare *La residencia* (*The House That Screamed*, 1969). In Mexico the popular silver-masked wrestler **Santo** (born Rodolfo Guzman Huerta) began a supernatural series, beginning with *Atacan las brujas* (*Santo Attacks The Witches*, 1965).

Thanks to international festivals, the world found out about the key Japanese movies of the period: *Onibaba* (*The Hole*, 1964, see Canon), *Kwaidan* (*Ghost Story*, 1964) and *Kuroneko* (*The Black Cat*, 1968). In France surrealist director **Jean Rollin** put up-front eroticism into a lyrical sex vampire series that started with *Le viol de vampire* (*Rape Of The Vampire*, 1967). From Germany there was the traditionalist horror *Blood Demon* (1967) and a succession of popular thrillers based on the work of Edgar Wallace that were dubbed *krimis*; in many the chilling and gruesome elements were substantial, and they shared stylistic ingredients with the Italian *gialli* thrillers, established by Mario Bava with *The Evil Eye* (1962). During a frantic new golden age Italy beat Mexico in the number of horror titles being

Amicus: the house that dripped blood

There were many Hammer pretenders but only one British company took on its market leadership and had its own identity. Formed by the American producers Milton Subotsky and Max J. Rosenberg and based in the UK, Amicus made its first horror movie in 1960 but it wasn't until the portmanteau classic *Dr Terror's House Of Horrors* (1964), starring Christopher Lee and Peter Cushing, that aficionados really took note. The successful reinvention of the moribund *Dead Of Night* anthology format – a collection of short stories with a connecting wraparound – led to films including *The House That Dripped Blood* (1970), but the biggest hit with the formula was *Tales From The Crypt* (1972), based on the EC Comics title. Directed by horror professionals such as Freddie Francis and Roy Ward Baker, and often written by *Psycho* author Robert Bloch, Amicus movies were always fun, quirky, interesting miniatures. But Subotsky clashed with the businessman Rosenberg and their increasingly public spats led to a loss of direction in the mid-Seventies that quickly became fatal.

produced – the star was usually **Barbara Steele** – and everything from vampires, werewolves and musclemen to sadism, disfigurement and necrophilia made its way to the rest of the world from Rome.

The Terror Of Dr Hichcock
dir Riccardo Freda, 1962, It, 88m

"The candle of his lust burnt brightest in the shadow of the grave" screamed the tagline for this compelling and provocative tale of necrophilia, shot in ravishing colours, and beautifully composed. Robert Flemyng is the bad doctor with a kinky taste for injecting women with an anaesthetic to simulate death in sex games; Barbara Steele is the second wife haunted by the spirit of the first. Freda's fetish fantasy is a superb showcase for Steele and all her dark desirability.

Carnival Of Souls
dir Herk Harvey, 1962, US, 81m, b/w

The first cult horror movie was Herk Harvey's $30,000 psychological chiller, featuring a woman who survives a car accident but is caught between life and death; she is then pursued by a cadaverous figure (Harvey) and a range of fatalistic symbols to a deserted pavilion where she watches a revelatory danse macabre. This compelling home movie exudes a uniquely eerie power, and the ghoul attack, pre-dating *Night Of The Living Dead* (1968), is cited as an inspiration by director George Romero.

Carry On Screaming
dir Gerald Thomas, 1966, UK, 97m

Even though horror films are close to parody already, for this comic effort the *Carry On* team sent up Hammer in a silly, funny romp about women who are kidnapped by a monster and literally petrified by zombie doctor Kenneth Williams before being sold as shop window mannequins. Harry H. Corbett is the bumbling cop investigating the disappearances at an old dark house that is home to a vampire, Dr Jekyll and a coffin-load of puns and farce.

The Seventies

Horror had been a poor relation to all other genres after its first golden era, in the Thirties, but was seized upon again by the major studios when the success of the Oscar-winning *Rosemary's Baby* filtered through to the higher echelons of power. With his modern witchcraft tale Roman Polanski made the genre respectable again by employing a religious perspective, a bigger budget and major acting talent.

When a wide audience responded enthusiastically to the care and attention lavished on an occult pop culture bestseller, the studios began new searches for crossover success. By playing on the theme of a lack of faith in godless times – the result of the Vietnam War, racial tension and the quest for alternative spiritual convictions – back-

The church

In horror movies churches very rarely offer the sanctuary they were designed for. Usually there are dangers lurking in every nave and cranny. In *The Omen* (1976) Father Brennan (Patrick Troughton) is killed when a lightning rod falls from the roof in a storm, spears him through the back and transfixes him to the spot, after he has given Robert Thorn (Gregory Peck) a warning about Damien; in *The Church* (1989), when priest Tomas Arana unlocks an ancient mystery in a basement crypt that was built on a pit of tormented souls buried alive as witches in the Middle Ages, a manifestation of Dante's *Inferno* erupts in the nave; and in *John Carpenter's Prince of Darkness* (1987) a strange cylinder of green liquid in a church basement enters the mouths of derelicts (including Alice Cooper) and infects them with an evil spirit. And all manner of psychotic priests have used the secrecy of the confessional to their advantage, most notably in *House Of Mortal Sin* (1975).

Harvey Stephens in *The Omen* (1976), one of the period's religious shockers

to-basics religious shockers eventually became front-runners. **William Friedkin**'s *The Exorcist* (1973, see Canon) and, later, **Richard Donner**'s *The Omen* (1976), and their sequels, might have been overly pious, but they, and **Steven Spielberg**'s equally trendsetting *Jaws* (1975, see Canon), delivered the gory set pieces usually seen in exploitation fodder to new and astonished eyes. Later **Ridley Scott**'s *Alien* (1979) shook up the rubber space monster formula by wrapping its blood-soaked highlights in classy production design.

The B-movie retreated into ever more bizarre sub-genres, such as Italy's flesh-eating zombie/cannibal fiestas and America's **blaxploitation**, the latter using mainstream stories more than making political statements, in *Blacula*, *Blackenstein* (both 1972), *Dr Black, Mr Hyde* (1976), *The House On Skull Mountain* (1974), which ghettoized *The Cat And The Canary*, and *Abby* (1974), the black *Exorcist*. The low budgets and minor stars in ever-sleazier schlock looked dated, but even Hammer's supernatural fairy tales were hokey when compared with the Friedkin juggernaut, and no amount of sexing up vampire flicks with lesbians (for example in *Twins Of Evil*, 1971) could compete with the tone and finesse of the major studios' output. In changing times Hammer lost its way and exhausted key franchises in one misjudged fiasco after another: when **Christopher Lee** strutted his groovy stuff in London in *Dracula AD 1972* he was instantly old-fashioned and when he was a property speculator in *The Satanic Rites Of Dracula* (1974) the flaws were compounded. Hammer's sad swansong was the completely banal *To the Devil … A Daughter* (1976), a misguided bid to beat *The Exorcist* at its own game.

Why didn't Hammer survive by exploiting the women-in-peril theme that erupted when

William Marshall in *Blacula* (1972), which like other blaxploitation movies was based on a familiar story

Dario Argento (see Icons) made the revolutionary *The Bird With The Crystal Plumage* (1970)? It remains a mystery. They tested the waters with a double bill of *Straight On Till Morning* (1972) and *Fear In The Night* (1972), but by the time a chance was there after **John Carpenter** introduced the world to **Michael Myers** (see Icons in both cases) in *Halloween* (1978, see Canon), and its copycat calendar chillers marked a return to the horror scene outside the Hollywood mainstream, they had already lost the plot.

But while Hammer did not enjoy success during the Seventies, in Britain former porn director **Pete Walker** created a gruesome and important collection of Home Counties horrors.

After testing the waters he directed three bona fide genre classics: *House Of Whipcord* (1974), which wallowed in sadomasochism, nudity and flagellation while purporting to be an attack on self-appointed guardians of moral propriety; *Frightmare* (1974), the first film to use bad review quotes on the poster to sell tickets; and *House Of Mortal Sin* (aka *The Confessional*, 1974), which featured a killer priest hiding behind Catholic Church piety and caused a tabloid sensation when Walker revealed he used real human blood.

Meanwhile another key figure in the history of horror was getting into his stride, in America: the enjoyably unclassifiable **Larry Cohen** shook up the genre with the cult hit *It's Alive* (1974), about mutant babies deformed by environmental pollution, and it was followed four years later by *It Lives Again* (and in 1987 by *It's Alive III: Island Of The Alive*). The similarly unconventional **David Cronenberg** (see Icons) made the intelligent sex-fest *Shivers* (aka *The Parasite Murders/ They Came From Within*, 1974, see Canon), which was an arthouse hit.

While Cohen's quirky, inspired films were notable for their irony and Cronenberg's *Shivers* was typical of his statements about contemporary society, each of Pete Walker's potent shockers exposed a malevolent netherworld of madness, obsession, moral obscenity and vindictive violence. And there was a similar, broader trend in America. While the blockbuster horror movie, for all its bluster and blood, was surprisingly conservative in its themes, its complete antithesis, apart from the rise of porno cash-ins like *Dracula Sucks* (1979), was the subversive American rural gothic in *The Last House On The Left* (1972) and *The Hills Have Eyes* (1977), both directed by **Wes Craven** (see Icons); and in the hugely influential *The Texas Chainsaw Massacre* (1974, see Canon) by Tobe Hooper (see Icons). All three

Lucio Fulci (1927-1996)

Anarchic horror specialist or reprehensible panderer indulging bloodthirsty like-minds? The jury is still out on the spaghetti sadism of Lucio Fulci, whose staggering output during the late Seventies and Eighties meant he nearly dethroned the master of Italian terror, Dario Argento. Although he directed many movies featuring graphic high-impact violence during the Seventies, such as *Don't Torture A Duckling* (1972), Fulci didn't get into his stride until *Zombie Flesh-Eaters* (1979), promoted in Italy as *Zombi 2*, which ripped off *Dawn Of The Dead* (*Zombi*, 1978) without George A. Romero's blessing. The eye-gouging, throat-ripping splatter show revitalized the Italian exploitation industry overnight and made Fulci a horror marquee name. The autobiographical *Nightmare Concert* (1990) featured Fulci playing himself as a troubled horror film director.

radical movies showed sensationalist images that had never been seen on screen before and each broke the accepted mould for what constituted horror. Even Linda Blair's foul-mouthed cursing in *The Exorcist* paled in comparison with a penis being bitten off and a girl being hung on a meat hook.

It took financially challenged radicals to rediscover the shocking power and bestial nature of the genre, which had also been evident in foreign films that reached America, such as the Australian survival horror *Night Of Fear* (1973) and, from Mexico, **René Cardona's** *Supervivientes de los Andes* (*Survive!*, 1976), the true story of plane crash survivors. But, with headway being made in special effects and prosthetic make-up by **Dick Smith** (*The Exorcist*) and **Tom Savini** (*Dawn Of The Dead*, 1978, see Canon), horror soon went through the taste barrier in Hollywood

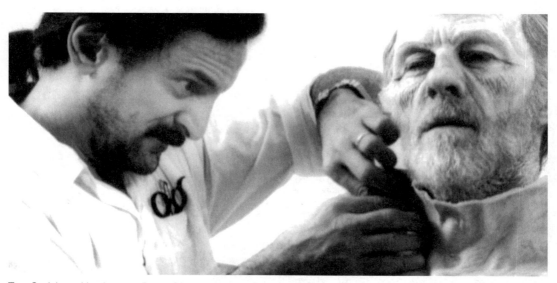

Tom Savini, working here on Bingo O'Malley for *Two Evil Eyes (1990)* after pioneering make-up work in the Seventies

— as exemplified by **Abel Ferrara**'s urban gothic *The Driller Killer* (1979), about a druggie maniac clearing winos from the streets — and in the Eighties it was firmly on the other side.

The Bird With The Crystal Plumage
dir Dario Argento, 1970, It/Ger, 98m

Who is the modern-day Jack the Ripper holding Rome in a grip of terror? Blocked writer Sam Dalmas (Tony Musante) knows that he's witnessed a vital clue – but what exactly was it? Argento's *giallo* trendsetter, scored by Ennio Morricone, is a glossily gory cosmopolitan whodunnit firmly entrenched in Hitchcockian paranoia and baroque style, which has echoes in films ranging from *Klute* (1971) to *Dressed To Kill* (1980).

The Devils
dir Ken Russell, 1971, UK, 111m

Ken Russell's adaptation of Aldous Huxley's non-fiction book *The Devils Of Loudon*, with sets by Derek Jarman based on those in *Metropolis* (1927), was hugely controversial and much censored. Oliver Reed gives his finest performance as a priest, Urbain Grandier, the erotic fantasy butt of the slanderous accusations of nun Sister Jeanne (Vanessa Redgrave). Laden with sexual perversion, demonic possession and gory torture, it's an excessive but brilliant study of madness, repression and bigotry.

Don't Look Now
dir Nicolas Roeg, 1974, UK/It, 110m

A tale of ordinary people who have suffered bereavement is at the heart of this arthouse mosaic of the mental, physical and spiritual complexities of real life. After the tragic drowning of their daughter, John and Laura Baxter (Donald Sutherland and Julie Christie) go to Venice, where she encounters a blind psychic conveying comforting messages from the other side; and soon John thinks he is seeing his daughter's ghost dressed in a red raincoat. It's a brilliant, engrossing, multi-dimensional examination of extra-sensory perception and human scepticism.

The Rocky Horror Picture Show
dir Jim Sharman, 1975, UK, 101m

This bright, breezy and camp adaptation of Richard O'Brien's hit stage musical, sending up *Frankenstein*, haunted house mysteries, glam-rock and pansexual stereotypes, is the Queen Mother of cult horror movies. Naïve newlyweds Brad and Janet (Barry Bostwick and Susan Sarandon) take refuge in a creepy castle where Dr Frank-N-Furter and other transsexual aliens are creating the perfect He-Man stud: cue fabulous entertainment, with smart horror references, electrifying musical numbers and infectious energy that created a midnight sing-along sensation.

The Eighties

Tired of seeing upstart independent companies making a fortune from shockers such as *Halloween* and *The Amityville Horror* (1979), **Paramount** were determined to exploit audiences' growing thirst for bloody horror entertainment, and picking up for distribution a cheaply made, obscure film about teenagers in jeopardy proved a canny move: *Friday The 13th* (1980) — and its subject

Troma

There are bad movies and there are Troma movies. Founded in 1974 by Lloyd Kaufman and Michael Herz, Troma was the home of *The Toxic Avenger* (1985), the crude shocker that put their crass crusading ethos on the map. Much was made in the Eighties horror press of the committed Troma team's approach to the genre: pick up a film for peanuts, annoy the director/producer with penny-pinching budgeting, gear the advertising to the appropriate crowd and start counting the cash. For the most part the movies, featuring buckets of blood, promiscuous sexuality and slapstick violence and including *Girls School Screamers* (1986), *Tromeo & Juliet* (1996) and *Terror Firmer* (1999), are almost unwatchable. Kaufman has said that they are all satires on contemporary issues.

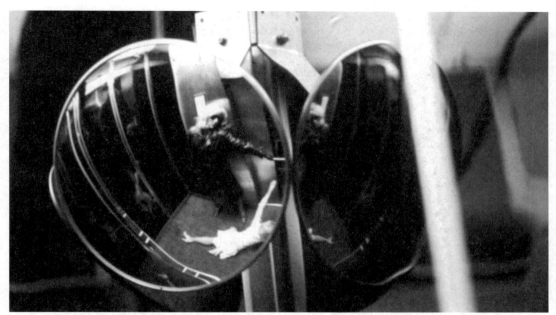

In Brian De Palma's *Dressed To Kill* (1980) the devil is in the detail

Jason Voorhees (see Icons) – became a huge commercial success, and was highly influential. Only three years earlier, when **20th Century Fox** had raked in the cash from releasing *Suspiria* (1977, see Canon), they had hidden behind a subsidiary corporation, International Classics Inc., but after Paramount's decision every major company followed suit, with Columbia, Warner Bros and MGM releasing *Happy Birthday To Me* (1980), *Wolfen* (1981) and *The Beast Within* (1982) respectively.

The "have promiscuous sex and die" theme of both *Halloween* and *Friday The 13th* subsequently got taken to its logical conclusion in a welter of "calendar date" horrors. Every holiday, tradition or event was called upon for movies ranging from *New Year's Evil* to *Mother's Day* (both 1980),

before the AIDS epidemic made the sexual content socially unacceptable. (In 1987 Larry Cohen was the first filmmaker to refer to AIDS through a vampire blood plague, in *A Return To Salem's Lot*.) Meanwhile assorted derivative psychopaths stalked numerous campsite/campus locations, in films including *The Burning*, *Night School* and *The Boogeyman* (all 1980).

Sequels to all the horror hits, including the groundbreaking *A Nightmare On Elm Street* (1985, see Canon), became *de rigueur*, the open ending being seen as a legitimate narrative structure, and these follow-ups proliferated to a degree not seen since Universal's heyday in the Thirties. Meanwhile an explosion in explicit horror gave rise to heated, if usually uninformed, debates over films such as *Don't Answer The Phone* (1980), for gross imagery, and *Dressed To Kill* (1980) by **Brian De Palma** (see Icons), for violence against women; the explosion was driven by more sophisticated, "the gore the merrier" special effects, which *An American Werewolf In London* (1981, see Canon) vividly showcased.

Technology also helped Stanley Kubrick when he tried his hand at horror: his use of the Steadicam in *The Shining* (1980, see Canon) was pioneering, though as a whole the film pleased mainstream cinemagoers more than die-hard horror fans. There was also in the early Eighties a revival of the three-dimensional process, fuelled by the unpredicted box-office success of *Friday the 13th Part 3 3-D* (1982), with other movies including *Parasite* (1982), *Amityville 3-D* and *Jaws 3-D* (both 1983). But lower-budget films also succeeded, such as *The Evil Dead* (1981, see Canon) from director **Sam Raimi** (see Icons), which became a cult zombie classic.

It was because of **home video recorders** that most of the vitriolic argument, mainly in the UK, was filtering into mainstream discussion. They had arrived on the market in the late Seventies and rapidly became a consumer staple, and while the major studios dithered about releasing blockbusters on tape because of piracy concerns, enterprising distributors filled the empty shelves of video rental stores with anything they could lay their hands on. This usually meant the controversial (*Possession*, 1981), and the lurid (*Nightmares In A Damaged Brain*, 1981), and European cannibal/zombie shockers (*Cannibal Apocalypse*, 1980), which would rarely have achieved a widespread cinema release because of censorship issues. Graphic horror scenes and mutilation shots were even used on the video covers for brazen promotion.

The overnight popularity of the VHS and

Betamax tape formats caught British authorities napping. There was no law about movies on video having to carry a rating certificate, so underage children along with genre enthusiasts were watching what was once deemed forbidden. Escalating tabloid furore and a gory back page advertisement in the January 1982 issue of *Television And Video Retailer* for *The Driller Killer* put the nail in the coffin of the exploitation bonanza, and eventually this led to video censorship guidelines on the statute books. Few other countries in the world were as affected by this issue.

Video had further effects on the horror film. Many low-budget movies made more money when released on video than in the cinema, so theatrical outings were often bypassed, giving rise

Video nasties

In Britain in May 1982 *The Sunday Times* carried a feature under the headline "How High Street Horror Is Invading The Home". It reported that because of the new industry's unregulated practices the video trade's biggest money-spinners were dubbed "nasties" and were as far removed from traditional horror suspense as possible, dwelling on graphic scenes of murder, rape, castration, sadomasochism and cannibalism. As other newspapers joined the *Daily Mail*'s "Ban the sadist videos" campaign, the Director of Public Prosecutions published an official list of the main offenders – which quickly became a shopping guide for some horror buffs. The rushed 1984 Video Recordings Act, outlawing videos without a governmentally approved certificate, failed to differentiate between the shoddy exploiter and bona fide masterpiece. And the issue of censorship did not go away, rearing its head in 1993 when a judge linked the infamous Jamie Bulger murder to *Child's Play 3* (1991).

to the "straight-to-video" tag that often implied that the product was down-market schlock. But the obvious next step was for companies to devote themselves to producing budget-conscious horror movies for the straight-to-video market alone with no intention at all of a cinema release. Enter, among others, **Charles Band**, producer of *Re-Animator* (1985, see Canon) and director of *Trancers* (1984), who launched Full Moon Video and pumped out a competent collection of chillers, including the above-average *Puppetmaster* (1989) series.

Also influencing the horror being watched in the West during the Eighties were new international markets. Towards the end of the decade came the first horror from Hong Kong to have a genuine impact outside its home, *A Chinese Ghost Story* (1987), produced by Tsui Hark. And from Spain, director **Agustin Villaronga**'s *Tras el cristal* (*In A Glass Cage*, 1987) controversially stretched the boundaries of the genre. That same year was also notable for the success of two vampire movies, **Joel Schumacher**'s *The Lost Boys* and **Kathryn Bigelow**'s *Near Dark* (see Canon), which not only showed the influence of AIDS but was also a rare horror to be directed by a female.

By then, in the light of the video horror backlash, with outcries from pressure groups, prudent studios had begun to cut from their franchise earners splatter scenes that were covered in full-page spreads in fan magazines before the films were released. The Hollywood powerhouses began to mount more watered-down horror – *Fright Night* (1985), *House* (1986) – or mega-budget family-friendly fear laden with special effects, such as *Gremlins* and *Ghostbusters* (both 1984). Yet against this conservative backdrop the occasional oddball or subversive horror would often cut through, and after the fears regarding

the video revolution receded in the latter part of the decade, these kinds of film, including *Hellraiser, Brain Damage, Henry: Portrait Of A Serial Killer* (all 1987), *Beetlejuice* and *Lady In White* (both 1988), all unshackled the genre from the corner it had painted itself into.

Friday The 13th
dir Sean S. Cunningham, 1980, US, 95m

The landmark slasher, about the reopening of a summer camp twenty years after a drowning and two murders there, propelled low-budget independent splatter into the big time and kicked off a franchise, as well as many imitators. The one-note plot – systematic slaying by a relentless killer – is empty-headed, but it's fast-paced and imaginatively graphic, thanks to the make-up king Tom Savini, who also thought of the ending. The sleepy climax at the lake steals wholesale from *Carrie* (1976, see Canon) – but it remains fabulously effective.

Hellraiser
dir Clive Barker, 1987, UK, 93m

Best known for his fright fiction, Barker proved he could direct in the film version of his novella *The Hellbound Heart*, a surreal and claustrophobic study in outrageously sadomasochistic horror in which owning an Oriental puzzle box leads to the thresholds of sensual pleasure and pain. An instant success, which brought a more sobering atmosphere to late Eighties horror, it launched Pinhead (Doug Bradley) on the growing "meet your favourite horror maniac" convention circuit, and Barker never bettered his delicious debut.

Angustia (Anguish)
dir Bigas Luna, 1988, Sp, 89m

The trickiest of chiller conceits is offered in this meditation on the medium of horror. While the viewer watches oedipal eye-gouger John, Luna cuts to an audience watching this take place within the slasher movie *The Mommy* (directed by Anul Sagib!). Then John goes into a cinema in which he blights the vision of members of the same "real" audience. Meanwhile in the other frame of action the shared audience is being held hostage. The final disclosure reveals the depth of Luna's grotesque reflections. It's a must-see.

Michael Rooker in the minimalist *Henry: Portrait Of A Serial Killer* (1987)

 ### Henry: Portrait Of A Serial Killer
dir John McNaughton, 1987, US, 83m

This underground study in slaughter psychology hits
home like a sledgehammer. Loosely based on the chilling
confessions of Henry Lee Lucas, it follows him and his
accomplices and forces the audience to identify with him
to a harrowing degree. Groundbreaking in its thematic use
of video (it was heavily censored for the sequence where a
family are brutalized on tape), its minimalist form is riveting
and the uncompromising glimpses into cold-blooded minds
are sickening rather than visually upsetting.

The Nineties

During the nineties video continued to mould the
horror film in unpredictable ways. An emerging
army of fanboys, rather than being limited by what
was showing in cinemas, was watching as many
horror titles as they could. An exhausting number
of horror films was available, and they weren't just
new releases; the video industry was pouncing on
entire back catalogues and thrusting them onto a
glutted market. The whole genre could be rented
or purchased on any High Street. And the **Digital
Versatile Disc**, far more friendly than the connoisseur collector's laserdisc, was poised to become
a new, improved home entertainment format,
which, to an even greater extent than the video,
meant that the money spent making a film could
be earned back without a theatrical release.

Horror on video was the cinematic equivalent
of junk food, and the steady diet was turning a

Guillermo del Toro

There are some directors who simply get the job done, but there are others, including Mexican-born Guillermo del Toro – a horror fan first, then a brilliant director – who truly care about creating popular art in their favourite genre. He has crafted some of horror's most unusual and elegiac works. *Cronos* (1993), a delicious modern twist to vampire legend, features an antiques dealer (Federico Luppi) discovering the secret to eternal life, and the typically understated set piece in which he licks blood from a white-tiled toilet floor is one of the most memorable moments of Nineties horror. *The Devil's Backbone* (2001), set in an orphanage during the Spanish Civil War, combines supernatural dread and sophisticated political commentary, and Toro's pet project *Hellboy* (2004) was the best film in the horror comic sub-genre.

Federico Luppi as an antiques dealer in *Cronos*

couch potato generation into horror trivia buffs with movie-making ambitions; this was best exemplified by video store clerk Quentin Tarantino, whose violent crime thriller *Reservoir Dogs* (1992) and vampire genre-bender *From Dusk Till Dawn* (1996) were driven by cult horror references.

And, pandering successfully to the cine-literate demographic raised on a decade of bloodletting and new-style boogey men, scriptwriter **Kevin Williamson** fashioned the self-reflexive *Scream* (1996, see Canon) for director **Wes Craven** and the post-modern *Halloween* homage hit the nail on

Drew Barrymore during her cameo in *Scream* (1996)

(1994). Each lengthy opus was directed by a well-known name – **Francis Ford Coppola** and **Kenneth Branagh** respectively – and each pretentiously included the authors' name in the title to suggest (erroneously) a more literary version. The failure meant that other staples were not adapted directly; instead, classic themes were placed in more modern retellings.

Coppola's conceit cleverly included references to silent era filmmaking techniques and traded on the new computer graphics industry that was allowing artists to put their wildest ideas on screen. Gone were the jerky stop-motion dinosaurs of "imagineer" Ray Harryhausen's *One Million Years BC* and in came the fluid, ultra-realistic *Jurassic Park* (1993) and *The Mummy (*1999), where creatures the world had forgotten could be seen in high-definition animation form. But just like foam latex prosthetics in the Eighties, in the Nineties computer-generated imagery was seen as the answer to everything, solved nothing if the story wasn't strong enough, and became overused to a distracting degree.

Other forms of horror were assimilated into mainstream cinema more than ever before. Following the success of *Fatal Attraction* (1987), in the early Nineties faux slasher titles proliferated, with *The Hand That Rocks The Cradle*, *Cape Fear*, *Sleeping With The Enemy* (all 1991), *Basic Instinct* (1992) and *Shallow Grave* (1994) all asking what a horror movie is. And this burgeoning sub-genre gave the decade its biggest anti-hero – Hannibal Lecter, whose "fava beans and Chianti" cannibal charmer in **Jonathan Demme**'s masterfully creepy *The Silence Of The Lambs* (1991, see Canon) earned **Anthony Hopkins** an Oscar. As had also happened after *Psycho* thirty years earlier, modern horror had returned to the real world from the supernatural and indestructible ones haunted by Freddy Krueger (see Icons) and his masked maniac kin.

the head, and could not be equalled. The same audience was reading comic books and flocked to Alex Proyas's *The Crow* (1994) and Stephen Norrington's *Blade* (1998) in such vast numbers that this new source of material started to be mined, moving horror further into the mainstream.

Meanwhile, although long series still had their place, the genre returned to its roots with two lavish studio productions, *Bram Stoker's Dracula* (1992) and *Mary Shelley's Frankenstein*

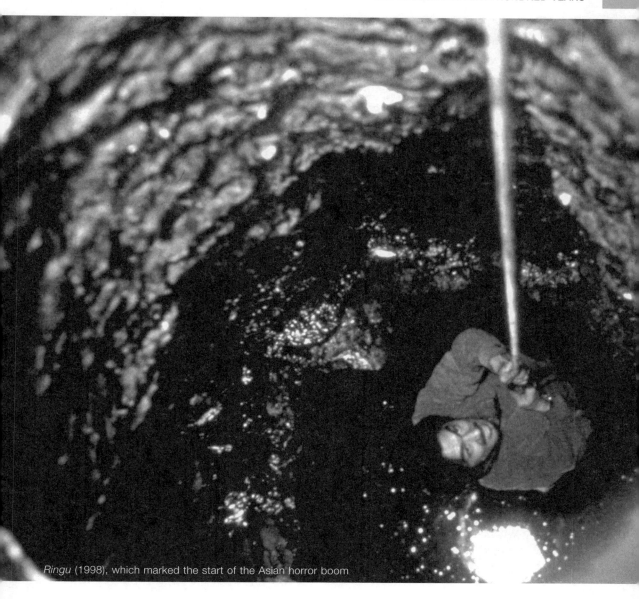

Ringu (1998), which marked the start of the Asian horror boom

And the real world continued to affect the genre. As the handover of Hong Kong to China in 1997 loomed, for example, many of the biggest names in horror there, such as Ronny Yu, went to America. The collapse of communism in Eastern Europe had proved less important for the genre, though it did inspire Christoph Schlingensief's *Das Deutsche Kettensägen Massaker* (*The German Chainsaw Massacre*, 1991), which had a theory about East Germans who disappeared. Later in the decade Spain returned to the international scene, with *Tesis* (*Thesis*, 1996), the debut of **Alejandro Amenábar**, and Álex de la Iglesia's *El día de la bestia* (*Day Of The Beast*, 1995), which showed that *The Exorcist* remained highly influential. From New Zealand came *Braindead* (1992, see Canon), the outrageous zombie shocker from **Peter Jackson** (see Icons) that was the most original work of the Nineties.

The end of the decade also saw the start of the Asian horror boom, after a period in which the region's horrors had been seen only in select arthouse cinemas, when **Hideo Nakata** and **Takashi Miike**, with *Ringu* (*The Ring*, 1998, see Canon) and *Audition* (1999) respectively, began to approach the sub-genre from an oriental perspective that harked back to the philosophy of producer Val Lewton. Many directors from the area, such as John Woo, had headed west for Hollywood careers, but Asian horror began its slow emergence from underground and its move to the multiplex because of those who stayed put. Meanwhile, Hollywood realized the truth of the adage that there are very few basic plots and up-and-coming filmmakers remade the films that inspired them; Gus Van Sant and Jan de Bont did this badly with *Psycho* (1998) and *The Haunting* (1999).

But it was *The Blair Witch Project* (1999) that propelled horror into the twenty-first century. Shot by amateurs on **digital camcorders** available in any technological equipment store, and using the power of the Internet for the first time to promote its supposed authenticity, the home movie horror made a fortune (and led to the establishment of online departments at PR companies). Its aesthetic has not been adopted, but it lit the way for many filmmakers in that the cheaper format was used to deliver equally professional results, in films such as *Collateral* (2004), by Michael Mann. And with the use of the Internet by horror geeks often making and breaking titles months before release, technology meant that more power lay with the people as the century drew to a close.

Candyman
dir Bernard Rose, 1992, US, 98m

"Look in the mirror, say his name five times and the Candyman will appear behind you," runs the urban legend in this triumphant adaptation of Clive Barker's *The Forbidden*. Virginia Madsen, who claims that she was hypnotized for some of the scenes, gives an amazing performance as a researcher who is looking into the legend of a hook-handed maniac when a murderer starts to bring dread to the Chicago ghetto.

Dust Devil
dir Richard Stanley, 1993, UK, 103m

African tribal myth is melded with politics in a mystical chiller powerfully linking black magic with the visual style of spaghetti Westerns. Hitch is an ancient shape-shifting demon collecting souls drawn to a drought-ridden town in the Namib Desert. The strength this evil medicine man is building is the reason that the country is on the brink of apocalyptic collapse – so thinks cop Ben Mukurob as the serial killer litters the wasteland with disfigured corpses.

Dellamorte dellamore (Cemetery Man)
dir Michele Soavi, It/Fr/Ger, 1994, 105m

Most horror movies are about the fear of dying; this dark tale is about the fear of living. Rupert Everett stars as a cemetery caretaker, Francesco Dellamorte, who tries to bury the living dead. When he meets She, mistakenly kills his perfect love, and is then cursed to see her face in every future female encounter, the zombie allegory turns into a chilling romance. It's the last truly great Italian horror.

The Blair Witch Project
dir Daniel Myrick & Eduardo Sanchez, 1999, US, 81m

The most successful independent production in history, this deliberately artless micro-budget fly-on-the-wall mockumentary details the attempt by three amateur filmmakers to uncover the facts about a legendary witch who kills anyone who enters her dark domain: the film is supposedly edited footage that was found a year after their disappearance. An exercise in creating atmosphere (screams in the night, twig sculptures) more than anything visceral, it's either the world's scariest movie or the biggest con trick that the public has ever fallen for.

From 2000

At the start of the millennium filmmakers continued to embrace the remake trend that Gus Van Sant and Jan de Bont had kicked off. There was a retooling of a William Castle gimmick picture, *Thir13en Ghosts* (2001), but the restyling then shifted to Seventies standards, with *The Texas Chainsaw Massacre* (2003) and *Dawn Of The Dead* (2004). The latter two movies were such blockbusters that every studio returned to their dusty vaults to look for titles to update that even people not interested in horror knew about, resulting in *The Amityville Horror*, *House Of Wax* (both 2005), *The Hills Have Eyes* and *The Evil Dead* (both scheduled for 2006).

The classic splatter titles were also driving all those in the horror industry's talent pool who, having grown up watching every famous and (more importantly) infamous title on video, realized that the best way of becoming a

director was still to make a low-budget horror movie that would more often than not earn its investment back in the ancillary markets such as television, cable and DVD. So Eli Roth helmed *Cabin Fever* (2003), a homage to *The Evil Dead*, Rob Zombie's *House Of 1000 Corpses* (2003) reworked *The Texas Chainsaw Massacre*, Tim Sullivan's *2001 Maniacs* (2005) followed *2000 Maniacs* and **Alexandre Aja's** *Switchblade Romance* (2003, see Canon) was a homage to *Death Weekend*. If films weren't being remade or referenced, they were being combined, and Universal's "versus" sub-genre was rekindled by

The Asian boom

By delving into the space between Western urban legend and Buddhism, at the turn of the century up-and-coming Oriental directors focused on Eastern concepts of spirituality and the supernatural that are not as undermined as they are in Occidental culture. When Hollywood acquired the rights to *Ringu* (1998) and the 2002 remake grossed a fortune, Asia was proclaimed "the next big thing" and, along with Hideo Nakata (*Dark Water*, 2002), Kinji Fukasuku (*Battle Royale*, 2000) and Takashi Shimizu (*The Grudge*, 2001), auteur directors quickly came to prominence. From Hong Kong, working in Thailand, there were the Pang brothers, (*The Eye*, 2002), from Korea there was Chan-wook Park (*Three … Extremes*, 2004), from Thailand there was Yuthlert Sippapak (*Buppah Rahtree: Scent Of The Night Flower*, 2003) and from the Philippines, Chito S. Rono (*Feng Shui*, 2004). Yet it was Takashi Miike who became the star of the Asian explosion, after years of haunting the festival circuit, primarily because he was its hardest worker. (He made seven features in 2001 alone!) The quality has been variable but much of his horror work is truly inspired, such as the zombie musical *The Happiness Of The Katakuris* (2001).

Thir13en Ghosts (2001), one of many remakes at the start of the new century

the face-offs *Freddy Vs Jason* (2003) and *Alien Vs Predator* (2004).

The *Dawn Of The Dead* remake in 2004 was also part of a return to the zombie fever that had infected horror movies in the late Seventies; contemporary opinion put the desire to see such gut-wrenching apocalyptic visions down to insecurity following September 11 and concerns about lives being too full of trivialities. After the surprise box-office hit *28 Days Later* (2002) from **Danny Boyle**, in which Britain is devastated by a rage virus, the undead started eating flesh again in ever increasing numbers: zombie master **George A. Romero**, with sobering skill, laced the fourth part of his socio-political series, *Land Of The Dead* (2005), with terrorist concerns, showing genius that

other films, such as *House Of The Dead*, *Undead* (both 2003) and *Choking Hazard* (2004) do not approach.

In Britain, thanks to tax breaks from the government, the early years of the new millennium proved very busy and varied for horror. Productions ranged from Stuart Urban's supernatural epic *Revelation* (2001), which *The Da Vinci Code* strikingly resembles, to Neil Marshall's werewolf update *Dog Soldiers* (2002), and from Roland Suso Richter's point-of-death chiller *The I Inside* (2003), to Craig Strachan's kitchen sink werewolf *Wild Country* (2005). Meanwhile the British comedy horror *Shaun Of The Dead* (2004) found favour with audiences worldwide thanks to its balanced blend of hardcore splatter and side-splitting comedy.

The Fantastic Factory

In 2000 Brian Yuzna, producer of *Re-Animator* (1985) and director of *Return Of The Living Dead 3* (1993), moved from Los Angeles to Barcelona following an invitation from top Spanish producer Julio Fernandez. Tired of paying too much for international horrors to distribute in Spain through his company Filmax, Fernandez bankrolled The Fantastic Factory, a studio label that was modelled after Hammer and designed to provide a steady stream of horrors. The enterprise started badly with Yuzna's *Faust: Love Of The Damned* (2001), but it picked up steam with Stuart Gordon's *Dagon* (2002) and Yuzna's *Beyond Re-Animator* (2003). It then hit its stride and lived up to its Hammer allusions with Paco Plaza's gothic reality mystery *Romasanta: The Werewolf Hunt* (2004), and the flow continues with Yuzna's *Rottweiler* and *Beneath Still Waters* and Luis de la Madrid's *The Nun* (all 2005).

This period also saw the video game movie finally take off – after a disastrous start in the Nineties, with *Super Mario Bros* (1993) and *Street Fighter* (1994) – *Resident Evil* (2002) spearheading the way forward. Before that zombie offshoot, directed by **Paul W. S. Anderson**, most video game movies failed because they couldn't replicate the interactive thrills created in the home or arcade, but horror, being such an emotionally charged genre, proved the best vehicle for the expectation. Increasingly large amounts of money were spent across all media, including computer game magazines, on mass-marketing campaigns for game-based films, including *Alone In The Dark*, *Resident Evil: Apocalypse* (both 2004), *Bloodrayne*, *Doom* (both 2005) and *Silent Hill* (scheduled for 2006). Meanwhile many studio-based horrors, including *The Mummy Returns* (2001), *Underworld* (2003) and *Van Helsing* (2004), were accused of appropriating the CGI-based video game look and manic feel.

Van Helsing (2004), which was clearly influenced by video games

Whether mediocre Western fare such as *White Noise* (2005) or American remakes of Asian hits, like *The Grudge* (2004), horror movies have been racking up enormous grosses, and the genre, after more than a hundred years of peaks and troughs, is more widely appealing and profitable than at any other time in its history.

Final Destination
dir James Wong, 2000, US, 98m

Survivors of a plane crash can't escape their true fate in this frightfully good supernatural premonition shocker. Every character surname is a nod to the heritage of horror – Chaney, Browning, Lewton, Hitchcock and so on – and each cleverly interlocking demise, drenched in an off-kilter atmosphere, evokes genuine scares. *Final Destination 2* (2002) was as smart, shuddery and gripping as its predecessor.

Jeepers Creepers
dir Victor Salva, 2001, Ger/US, 91m

Shocking and sensational, this superbly orchestrated flesh-snatching saga created a classic monster for the new millennium. The Creeper is a winged demon of folklore reborn for 23 days every 23rd spring to sniff out tasty body parts – and he wants Darry Jenner's eyes in a graphic, gripping variation on the psycho-from-Hell formula. In *Jeepers Creepers 2* (2003) The Creeper lays siege to college kids on a stranded bus and *Jeepers Creepers 3* (scheduled for 2006) shifts into the future.

The Others
dir Alejandro Amenábar, 2001, Sp/US, 104m

The Santiago-born director's English-language debut features Jersey housewife Grace Stewart (Nicole Kidman) and her two light-sensitive children waiting for her soldier husband to return from World War II. Relying on deliberately old-fashioned bumps in the night for its

spiralling spookiness, Amenábar, who appears as a dead man in a photograph, evokes the spirit of *The Innocents* for his neo-classic terror that relies on gothic mood and high-strung performance.

Saw
James Wan, 2004, US, 102m

Two men wake up chained to opposite walls in a filthy cell and a tape-recording tells one that unless he kills the other and commits suicide his family will be slaughtered. So begins this devious nerve-jangler, laden with sneaky twists and wincing turns. The gruesome games in this dazzling razor-sharp puzzler are the work of the infamous "jigsaw killer", who places his victims in life-or-death scenarios to teach them the value of being alive.

Night Watch
dir Timur Bekmambetov, 2004, Ru, 114m

The highest grossing Russian movie ever – and it's a horror! This fast-paced epic, based on the first part of Sergei Lukyanenko's bestselling trilogy, has hunters pursuing nocturnal demons in strict observance of an old treaty signed by the forces of light and darkness, and a "Great Other" who will determine the outcome. The stylized subtitling for export versions of this fast-paced SFX extravaganza often becomes an artistic statement itself: when a vampire strikes, for example, the red text drips off the screen.

Wolf Creek
dir Greg McLean, 2005, Aust, 95m

Two female British tourists and a Sydney surf dude visit the meteor crater in Wolf Creek National Park. When their car breaks down, bushman Mick Taylor (John Jarratt, in a blood-freezing portrayal of evil incarnate) offers to help, but lures the trio into a worst-case scenario of humiliation, torture and gory death. Harrowing, grisly, full of white-knuckle suspense, and based on a true story, McLean's impressive debut inevitably draws comparisons with *The Texas Chainsaw Massacre*.

Devon Sawa as Alex Chance Browning in the survival shocker *Final Destination* (2000), in which the characters' names acknowledge horror's heroes

The Canon: 50 horror classics

An iconic image from *The Exorcist* (1973), a
landmark film that inspired many cash-ins

The Canon:
50 horror classics

An American Werewolf In London

dir John Landis, 1981, UK, 97m

cast David Naughton, Jenny Agutter, Griffin Dunne, John Woodvine, Brian Glover, Rik Mayall *cin* Robert Paynter *m* Elmer Bernstein

Among the public there was a lycanthropic battle royal in 1981, between **Joe Dante**'s *The Howling*, with make-up designed and created by Rob Bottin, and **John Landis**'s *An American Werewolf In London*, with make-up by Rick Baker. But for the devoted fright fan there was no contest. Landis's creature feature won paws down and Baker won an Oscar for his prosthetics and groundbreaking werewolf transformation.

The astonishing transformation of David Kessler (David Naughton), devised by Rick Baker

"From the director of *National Lampoon's Animal House* – a different kind of animal" roared the promotional trailer for Landis's pet project, which he wrote in 1969, long before he had even turned director with *Schlock* in 1973. "The movie is very scary, extremely violent and upsetting," said Landis. "It is very Greek in that respect: you get to like people, and then you watch them destroyed. Primarily I wanted to scare the shit out of you." Landis achieved that aim with a brilliant meld of enjoyable laughs and hair-raising terror that set the standard for the modern werewolf movie. The unrelated cash-in *An American Werewolf In Paris* (1997) was hopeless.

Young Americans David Kessler (**David Naughton**) and Jack Goodman (**Griffin Dunne**) are attacked by a werewolf while backpacking at night on the English moors. The last thing that David remembers from before he passes out is the sight of Jack's mangled body as the snarling creature then turns towards him…

Three weeks later David wakes up in a London hospital and, although he is told that Jack's body has been sent back to the States for burial, he is visited repeatedly by his friend's ghost, urging him to commit suicide to stop himself from turning into a wolf-man at the next full moon. Believing Jack to be just a hallucination, David moves in with his new lover, nurse Alex Price (**Jenny Agutter**). But, sure enough, he turns into the predicted werewolf and roams through London committing brutal murders. It all reaches a stunning climax in a Piccadilly Circus cinema, where David's mutilated victims urge him to take his life, and London's West End is then the scene of a massive car pile-up.

The superbly cast Naughton and Dunne ground the movie effortlessly with their easy sparring, which is peppered with witty dialogue; and their likeability means that the grisly flow of their predicament can be identified with. The David and Alex romance is sweet without being cloying and another reason why audiences sympathize with David and want him to overcome the curse. The film has many in-joke horror references (David's mention of Lon Chaney Jr's *The Wolf Man*), and Landis also has great fun with the soundtrack – all the songs feature the word "moon" in the title.

But it's mainly for Rick Baker's incredibly realistic creation of a metamorphosis from man to beast that Landis's lycanthropic landmark will always be remembered. David's bones and muscles bend and reform, his flesh moves, his backbone ripples, his face distorts as his jaw extends and his hair sprouts everywhere. It's absolutely astonishing.

Black Sunday
(La maschera del demonio)

dir **Mario Bava, 1960, It, 88m, b/w**
cast **Barbara Steele, John Richardson, Ivo Garrani, Andrea Checchi, Arturo Dominici** *cin* **Mario Bava** *m* **Roberto Nicolosi**

Filming in sepulchral black and white, acclaimed Italian cinematographer **Mario Bava** turned director with *Black Sunday* and created one of the most beautiful and disturbing of all horror films. Opening with a legendary shock – a spiked mask hammered onto the face of a cursing witch, an image considered so potent that the film was banned in Britain for seven years – Bava's chiaroscuro masterpiece also crowned former Rank starlet **Barbara Steele** as the queen of Italian horror.

Based on Bava's favourite ghost story from Russian folklore, *The Vij* by Nikolai Gogol, it revolves around the one day in every century when, according to superstitious tradition, Satan is allowed to freely walk the Earth and witches return to haunt their descendants. Put to gruesome death by the Inquisition of a province in Middle Europe, Princess Asa (Steele) and her lover Javutich (**Arturo Dominici**) are accused of witchcraft and vampirism and burnt at the stake by her brother. Two hundred years later, doctors Kruvajan (**Andrea Checchi**) and Gorobek (**John Richardson**, who in 1966 starred in *One Million Years BC*) are travelling to Moscow when their carriage breaks down next to the graveyard where Asa's coffin rests. Removing the mask from her face and finding it horrifically pitted, Kruvajan accidentally cuts his hand and the spilt blood begins its reviving process on the vengeful witch. Outside the cemetery Gorobek meets and becomes smitten by Princess Katia (Steele again), the daughter of Prince Vajda (**Ivo Garrani**); he fears for her safety because of the resemblance to her demonic ancestor. His concerns are well founded because the resurrected Asa summons Javutich from his grave, and inducts Kruvajan to her dark side, to help her exact terrible revenge and take over Katia's identity.

Bava's malefic world is a magnificently art-directed spectral landscape of dark mountains set against moody skies, mist-shrouded forests where branches clutch at travellers, and ornate black coaches floating in slow-motion past scenes of decadent decay. Abetted by a restless moving camera that travels through cobwebby sets crawling with insects – most effective when Javutich is followed down a secret passageway leading to Asa's tomb – Bava conveyed every tense emotion in visual terms, thanks to his technical background. The resulting ambience of a nightmare fairy tale is an undisputed and unsurpassed pinnacle of visionary poetry that would influence the work of many self-confessed rabid fans, including **Joe Dante**, who directed *The Howling* (1980), and **Tim Burton**, who directed *Sleepy Hollow* (1999). Bava stated: "Filmed entirely with a dolly because of time and money, the photography in a horror film is 70 percent of its effectiveness; it creates all the atmosphere."

Most of the other 30 percent came from horror icon Barbara Steele in her quintessential performance. Steele's otherworldly persona is captured perfectly by Bava's camera, which successfully brought out her dark vampire/sexy virgin duality. In casting Asa/

Barbara Steele (1937-)

Steele by name, steely by nature, the first femme fatale to be crowned the undisputed queen of horror left the Rank Organisation's "charm school" and fled to Rome after her talent was wasted in harmless fluff such as *Bachelor Of Hearts* (1958). Yet she had no idea that she'd soon be typecast as the sultry siren of supernatural shockers. Employed for her smouldering dark looks and brooding sexuality, Steele made her incredible debut as both vampire and victim in *Black Sunday*, and in her Italian career playing roles of good and evil would be a constant. Her incandescent beauty and screen presence won her a royal sobriquet to savour, but her working-class accent was dubbed over in most films, including *The Pit And The Pendulum* (1961). Riccardo Freda's kinky *The Terror Of Dr Hichcock* (1962) and its follow-up *Lo spettro* (*The Ghost*, 1963) are two of the best movies she appeared in, but she was rightly convinced that horror was sabotaging her mainstream career – Fellini cast her in *8 1/2* (1963) and then cut her out – and she backed away from numerous projects; although her attitude towards her classification has softened, it's a stance that her legion of horror admirers has grudgingly accepted. She resurfaced in America for supporting roles in *Piranha* (1978) and *Silent Scream* (1980) and then moved into the production arena, where she was involved in the *Dark Shadows* TV horror soap in 1990.

Katia so well, Bava took hold of a horror cliché and remoulded it in baroque Italian terms – and that was the key to *Black Sunday*'s success. From the fog-shrouded mausoleums to the shadowy castle interiors, Bava elevated tired motifs and the new renditions sparkled.

Braindead

dir Peter Jackson, 1992, NZ, 104m

cast Timothy Balme, Diane Peñalver, Elizabeth Moody, Ian Watkin, Brenda Kendall *cin* Murray Milne *m* Peter Dasent

The goriest zombie horror ever made bar none. **Peter Jackson** raised the blood bar to dizzying heights with his groundbreaking masterpiece *Braindead* and no one has tried to match him. They couldn't. Jackson's landmark splat-stick black comedy, in which custard pies are replaced with fountains from assorted body parts, was the most original and astounding work of the 1990s and there will never be a bloodier, more hilarious, more outrageous, gross-out zombie shocker.

Jackson goes all the way, then beyond and then even further than you might have thought possible in this extraordinary accomplishment, which he scripted with his future wife **Frances Walsh** and **Stephen Sinclair**; the trio had worked on the screenplay for Jackson's *Meet The Feebles* (1989) and went on to glory with his *Lord Of The Rings* films (2001-2003). "It's a rot-infested romance", explained Jackson. "A social metaphor for a pretty universal theme. Here's this guy who lives at home with his domineering mother and at some point there's going to be another woman in his life. It's set in the Fifties to make that more believable and the scary tension is the contrast between the two women who want his attention taken to the ultimate crazed, splatter limits."

The sequence before the credits barely hints at the carnage to come. In the low-rent style of Indiana Jones, a hunter (Jackson himself) evades natives to get a sacred Sumatran rat-monkey, for delivery to Wellington Zoo in New Zealand. However, the vicious creature bites him, and every infected body appendage is hacked off because the simian carries a virus that turns victims into the living dead. The demon monkey, brought to life in jerky stop-motion à la *Jason And The Argonauts* (1963) in homage to veteran special effects man Ray Harryhausen, also sinks its toxic fangs into Vera Cosgrove (**Elizabeth Moody**) when she follows her browbeaten son Lionel (**Timothy Balme**) to the zoo for his clandestine date with shop girl Paquita (**Diana Peñalver**).

When the putrefying venom transforms his mother into a rabid flesh-eater, Lionel keeps some semblance of normality in their lives by faking her funeral. But as Vera's victims grow in numbers, the strain on Lionel matches the one on the cellar door padlocks that are holding his new undead "family" at bay. Then slimy uncle Les (**Ian Watkin**) arrives to lay an inheritance claim on the house; and when he throws a huge celebration party – just as Lionel accidentally injects animal stimulant into his rotting "guests" instead of poison – the scene is set for atrocious splattering on the grandest of scales.

Father McGruder (Stuart Devenie) in Peter Jackson's astounding *gore de force*

Braindead is Jackson in show-stopping form and is suffused with his unique immature charm and weird world vision. His flamboyant *gore de force* includes kung-fu priests, shots from the point of view of a severed head, murderous spinal columns, Godzilla-size Vera trying to push Lionel back into her womb and weapons ranging from blenders and ornamental flying ducks to lawnmower blades and umbilical cords – and this is the tip of a blood-soaked iceberg that is unparalleled. Brilliantly brought to life by designers **Bob McCarron** and **Richard Taylor**, it was a showcase opportunity for artists that will never be repeated. The comic highlight is Lionel trying to pacify zombie baby Selwyn in a park by beating him into submission. The gory highlight is, well, the rest of the movie.

The Bride Of Frankenstein

dir **James Whale, 1935, US, 80m, b/w**
cast **Boris Karloff, Colin Clive, Valerie Hobson, Ernest Thesiger, Elsa Lanchester, Dwight Frye, Gavin Gordon** *cin* **John Mescall** *m* **Franz Waxman**

The finest of all the Frankenstein movies proved that a sequel could be better than the original. With its directorial style, visual design and literate scripting, yeoman performances from never-better **Boris Karloff** and **Ernest Thesiger**, superior score from Franz Waxman, and classy minute detail, *The Bride Of Frankenstein* is practically unsurpassed.

The offbeat Grand Guignol fairy tale laid down in *Frankenstein* (1931) is given an injection of dynamism and a richer, quirkier, wittier and more lavish texture. Whereas the original had been something of a novelty act at the dawn of sound, and the first American movie with the type of mad scientist usually seen only in badly distributed weird German movies, the sequel emphatically marked the peak of Universal's horror cycle.

After a prologue where author Mary Shelley (**Elsa Lanchester**) is persuaded by Lord Byron (**Gavin Gordon**) to continue her

Elsa Lanchester in a brief but
almost show-stealing performance

famous story, it's revealed that the Monster (Karloff) didn't die in
the mill fire but escaped further villager hounding by taking refuge
with a blind hermit (**O. P. Heggie**) who teaches him how to talk.
(Karloff's 44–word vocabulary came from the test papers of the child
actors at Universal's on-site school.)

Recognized by hunters, the Monster then falls under the evil
influence of Dr Pretorius (**Ernest Thesiger**), the former teacher
of Henry Frankenstein (**Colin Clive**) who wants to create a race
of monsters and has been growing experimental homunculi from
cultures. The Monster and Pretorius then force the still recuperating
Frankenstein to create a mate to ease the Monster's loneliness. But
when the moment arrives for him to claim his bride (**Lanchester**

again), she flinches in terror and the grief-stricken creature destroys himself and everyone else after permitting Frankenstein to join his wife Elizabeth (**Valerie Hobson**) in safety.

Neither **James Whale** nor his cameraman John Mescall strove for any realism at all in this completely set-bound visualization of the second half of Shelley's novel, about the Monster's need for female companionship. The claustrophobic castle, the candle-lit chambers, the bleak expressionistic forest and the electric look of the non-specific period laboratory are all stunningly realized at off-kilter angles to suggest Frankenstein and his creation's mutual derangement.

The big moment when the synthetic Bride begins to breathe is spellbinding. Basing her birdlike movements on the quick darting of swans, and dressed in a white shroud, perched on 30-inch stilts, with a bushy Nefertiti hair-do accompanied by lightning streaks, Lanchester nearly manages to steal the film from under Karloff's nose in her brief yet bravura showcase. She was highlighted by the ghostly hollow ring of wedding bells and timpani to suggest her beating heart by Franz Waxman, one of the first composers to use musical leitmotifs for his screen characters. (He successfully sued Rodgers and Hammerstein for stealing his eerie three-note "Bride's Theme" for their "Bali Hai" song in the hit musical *South Pacific*.)

While the film evokes a genuine pathos among its high-tone chills, displaying Whale's trademark of bold, macabre humour, his distaste for religion is equally brazen in the symbolic use of the Monster in parallels with Christ. And the intolerance subtext can easily be read in terms of his own homosexual experiences in closeted Hollywood. Karloff, for his part, gives his best and most powerful performance, once again under Jack Pierce's tremendous make-up design, expressing the Monster's complexity and soul. Breathtaking in its emotional and visual scope, *The Bride Of Frankenstein* fully deserves its lofty status as a genre institution.

The Cabinet Of Dr Caligari (Das Kabinett des Dr Caligari)

dir **Robert Wiene, 1919, Ger, 82m, b/w**
cast **Werner Krauss, Conrad Veidt, Lil Dagover, Friedrich Feher, Hans Heinz von Twardowski** *cin* **Willy Hameister**

Two Eastern Europeans changed the face of early silent cinema and in doing so created the first horror film of real artistic quality when, in 1919, the Czech **Hans Janowitz** and the Austrian **Carl Mayer** sold a film script to **Erich Pommer**, director of the pioneering Decla Film Company in Berlin, based on events from their turbulent lives.

The Cabinet Of Dr Caligari, which showed that a film's design could express mental states

Strolling down the Reeperbahn in Hamburg in 1913, Janowitz saw a respectable gentlemen emerge from behind bushes, adjust his clothes and merge into the evening crowd. The next day, newspapers carried a story about a young girl who had been raped and murdered in exactly the same place. Convinced that he'd seen the murderer, Janowitz attended the girl's funeral and saw his suspect again. The killer was never apprehended and Janowitz became obsessed by the possibility that casual assassins were freely roaming the streets laughing at the authorities.

When he met fellow writer Mayer, who shared his desire for a career in film, Janowitz had just been discharged from the army, because a psychiatrist had attributed his rebellious attitude to mental instability. For recreation the friends would go to funfairs and one night they attended a "Man and Machine" sideshow, in which a stooge carried out feats of strength and foretold the future while supposedly in a trance. This attraction, Janowitz's fixation with the murder and Mayer's bitterness at regimentation were transferred to paper in a savage indictment of bourgeois hypocrisy. Their script, referring in its title to an officer character described by Stendhal, dealt with a travelling magician, Dr Caligari (**Werner Krauss**) and the somnambulist assistant Cesare (**Conrad Veidt**), who is kept in a coffin-shaped cabinet and who, through hypnosis, is led to kidnap and murder.

The film was due to be directed by future *Metropolis* visionary **Fritz Lang**, whose planned triptych including *The Spiders* (1919) was taking a long time to complete, but the project was eventually handed over to **Robert Wiene**, who, although not a name of note in cinema, was conversant with Berlin's bustling art scene. And the big story during this period after World War I was Expressionism, a movement seeking to restore man to the centre of his universe, in contrast to the old orders, where nature was the focus. Accordingly, objects, light and shadows were reshaped into an individual world-view, and the best exponents of this chaotic art form were the avant-garde group *Der Sturm*; so Wiene hired its principal purveyors, **Walter Reiman**, **Walter Röhrig** and **Hermann Warm**, as designers. This was not only to make his film a timely conversation piece but also because electricity cost a fortune, and the canvas set with painted highlights saved money.

To explain this stylized look Wiene changed the script, adding a framing device that made the story the ravings of an asy-

Asylums

It's a primal fear to be considered insane and unable to prove the contrary, and to be locked up for life in a madhouse, and *Bedlam* (1946), *Shock Corridor* (1963) and *The Dead Pit* (1989) concern precisely those worries. The lunatics taking over the asylum, taken from Edgar Allan Poe's *The System Of Dr Tarr And Professor Fether*, is a common horror theme, as used in *The Monster* (1925), *Dr Tarr's Torture Dungeon* (1971) and *Don't Look In The Basement* (1972), and plot twists revolving around who is sane and who isn't are central to *The Cabinet Of Dr Caligari* (1919) and *Asylum* (1972). But most frequently madhouses are places where psychopaths escape from, as is the case in films ranging from *The Cat And The Canary* (1927) to *Halloween* (1978). Don't any of them have decent security?

lum inmate. Janowitz and Mayer were furious. It obliterated their political polemic: that a Caligari-esque Prussian establishment was turning the German population into zombie-like Cesare figures. But *Caligari*'s influence, as one of the most timeless artefacts of the twentieth century, would have nothing to do with any outdated messages. Wiene's madman's vision of the world was the first movie to suggest psychological horror as an alternative to physically frightening shocks and demonstrated that visual design could express emotional fracture and mental states – the standout sequence is the heroine Jane (**Lil Dagover**) being abducted by Cesare and carried over weirdly angled hills, roads and steps. Even more important was that *Caligari* showed how the new medium of film could capture dark fantasies more potently and dramatically than had ever been thought possible.

Cannibal Holocaust

dir **Ruggero Deodato, 1979, It/Col, 98m**
cast **Robert Kerman, Francesca Ciardi, Perry Pirkanen, Luca Barbareschi, Salvatore Basil, Gabriel Yorke** *cin* **Sergio d'Offizi** *m* **Riz Ortolani**

Banned in 33 countries and the cause of protests that forced director **Ruggero Deodato** to defend his filmmaking methods in Italian law courts, *Cannibal Holocaust* is arguably *the* most shocking and horrifying movie ever made.

Produced at a time when graphic American stalk–and–slash was taking over the global marketplace, *Cannibal Holocaust* was part of the Italian reaction: hitting back with a brand of "realistic" horror drawn from their film culture. Animal torture and killing had been a mainstay of the country's exploitation industry since the worldwide success of the shockumentary *Mondo Cane* (1962) – which, amazingly, was Oscar-nominated – and its copycat ilk, including *Africa Addio* (1966) and *Savage Man … Savage Beast* (1981).

During the Seventies documentary work akin to images in *National Geographic* and footage that was often staged got edited into racist exotic dramas that were purportedly to show the difference between civilization and the rest of the world. *Cannibal Holocaust* wasn't the first in this unsavoury development; *Deep River Savages* (1972), *Prisoner Of The Cannibal God* (1978) and Deodato's *Last Cannibal World* (1977) popularized authentic violence. But they didn't have the literary device – later used by *The Blair Witch Project* (1999) – that sent Deodato's visceral epic, which in truth had no message, into the shock stratosphere.

A film crew led by Alan Yates (**Gabriel Yorke**) goes missing in South America while shooting a documentary on tribal cannibalism. Anthropologist Professor Monroe (porn star Robert Bolla, appearing here under his real name of **Robert Kerman**) is assigned the task of leading an expedition into the "Green Inferno" to establish their fate. In the Colombian jungle they witness various nasty rituals and eventually find sealed cans of film shot by the Yates party being kept by the feared Tree People.

The rest of the film consists of the found footage providing details of the film crew being hunted down, mutilated and eaten. Complete with amateurish zooms, scratches, graininess and lab marks, it unfolds in front of stunned New York television executives who predict massive ratings should they air it. It's because Deodato imitates the cynical art form he seeks to condemn that his barrage of barbaric set pieces is so challenging, so morally repugnant and so horrifying.

All of the animal butchery is real (the hardest to watch is the live turtle being cut into pieces) but most of the human atrocity is faked (the castration, a native having her unborn baby forcibly aborted by hand, a woman vertically impaled on a ten-foot pole). However, just before the main carnage, Deodato plays his trump card – Monroe shows real-life archival footage of a firing-squad execution as an introduction to Yates's "style". This bravura coup de theatre helps to lend nerve-shredding authenticity to the cruelty then provocatively paraded on screen.

So is this mutilation extravaganza a powerful visionary work using the "violence as art" idiom of Italian horror, or the definition of unethical obscenity sarcastically masquerading as a meditation on man's capacity for evil? No matter which side of the fence you fall on, *Cannibal Holocaust* is a procession of extreme imagery that proves unforgettable.

Carrie

dir **Brian De Palma, 1976, US, 98m**

cast **Sissy Spacek, Piper Laurie, Amy Irving, William Katt, John Travolta, Nancy Allen** *cin* **Mario Tosi** *m* **Pino Donaggio**

Sissy Spacek as Carrie, at the end-of-term prom

Based on **Stephen King**'s debut novel, **Brian De Palma**'s modern gothic fairy tale significantly improved upon the 1974 bestseller. De Palma expanded its scope by positioning his *Cinderella*-in-the-abattoir as a religious morality tale dealing with the bigotry, peer pressure and bullying that can be found in any high school. Portraying Carrie White as a kindly figure and making it clear that her telekinetic power is more a stigma for her than a saving grace made the character doubly sympathetic; thanks also to **Sissy Spacek**'s heartrending and subtly shaded performance – the staring Carrie, rigid in her bloodied ball gown, quickly became an iconic image – this unforgettable package of pop psychology and psychic phenomena is a transfixing and viscerally moving experience.

Constantly chastised and physically abused at home by her religious fanatic mother Margaret (**Piper Laurie**), Carrie finds no respite from her miserable existence at Bates High School either. There she's mocked mercilessly for being such a shy wallflower, especially after a menstrual incident in the showers. This episode gives Carrie's bitchy classmate Chris Hargensen (**Nancy Allen**) the idea of engineering, with her scheming boyfriend Billy Nolan (**John Travolta**), that Carrie be crowned "Prom Queen" at the end-of-term festivities and drenched in pig's blood from a bucket rigged in the gymnasium rafters. This macabre practical joke tips Carrie over the edge, causing her paranormal powers to erupt into a blazing inferno of death and destruction.

Laurie is as striking as Spacek – both actresses were nominated for an Oscar – and her symbolic crucifixion by kitchen utensils is a thrilling highlight that matches the overwhelming shock of the bloody gym massacre. A wonderfully romantic moment is accentuated by the fabulous music of **Pino Donaggio**: troubled about her uncaring treatment of Carrie, Sue Snell (**Amy Irving**) asks her boyfriend Tommy Ross (**William Katt**) to be Carrie's dance partner, and while the camera revolves around the actors, who are themselves

King of Horror

Not only did *Carrie* begin a trend of using the innovative shock ending as a selling point; it also turned **Stephen King** into a household name. Since that debut novel in 1974, he has become one of cinema's most frequently adapted authors and one of the best-selling writers in the world. While movies on the conveyor belt of adaptations have included the good (*The Dark Half*, 1992), the bad (*The Mangler*, 1994) and the ugly (*Stephen King's Thinner*, 1996), aside from *Carrie*, only the following have achieved any lasting standing:

• *The Shining* (1980). Stanley Kubrick's version of King's 1977 terror tome is a disappointment for fans of the book who felt that Kubrick took the easy scare option, but its reputation has grown consistently and many now consider it a modern horror masterpiece.

• *The Dead Zone* (1983). In David Cronenberg's loyal and restrained rendering of King's psychic tale from 1979, Christopher Walken can see a person's past, present and future just by touch. Performances from Walken and Martin Sheen are highlights in one of Cronenberg's biggest commercial and critical hits.

• *Misery* (1990). Rob Reiner's adaptation of King's 1987 success won an Oscar for Kathy Bates, as a deranged fan keeping captive, and "hobbling", a best-selling author (James Caan). Reiner only got the rights to the novel because King loved his compassionate treatment of *Stand By Me* (1986).

• *Dolores Claiborne* (1995). Kathy Bates returned to King's universe as the title character under suspicion of murder, in Taylor Hackford's sparkling rendition of the 1992 chiller – the best psychological thriller Alfred Hitchcock never made.

• *Apt Pupil* (1997). After discovering that his neighbour (Ian McKellen) is an SS war criminal, Todd Bowden (Brad Renfro) wallows in Nazi death-camp horror in Bryan Singer's expansion of King's 1982 short story from *Different Seasons*. (*Stand By Me* and *The Shawshank Redemption*, 1994, came from the same source.) Aborted once during production a decade earlier, Singer's exploration of the evil lying hidden in the mundane and everyday is the most controversial and underrated King adaptation.

on an unseen revolving platform, it highlights the dizzying swirl of awakening emotions and possibilities felt by both characters.

De Palma also uses blood motifs for visual and verbal texture and his signature split-screen technique to overload the senses during the climactic scenes of frenzied panic. In other ways he was deliberately understated. "More telekinesis had been planned," said Spacek. "Brian wanted to play it down. The crying too – I didn't want Carrie to be this wimp, so anytime she cried she bottled it in. There was never any release, she was like a time bomb, until finally she explodes."

It's *Carrie* that the horror world has to thank for the much-copied shock ending. The jolt when Carrie's hand suddenly springs out of her rocky grave led to hefty business through word-of-mouth and marked out both De Palma and King as rising talents. Filmed in lyrical slow-motion to lull the viewer into an other-worldly false sense of security, it caps De Palma's best film.

The Cat And The Canary

dir Paul Leni, 1927, US, 86m, b/w
cast Laura LaPlante, Creighton Hale, Lucien Littlefield, Forrest Stanley, Arthur Edmund Carewe *cin* Gilbert Warrenton

Talon-clawed hands appear from the wainscoting to reach for the heroine's throat, bodies lurk in secret passageways, panels slide open in walls, dark corridors billow with breeze-blown curtains, torch beams waft through deserted rooms and relatives gather in a creepy mansion to hear the reading of a will. All these subsequently hoary clichés, and more, are contained in the most famous of all spooky spoofs, German director **Paul Leni**'s charmingly scary, genuinely amusing old dark house mystery based on the popular 1922 play by **John Willard**.

During the 1920s the Broadway stage developed its own genre of thriller comedies that took place in gloomy environments with only one set. *The Bat* in 1920 was the first spine-tingler to run for more than 500 performances – and became a film in 1926 – and many lesser efforts followed in the attempts to challenge it, includ-

Laura La Plante as Annabelle, who to gain a fortune must not appear insane

ing *The Monster*, *The Last Warning* and *The Gorilla.*, all of which were adapted for the cinema.

But while Willard's supernatural shenanigans, ultimately revealed to be contrived machinations, might not have matched *The Bat* in terms of theatrical success, the adaptation became synonymous with sinister screen satire. It had an enormous effect on the horror genre because Leni brought his stylistically weird and wonderful sensibilities, as seen in *Waxworks* (1924), to drawing-room America, and even Alfred Hitchcock cited it as an influence.

On the twentieth anniversary of his death at midnight, the will of eccentric millionaire Cyrus West is read out to his surviving relatives in the dusty confines of his hilltop mansion overlooking the Hudson

River. Obsessed with hereditary insanity, he identifies distant relative Annabelle (**Laura La Plante**) as his sole beneficiary. But if she should show any signs of mental imbalance, a second envelope will be opened and another heir named. As the greedy relatives do their best to pass off Annabelle as insane, it's announced that a criminal called The Cat has escaped from a nearby asylum. That night the mansion teems with mysterious off-screen murders and cowardly family members shivering under bedcovers, until dawn breaks and it's revealed that The Cat is the second heir, cousin Charlie (**Forrest Stanley**), who is hoping to drive Annabelle crazy.

Beginning marvellously with a hand wiping away cobwebs from the credits, the film's ominous mood is established immediately by the cringing, dying West being surrounded by shadows turning into enormous medicine bottles. These then transform into the house battlements and the interior mechanism of a clock is shown with the cogs turning to meet midnight – the first time it will have chimed since West's death.

It's this eye-catching opening that puts the grim chill in *The Cat And The Canary* and grounds perfectly the ensuing ghastly goofiness. Leni captures every detail, and uses points of view that were unusual at the time, such as that of the murderer peering from behind a portrait. So successful was this approach, it became the cornerstone of Universal's horror technique. Of the five remakes, the 1939 Bob Hope comedy vehicle is the best – because it relies heavily on Leni's delightfully atmospheric original.

Cat People

dir Jacques Tourneur, 1942, US, 73m, b/w

cast Simone Simon, Kent Smith, Tom Conway, Jane Randolph, Elizabeth Russell *cin* Nick Musuraca *m* Roy Webb

A new artistic approach was applied to horror in **Val Lewton**'s first production and the genre would never be the same again. In **Jacques Tourneur**, son of French silent director Maurice Tourneur, Lewton found a director with the same senses of graceful style and scintillating mood aesthetics as his own, and one who would realize his ambitions perfectly in the pair's most popular evocation of the silent and the unseen.

Saddled with a title that the RKO front office had tested with positive results, and inspired by French fashion magazines picturing models with heads of cats, Lewton's team constructed an ambiguous variation on the werewolf legend. New York fashion designer Irena Dubrovna (**Simone Simon**) is convinced that she descends from a Serbian race of women that Balkan folklore says are capable of shape-shifting into dangerous cats when their passions are aroused. Her obsession beguiles navy man Oliver Reed (**Kent Smith**), who courts and then weds Irena, despite her fears preventing consummation of the marriage.

Frustrated, Oliver sends Irena to psychiatrist Dr Judd (**Tom Conway**), who convinces her that she's just paranoid while clearly turned on by her erotic fantasies, and turns to jealous co-worker Alice (**Jane Randolph**) for sympathy. The stage is set for ominously sexual fuses to blow and for subliminal hints of something too evil for words slinking in the darkness.

Saturating the film with feline artefacts – statues, paintings and furnishings – all designed to underscore subconsciously Irena's fixation, Tourneur artfully keeps us guessing as to her actual orientation. Is she frigid (as an opening quote from Freud suggests), a repressed lesbian (at her wedding reception a strangely cat-like woman addresses her as "my sister" in a voice dubbed by Simon) or indeed an unwilling cat woman?

Tourneur's tasteful teases became moments of classic horror in their own right: Irena trying to coax the canary, a gift, out of its cage, the paw-like batting of her hand suggesting something else entirely; Alice being stalked by something ghastly and unseen as she walks by Central Park, ending with a magical moment when the doors of a bus hiss open to offer safe refuge. (So delighted was Lewton with that jolt – it never fails to catch its audience unaware – he termed all his frissons from then onwards "busses".) Later, in one of the most iconic sequences in horror history, Alice is in a basement swimming pool when the lights go out, a cat shadow shimmers on the wall and she finds her robe clawed to shreds at the water's edge.

Rational calm counter-pointed by elliptical horror fantasy: that's what makes *Cat People* so fear-inducing. But Tourneur was such a master of manipulating the imagination, he allowed audiences that he held in the sweaty palm of his hand the ultimate terror indulgence – the freedom to frighten themselves.

The Curse Of Frankenstein

dir Terence Fisher, 1957, UK, 82m

cast Peter Cushing, Christopher Lee, Hazel Court, Valerie Gaunt, Robert Urquhart *cin* Jack Asher *m* James Bernard

"All new and never dared before" hyped the blood-red poster for the turning point in postwar British horror. With *The Curse Of*

Peter Cushing, playing the Baron, opposite friend and co-star Christopher Lee, the Creature

Black Park

The most famous location in horror movies is this large country park on the outskirts of London, wedged between Iver Heath, Slough, the M40 and Pinewood Studios. Used for a host of movies ranging from the *Harry Potter* series to the *Carry On* comedies, Black Park was the main forest backdrop for literally every Hammer horror, from *The Curse Of Frankenstein* (1957) and *The Brides of Dracula* (1960) to *Kiss Of The Vampire* (1963) and *Twins Of Evil* (1971). It was handily nearby the House of Horror's home of operations, Bray Studios, and saw everything from coaches trundling down muddy pathways to nubile, semi-naked heroines being chased.

Frankenstein, Hammer sparked off a money-spinning worldwide renaissance of the genre; the international fear careers of two of its best-loved practitioners, **Peter Cushing** and **Christopher Lee**, were launched; and journeyman director **Terence Fisher** found his forte. It's hard now to imagine what a sea change was represented by this remodelling of Mary Shelley's classic novel as a gory drawing-room melodrama. Yet it was a sensational novelty to have all the blood in vivid Technicolor – and to cause such disgust. "For sadists only" wrote one critic, while another went as far as apologizing to America for exporting such repulsive degradation.

Hammer had already been producing successful science-fiction movies such as *The Quatermass Xperiment* (1955) when they hit upon the idea of redoing the classic monster catalogue in colour and in a more graphic style. Universal were not pleased when alerted to the fact that this upstart British company planned to remake *Frankenstein* – as a vehicle for the ageing Boris Karloff, star of their own 1931 landmark. They threatened to take legal action if Hammer appropriated any element unique to their version, and in particular Jack Pierce's copyrighted monster make-up. So Jimmy Sangster went back to Shelley for his script, and rather than making the monster the central focus, as it had been in James Whale's film, he shifted the focus to Baron Victor Frankenstein (Cushing) and his fiercely driven quest to create the perfect being.

The Curse Of Frankenstein begins with narration by the Baron from a prison cell as he awaits the guillotine for his unspeakable crimes against humanity. He tries to convince a priest brought in to listen to his confession that it wasn't he who committed the murders for which he's being condemned but the Creature (Lee), which he and his assistant Paul Krempe (**Robert Urquhart**) assembled from body parts. In flashback we see how Victor's intense passion and megalomania grow as the Creature is brought to life, is given a crash course in behaviour and breaks its bonds to cause uncomprehending murder.

Putting the action in the novel's original setting, Fisher's directorial verve gave it the patina of a witty fairy tale and a high scare score. The Creature's introduction is memorable: a rapid track into a disfigured face before, on coming abruptly to life, he tries to strangle his creator. And the impact was greater because of make-up man **Phil Leakey**'s frantic last-minute design for the Creature, amid panic about copyright infringement, which was a corpse-like collage of mortician's wax, rubber and cotton wool that took three hours to apply to Lee's face.

"It was the first time I worked with Peter," recalled Lee. "I told him, 'I haven't any lines in this,' and he said, 'You're lucky! I've read the script.'" But although he has barely fifteen minutes of screen time, Lee still makes an indelible impact as the man-made being without any control over his actions. However, the movie inevitably belongs to Cushing who, hardly ever off the screen, is superb in delivering Victor's delight and wonder in the new medical avenues that he's opening, and his lack of regard for the pain and suffering he's causing to those around him.

Dawn Of The Dead

dir George A. Romero, 1978, US, 126m
cast David Emge, Ken Foree, Scott H. Reiniger, Gaylen Ross, David Crawford *cin* Michael Gornick *m* Goblin, Dario Argento

Ten years after *Night Of The Living Dead* (1968), director **George A. Romero** resurrected his zombie flesh-eaters for the second segment of what he had decided would be a trilogy. (*Day of the Dead* followed in 1985 and twenty years later the series came to include *Land Of The Dead*.) The result was an audacious horror masterpiece which, thanks to its shopping mall setting and brainwashed zombie "consumers", immediately represented the materialism of Seventies America. One of the most profitable independent film productions ever made, it earned Vietnam combat photographer and make-up artist **Tom Savini** the title "the King of Splatter" and sent critics of the genre reeling with its clammy "No Exit" grimness, and its potent social message told in an intelligent horror vernacular. It was even called "the *Gone With The Wind* of gore" because of its unusually epic length for a horror film, of more than two hours.

With society teetering on the verge of collapse because of human pettiness and lack of cooperation more than the rampant zombie plague, television broadcaster Fran (**Gaylen Ross**), her daredevil helicopter pilot boyfriend Stephen (**David Emge**), their

SWAT friend Roger (**Scott H. Reiniger**) and heroic black police trooper Peter (**Ken Foree**) take refuge in a huge shopping mall relatively devoid of the undead. While the men can't resist looting the deserted stores for luxuries, Fran is the only one who recognizes that the precinct represents a lifestyle that must be forsaken if they are to survive the onslaught of cannibal cadavers.

The foursome's fragile false sense of security is further shattered when a gang of nomadic Hell's Angels (led by Savini) break in through the doors and let in the gathering hordes of the living dead. Fatally wounded in an elevator, Stephen leads the zombies straight to his former friends. Peter, originally planning to sacrifice himself so that Fran can escape in the helicopter, changes his mind and both fly off into an uncertain future.

This was the first horror film to suggest the possibility of moving beyond impending apocalypse towards creating a new social order. "The mall was a temple to the 'me' generation of the time," Romero explained. "The stores were symbolic cathedrals meant to appear as an archaeological discovery revealing the gods and customs of a civilization now gone."

But this subtext didn't matter to the hardcore splatteratti, who mainly regarded the whole bloody business as a horror comic; the sheer sensationalism of the graphic gore popped the pupils unnervingly. The film was seen first in Italy after co-producer **Dario Argento** released it in a cut that accented the operatic violence, such as the zombie walking into the helicopter blades and getting his cranium severed; when Romero unleashed his longer, un-rated cut on America eight months later, the throwaway details dear to his heart were kept in but the blade sequence was excised.

Far from being the disaster that everyone was expecting, the 2004 *Dawn Of The Dead* remake by Zack Snyder, which had a scale and budget denied to Romero, though geared more towards high action was an engaging roller-coaster ride through gripping gory terror.

Diabolique
(Les diaboliques)

dir Henri-Georges Clouzot, Fr, 1954, 114m, b/w

cast Simone Signoret, Véra Clouzot, Paul Meurisse, Charles Vanel, Pierre Larquey *cin* Armand Thirard *m* Georges Van Parys

Before Alfred Hitchcock's *Psycho* (1960) raised the horror thriller to new heights of suspense, **Henri-Georges Clouzot**'s chiller was considered the most frightening and artistic nightmare that the genre could produce. In France Clouzot was even dubbed "the Gallic Hitchcock" for this brilliant follow-up to *The Wages Of Fear* (1953). And Hitchcock paid attention to the themes of *Diabolique*, because of the critics' reviews; and because he had been beaten by the Frenchman to the rights to the novel on which it was based, *Celle qui n'était plus* (*The Woman Who Was No More*), by **Pierre Boileau** and **Thomas Narcejac**. And so the horror world has this clever classic to thank for *Psycho*, for *Diabolique* foreshadowed it in many ways; it centred on a murder in a bare bathroom, for example, and benefited from a smart publicity campaign that urged moviegoers not to watch unless they did so from the very beginning.

A dark puzzle picture employing the apparatus of terror within the context of a detective story, *Diabolique* focuses on the relationship, implied at times to be lesbian, between the sickly Christina Delasalle (**Véra Clouzot**, the director's wife) and the stiff, ice-cool Nicole Horner (**Simone Signoret**), the wife and mistress, respectively, of Michel Delasalle (**Paul Meurisse**). The head of a boys' school that has his name, Delasalle is unkind towards his teach-

Nicole (Simone Signoret) gets her revenge – or does she?

ers and his pupils, and abuses his fragile wife in front of his mistress (who herself hides behind dark sunglasses), and even in front of the schoolboys, when he asks her to swallow a bone.

The plan of the two women to murder him, as organised by Nicole, to take place at her home far away, seems justified. But Christina – whose religious beliefs frequently put doubts in her mind – gets nervous, so it is her partner who terrifyingly drowns a drugged Michel in the bath. And then the corpse vanishes. Before long Inspector Fichet (**Charles Vanel**) is making them nervous, and after mysterious appearances and disappearances, including a sighting reported by one of the almost ubiquitous schoolboys, an ill Christina is forced to take to the long, dark corridors to put her mind at rest.

Clouzot crafted a gripping scenario loaded with subtle insights into the basest aspects of human nature, which are often conveyed through movements of the eyes and snippets of dialogue about lies and responsibility. Handled particularly masterfully is the unnerving final sequence, which reaches a climax when Michel's corpse appears to rise from the bathtub, witnessed by the traumatized Christina, and which features the fiendish revelation. (After the end credits came the plea, "Don't be diabolical yourself. Don't spoil the ending for your friends by telling them what you've just seen. On their behalf – Thank you.") And the darkness is not disturbed by the seamlessly incorporated irreverent humour; both are present in tense scenes when the body is almost discovered. The black-and-white cinematography, frequently focusing on water, captures the foreboding that makes the clever *Diabolique* – unlike the remake of 1996 starring Sharon Stone – a pinnacle in cinematic dread.

Dracula

dir Tod Browning, 1931, US, 85m, b/w
cast Bela Lugosi, Helen Chandler, David Manners, Dwight Frye, Edward Van Sloan, Herbert Bunston, Frances Dade
cin Karl Freund

"I … am … Dracula. I bid you … welcome" is probably the most famous line of dialogue in horror history. *Dracula* brought Universal

Tod Browning's *Dracula* influenced every vampire film that followed it

monsterdom into the big time, made a movie star out of Hungarian stage actor **Bela Lugosi** and catapulted director **Tod Browning**, "the Edgar Allan Poe of Cinema", to the frontline of fear-making. Restoring the true meaning of the word "vampire" to the language – in the silent era "vamp" had tended to stand for predatory females played, for example, by Theda Bara – "the strangest love story of them all", as the poster had it, presented Count Dracula being undead as a supernatural fact. There was no final revelation that everything was an elaborate con, as it was in Browning's *London After Midnight* four years earlier, nor the kind of cheating that existed in *The Cat And*

Blood

Sucked by vampires, spilt by murderers, bathed in by mad countesses, and used as paint by crazed artists and as ink in Devil pacts, the fluid that keeps us all alive is the life force of the horror movie. Though its nicknames have ranged from tomato ketchup to **Kensington Gore**, like words such as "curse", "castle" and "monster" the word "blood" in a title conveys exactly what the movie is about. But while gallons are often splashed about to cover up deficiencies in low-budget B-movies, less is often more powerful: the smudge on Renfield's finger in *Dracula* (1931), the trickle in *The Texas Chainsaw Massacre*. In black-and-white movies the most common blood substitute was chocolate syrup – *Psycho* used the Shasta brand – and in colour movies, blood could be anything from scarlet to crimson depending on the film stock or the secret recipes of the make-up men. For the exploitation horror brigade Cochineal and Karo corn syrup were favourites.

The Canary, as was the vogue. Browning's script acknowledged that audiences were now ready to deal with fully-fledged horror, and the film's instant smash-hit status stabilized Universal's finances during the Great Depression.

For Browning, *Dracula* was the culmination of an obsession with the shadowy horror themes that the American cinema had long resisted. One of the few Hollywood players conversant in developments in other cultures, Browning was familiar with English gothic literature and knew of Robert Wiene and F. W. Murnau's pioneering movie work in Germany. He and his cinematographer Karl Freund almost certainly perused *Nosferatu*, as there are numerous parallel shots in *Dracula* – notably Orlok and Dracula studying their foreign leases, and a cut hand stimulating the vampire's bloodlust. Browning's genius was in taking this melting pot of influences from around the world and forging a new baroque style, American Gothic.

Based on the 1927 hit stage version of *Dracula* by Hamilton Deane and John L. Balderston, adapted from the Bram Stoker novel, Browning's classic chiller opens in high style with Renfield (**Dwight Frye**) travelling to Castle Dracula in Transylvania to sell the lease of Carfax Abbey in Yorkshire to the deceptively urbane Count (Lugosi). Later the ship *Vesta* arrives in Whitby Harbour near Carfax Abbey and Renfield is found aboard the eerily deserted vessel raving mad, eating rats and insects. As Renfield is placed in the asylum of Dr Seward (**Herbert Bunston**), Dracula begins his nocturnal exploits and turns Lucy Weston (**Frances Dade**) into a vampire. Her friend Mina Seward (**Helen Chandler**) then catches his attention, and when her health deteriorates her father calls in a specialist, Dr Van Helsing (**Edward Van Sloan**), who diagnoses her sudden anaemia. Realizing what's happening Van Helsing tells Mina's fiancé Jonathan Harker (**David Manners**) and Dr Seward all about vampirism and prepares them for the desperate measures to be taken to prevent Mina from becoming one of the undead.

Although Dracula's demise coming as only an off-screen groan is hardly a fitting end for the powerful nobleman, and although the Transylvanian beginning is so brilliantly staged that the rest of the movie seems to remain in awe of it, Browning shaped the way that every vampire movie would be made afterwards. Its standing as a memorable genre milestone cannot be overstated, even though, like most of its contemporaries, it's the quaint charm more than the transfixing horror that it is now famous for. Yet *Dracula* was an influential piece of cinematic mood-making, with Freund's eerie photography helping to scale up the unease; and, having perfected his performance through countless appearances in the stage hit, Lugosi is the definitive monochrome Count Dracula. With his formal dinner suit, black cape, cultivated demeanour, cruel smile and East European accent, he claimed the part of the Prince of Darkness as his own, and Lugosi's enduring image casts a weighty shadow to this day.

Dracula
(aka Horror Of Dracula)

dir **Terence Fisher, 1958, UK, 82m**

cast **Peter Cushing, Christopher Lee, Michael Gough, Melissa Stribling, Valerie Gaunt** *cin* **Jack Asher** *m* **James Bernard**

Epochal in its impact and unequivocally the best Hammer horror ever made, *Dracula* sexually liberated the horror movie, allowing it to become more sensually provocative; it was also more graphically violent after the company tested the bloody waters in their breakout success *The Curse Of Frankenstein* the previous year. Director **Terence Fisher**'s shocker might not be the most faithful adaptation of Bram Stoker's novel; but, sparsely and crisply scripted by Hammer veteran Jimmy Sangster, who set the story in the cod Mitteleuropa that Hammer would soon make a notorious cliché, it remains one of the finest renderings of the Dracula theme. Of the well-mounted scenes hardly any are without rousing action, erotic frisson or unforgettable suspense and Fisher's masterly direction set an unmatched standard in romantic gothic horror.

When Jonathan Harker (**John Van Eyssen**) dies at the teeth of Count Dracula (**Christopher Lee**), an attempt is made by his close friend Dr Van Helsing (**Peter Cushing**) to track the vampire king down. But he eludes all capture and shows up in London, promptly killing Harker's fiancée Lucy (**Carol Marsh**). After Van Helsing frees Lucy's immortal soul, Dracula retaliates by kidnapping Mina (**Melissa Stribling**), wife of Lucy's brother Arthur Holmwood (**Michael Gough**). A chase across Europe ensues, with Arthur and Van Helsing pursuing the bloodsucker and his enslaved victim back to the undead demon's Transylvanian castle.

Peter Cushing, as the heroic Van Helsing, is one of the film's greatest strengths, projecting genuine intelligence, and a dogged determination to eradicate evil. (He later admitted that of all the roles he played, this one required the least amount of acting.) Dracula is introduced by Fisher as an imposing figure at the top of a staircase — without any footstep sounds, to add to the royal fiend's supernaturalism — and it is one of the greatest entrances in horror history. Christopher Lee's overall performance was one of immense

Terence Fisher's *Dracula*, the best Hammer horror, showed masterly directorial skills

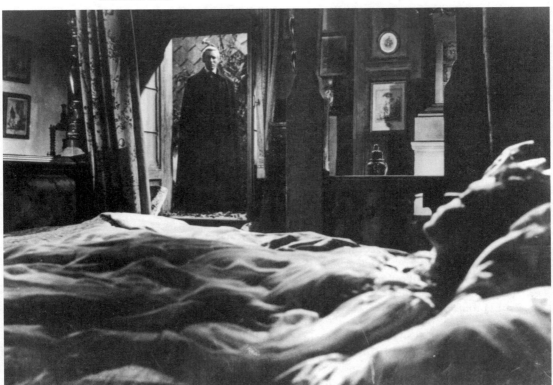

stature that was cruel, predatory and, most importantly, seductively charming – all with only thirteen lines of dialogue. "It was a milestone in my career", he said. "And it has proved to be a mixed blessing. But I always tried to impress on the audience the majesty and dignity of this immortal character as well as the savagery, ferocity and, above all, great sadness."

The film was packed with hugely effective moments showing what could be done on a low budget when everyone's flair and elegance was used well; and the best was kept until last and would prove so popular through word-of-mouth that it was reprised at the beginning of the first official sequel, *Dracula, Prince Of Darkness* (1965). This was the sequence where Van Helsing and Dracula fight tooth-and-nail throughout the castle, with the battle ending in the massive library; using two candlesticks to form the sign of the cross, Van Helsing leaps across the room, pulls the curtains from the window and forces Dracula into the rays of the rising sun, where he disintegrates into ash. It was a thrilling end to a blood-curdling smash that grabbed the horror world by the jugular, and Hammer never looked back. "The filming of *Dracula* went like a dream," said Fisher. "Everything worked."

The Evil Dead

dir Sam Raimi, 1982, US, 86m
cast Bruce Campbell, Ellen Sandweiss, Betsy Baker, Hal Delrich, Sarah York *cin* Tim Philo *m* Joseph LoDuca

Stephen King raved after the premiere of *The Evil Dead* at the Cannes Film Festival – "the most ferociously original horror movie I have ever seen" – but British moral guardians sounded the alarm when it was released because of its supposedly harmful psychological effects. The Maine man was right about its originality and, as usual, the self-appointed arbiters of public taste got it wrong. Made as a calling card that announced the arrival of three tyro filmmakers on the independent scene, the no-budget zombie bloodbath from director **Sam Raimi**, producer **Robert Tapert** and star **Bruce Campbell** soon gained its well-deserved status as a cult classic. Through combining a haphazard narrative, gushes of gore to cover every glaring fault and

A scene created to help market *The Evil Dead* (1982), which became a calling card for Sam Raimi an inventive style borne out of poverty-stricken necessity – Raimi jokingly dubbed the dizzying fast tracking shots "Shakicam" – *The Evil Dead* became a frighteningly atmospheric, cunning innovation with a wry sense of humour.

Five college students, Ash (Bruce Campbell), Cheryl (**Ellen Sandweiss**), Scotty (**Hal Delrich**), Linda (**Betsy Baker**) and Shelly (**Sarah York**), arrive at a rickety cabin deep in the Tennessee backwoods for a weekend of sex and drugs. There they discover the Necronomicon, a fictional book of the dead, that puts a curse on whoever reads it, and a tape-recording of weird incantations. The magic spell awakens a terrifying life force in the forest, and one by one the characters become violently possessed by ferocious demons. The only way to break the hex is by dismemberment and decapitation, which leaves Ash as the reluctant hero, barricading every door and making a last stand against the satanic intruders.

It might have an anaemic plot and no characterization, but Raimi delivers on all delightfully disgusting and creepy claustrophobic levels. The unsubtle bloodletting is extreme and frequent, funny and repulsive. Pencils, knives, clocks, chainsaws, trees, writhing vines, vices, fingernails and more are used as weapons of messy destruction. Informed by Raimi's love of the Three Stooges as much as down-and-dirty shockers such as *The Texas Chainsaw Massacre* (1974) – the scene where the light bulb fills up with blood is his student horror appropriation of the trio's comedy sketch "A Plumbing We Will Go" – *The Evil Dead* is gory and goofy in equal pulse-pounding parts.

"We made it for our local Detroit drive-in crowd," said Raimi, who went on to direct *Spider-Man* (2002). "We wanted to make a film that would stop people kissing in their cars and turn their attention to the screen. Since we never got any girls we figured it was only fair to make a film so other people didn't get them either!"

The Evil Dead was followed by *Evil Dead 2: Dead By Dawn* (1987), not so much a sequel as a big-budget version of the original, and *Army Of Darkness* (1992), which was way too manic and camp (and which because of its thirteenth-century time travel plot had the working title "The Medieval Dead"). While Bruce Campbell's Ash evolved into a more gung-ho action hero as the series progressed, it's his ultra-game performance here, coupled with Raimi's keen-as-mustard direction, that gives *The Evil Dead* its still contagious heart and soul.

Bruce Campbell

The nearest that latter-day horror has to a journeyman star in the old tradition, Bruce Campbell is the king of the un-credited cameo. The countless movies in which he has appeared briefly or as just a voice include those of his friends the Coen brothers, but he is perhaps most famous for the role of Ash in best friend Sam Raimi's *The Evil Dead* and its two sequels. Campbell's square-jawed classic matinee-idol looks – his autobiography is titled *If Chins Could Kill* – have graced *Maniac Cop* (1988), *Darkman* (1990), *Sundown: The Vampire In Retreat* (1991) and – one of his finest hours – cult horror comedy *Bubba Ho-Tep* (2002), in which he portrayed Elvis Presley as a bitter, lonely old man living out his life in a rural Texas nursing home. "There is a large element of me in every role I do," he once said. "Actors who say they can dive inside a character are either schizophrenic or lying."

The Exorcist

dir **William Friedkin, 1973, US, 122m**
cast **Ellen Burstyn, Linda Blair, Max von Sydow, Lee J. Cobb, Jason Miller,** *cin* **Owen Roizman** *m* **Jack Nitzsche**

With the most talked-about, widely shocking and controversial fear-inducer ever, director **William Friedkin** took horror into the big-budget arena and inspired numerous cash-ins. *The Exorcist* did for the genre what *2001: A Space Odyssey* (1968) did for science fiction: it legitimized horror in the eyes of the world and the film industry, which previously considered such movies as giggles or drive-in fillers. It therefore made history in a way that few films, especially horrors, ever do.

The Exorcist also became a cultural happening. People left screenings shaking, nauseous and screaming. Some sought psychiatric help because of the film's overwhelming impact and there were claims that it led to a rise in church attendance. Even the Pope reacted; he delivered an address on the Devil, saying "evil is not merely a lack of something, but an effective agent, a living spiritual being, perverted and perverting … a terrible reality". That was the only rave review that Warner Bros needed to have their satanic sensation enter the record books.

Based on true events occurring in 1928 and 1949, Friedkin's adult horror was scripted by **William Peter Blatty** – he won an Oscar – who adapted his own bestseller set in Georgetown, where actress Chris MacNeil (**Ellen Burstyn**) is living with her 12-year-old daughter Regan (**Linda Blair**) while shooting a movie. The world around them is shown to be falling apart: there's poverty, decadence, youths on the rampage, political turmoil, divorce for Chris and a crisis of faith for Father Damien Karras (**Jason Miller**), who is suffering from guilt because he couldn't care for his old dying mother.

And so the chaotic stage is set for the Devil to make a dramatic entrance. Lucifer takes possession of Regan and soon she's projectile vomiting, rotating her head, levitating and uttering inhuman obscenities during violent tantrums. When the medical world can't offer a rational solution Chris turns to the Church and Karras agrees to assist in an exorcism, performed by the mysterious globe-

The arrival of Father Lankester Merrin (Max von Sydow)

trotting priest, Father Lankester Merrin (**Max von Sydow**).

Unbearably intense because of its revolutionary special effects make-up work by **Dick Smith** and **Rick Baker**, shocking language and sexual imagery – Regan stabbing at her crotch with a bloodied crucifix is a key horror moment – its high point comes when the two priests eventually engage in a battle between good and evil. It's here that the well-developed parallel storylines converge – Regan struggling against the spirit that has taken over her body and Father Karras confronting his own demons.

Friedkin pulled off what had seemed impossible with *The Exorcist*: he incorporated state-of-the-art special effects into the narrative completely naturally, so they made the fright even more powerful. And he conveyed a fear rarely tackled in horror – the innocent becoming the monster rather than those around her. It was followed by *Exorcist II: The Heretic* (1977, bad), *The Exorcist III* (1990, good) and *Exorcist: The Beginning* (2004, ugly).

Eyes Without A Face
(Les yeux sans visage)

dir Georges Franju, 1959, Fr, 90m, b/w
cast Pierre Brasseur, Alida Valli, Edith Scob, Juliette Mayniel, François Guérin *cin* Eugen Schüfftan *m* Maurice Jarre

In **Georges Franju**'s unflinching surrealistic masterpiece, the usually elusive alliance of poetry and terror combined with sensational force; and handling the brutalizing horror with a sly velvet touch, *Eyes Without A Face* owes as much to the B-movie carnival sensibility of William Castle as it does to the hypnotic imagery of Jean Cocteau and Luis Buñuel. Famed for taking his camera into the abattoirs of Paris for the documentary *Blood Of The Beasts* (1949) to show the truth of conveyor-belt death, Franju set out to challenge medical ethics in his only venture into horror movies, and he had to approach the issue with surgical precision – the issue that the film itself features so controversially. "When I shot *Eyes Without A Face*," he said, "I was told, no sacrilege because of the Spanish market, no nudes because of the Italian, no blood because of the French and no martyred animals because of the English. And I was supposed to be making a horror film!"

By his reckless driving, brilliant plastic surgeon Dr Genessier (**Pierre Brasseur**) is responsible for disfiguring his daughter Christiane (**Edith Scob**). To make amends, he experiments with facial tissue skin grafts that continually fail to take. The reluctant donors are all Sorbonne students resembling Christiane, who are found in the Paris streets by the doctor's devoted nurse-cum-mistress Louise (**Alida Valli**) and lured back to his laboratory. Eventually, Christiane rebels against the constant operations, accepts that her face will always be an emotionless mask, stabs Louise to death and sets dogs on her father that ferociously tear his face off in revenge for the inhumane tests carried out on them.

Working with an adaptation by **Pierre Boileau** and **Thomas Narcejac** (the authors whose stories led to *Diabolique* and *Vertigo*) of the novel by **Jean Redon**, Franju transforms shock into high art by extending its melodramatic horror concerns into mythological malaise through superb atmospheric imagery. The prison of caged dogs, the shadowy rooms of the exquisite mansion used as cheap-rent student bait and leather-clad Louise stalking her prey in a Citroën through the Latin Quarter like a sinister scuttling beetle are heart-palpitating details that sear into the psyche.

Edith Scob is perfection as Christiane. In the extended climactic sequence where she walks through rooms ethereally – dressed in a full-length white nightgown and blank because of the luminescent white wax mask fashioned by her father's guilt – and liberates his black zoo of test creatures and a flurry of doves, the shimmering fairy-tale grace of her one-inexpressive-face-fits-all demeanour is stunning.

Franju's esoteric frightener is notorious for one particular scene, in which, without customary shock tactics, the minutiae of a skin-grafting procedure is shown in every queasy detail. (This led the film to be exploitatively re-titled *The Horror Chamber Of Dr Faustus* in America so it could be identified with the scalpel-and-formaldehyde bargain basement.) Although directing with unnerving realism, Franju's focus is on Genessier, the labour of true love it represents to him and the guilt he can never eradicate.

It is one of horror cinema's most enduring images; a moment of pure Grand Guignol elegance.

Frankenstein

dir **James Whale, 1931, US, 71m, b/w**

cast **Boris Karloff, Colin Clive, Mae Clarke, Edward Van Sloan, Dwight Frye, Marilyn Harris** *cin* **Arthur Edeson** *m* **David Broekman**

The success of *Dracula* (1931) dispelled any doubt in Universal's mind about the marketability of monsters, and their next diversion went on to become the most famous horror film of all time. *Frankenstein* not only made a star out of **Boris Karloff**; it also fixed an image of the Monster's look in popular culture that has never declined.

With his legs stiffened by steel struts and two pairs of trousers, his arms made to look longer by a shortened jacket, his feet in asphalt-spreader boots and his head transformed by make-up man Jack Pierce's scars, waxen eyelids and electrical neck bolts, Karloff's first entrance is a masterful reveal.

Director **James Whale** focuses on shambling footsteps, a slowly turning dark figure in a doorway and then a series of increasingly closer shock cuts as the monster's frightening visage fills the entire screen. Karloff said that the part, which was turned down by Bela Lugosi when he realized it contained no lines, "was what we call a natural. Any actor who played it was destined for success." But it was Karloff's sensitive portrayal and the range of emotions he beautifully conveyed without dialogue that contributed to the horror, that grows as his warmth and wonderment when newly born turns to murderous incomprehension at being rejected for looking grotesque.

Karloff's success in making the Monster both fearsome and tender is highlighted in the most controversial and heavily censored scene, with Maria (**Marilyn Harris**), the little girl he meets by the lake who doesn't recoil at his appearance. The two share a gentle bond, but he inadvertently drowns her in a poignant moment of playfulness. Yet her death is the result not of any innate savagery on his part, but of his failure to understand that not all delicate beautiful things, like the flowers he picked beforehand, can float.

Although adapted from Peggy Webling's hit London play rather than the novel by Mary Shelley, Henry Frankenstein (**Colin Clive**) is still obsessed with the concept of creating artificial life. After leaving school because the scientists there would not permit him to continue his experiments, he retreats to an isolated Bavarian castle, where he uses corpses stolen from graves to further his work. One dark and electrically stormy night, he succeeds in bringing life to a crudely stitched together collection of body parts. But his hunch-backed assistant Fritz (**Dwight Frye**) mistakenly stole a criminal

The Monster (Boris Karloff) and Maria (Marilyn Harris) in the film's most heavily censored scene

brain instead of a normal one from a medical college, and the Monster soon shows signs of aberrant and animalistic behaviour. Everything comes to a head on Henry's wedding day, when the Monster embarks on a killing spree, terrorizes his bride Elizabeth (**Mae Clarke**) and ends up in a burning mill.

The most justifiably memorable scene is Henry in his spectacularly elaborate art–deco laboratory animating his creation with lightning flashes and screaming, in orgasmic exultation, "It's alive!" In a terrific performance Clive makes Frankenstein a complicated and sympathetic character, conveying his obsessed brilliance and tragic heroism in broad strokes. Both Clive and Karloff would suffer forever from the public confusion of Frankenstein and his Monster.

Frankenstein was also notable for revolutionizing movie advertising. Until this point no studio had used the ploy of frightening audiences into buying tickets, but the intriguing poster publicity carried a "friendly warning" from a studio copywriter advising the weak-hearted not to watch, and people then went to find out if they could take it. In addition, **Edward Van Sloan**, who played Frankenstein's old teacher Dr Waldman, filmed a speech to precede the opening credits saying that the entertainment would thrill, possibly shock and even horrify. Few left their seats and even reports of the mild hysteria quelled by smelling salts administered by concerned cinema managers were fanned into further promotional opportunities.

Freaks

dir Tod Browning, 1932, US, 64m, b/w

cast Harry Earles, Olga Baclanova, Wallace Ford, Leila Hyams, Henry Victor *cin* Merritt B. Gerstad

Hot from his *Dracula* triumph for Universal, **Tod Browning** moved back to MGM, where he had enjoyed success with Lon Chaney on films such as *The Road To Mandalay* (1926) and *West Of Zanzibar* (1928), and directed the most personal, controversial and unusual horror film of all. It was **Harry Earles** who suggested that Browning take a look at the story *Spurs*, written by Clarence Aaron "Tod" Robbins. Earles had played tiny Tweedledee in both versions of *The Unholy Three* (1925, 1930), also written by Robbins, and he thought his friend would be interested in the circus-set horror show because he had made his start under the big top and had already used it as a setting in his silent movies.

Browning loved the story. Here was a chance to present a world that was important to him, where sideshow freaks were the norm. The viewer, he thought, might feel fear and pity at first, but that would soon give way to respect, understanding and amazement at the way that they function in spite of their handicaps. This, along with the macabre moral and the ultra-horrific punch line, was exactly the route that Browning was convinced he should follow to push public tolerance further than even he had dared previously.

The stars of *Freaks*, which provides a portrait of circus life

Cleopatra (**Olga Baclanova**), a normal trapeze artist, sets her sights on rich midget Hans (Earles) and agrees to be his bride. Together with her strongman lover Hercules (**Henry Victor**), she plans to wed and then kill her husband for his wealth. But the odd affair arouses the anger of the freak circus population – The Boy with Half A Torso (**Johnny Eck**), The Living Torso (**Prince Randian**), The Armless Wonder (**Martha Morris**), The Siamese Twins (**Daisy and Violet Hilton**), The Human Skeleton (**Peter Robinson**), The Bearded Lady (**Olga Roderick**), The Bird Girl (**Koo Koo**), The Half Woman/Half Man (**Josephine-Joseph**), The Snow Twins (**Elvira and Jennie Lee**) and The Pinhead (**Schlitze**) – who know few outsiders and love even fewer.

Gradually they come to accept the idea, even though Cleopatra gets drunk at her wedding reception, drops her guard and lets her new "family" know exactly what she thinks about them. When they keep their eye on Cleopatra after the outburst, her venal plan is finally uncovered, and they plot a terrifying revenge. In one of the most legendary and disturbing shock moments of the burgeoning genre, the group gather in the rain one stormy night and crawl in the mud, the knives in their mouths glinting in the lightning, to transform Cleopatra by crude surgery into a half-woman, half-chicken freak.

Browning pits the physical beauty of both Cleopatra and Hercules against the accidental deformities of nature and lets the audience decide who the most repugnant characters are. Moreover, camera angles at low level convey a sense of normality until a "normal" person walks into frame: such simple techniques offset all arguments about gratuitous voyeurism, and despite its reputation as a full-on shocker, *Freaks* is mainly an absorbing portrait of daily circus life.

Nevertheless, it was greeted by audiences with wholesale revulsion and on initial release critics called it everything from "an abomination" to "loathsome, obscene, grotesque and bizarre". Hastily pulled from release, put in a vault and forgotten about by MGM as a knee-jerk reaction, and banned for 31 years in Britain, *Freaks* was ignominiously dragged around the cheap grind-house circuit of the southern US by exploitative producer Dwain Esper in the Forties under the more alluring title *Forbidden Love*.

But *Freaks* was rediscovered in the light of the Thalidomide tragedy at the start of the Sixties, and was programmed at the 1962 Venice Film Festival. After the headlines regarding the morning sickness drug that triggered birth defects, a film could be seen that treated blighted individuals with tenderness and compassion. Its reputation growing as a misunderstood masterpiece, *Freaks* was then picked up by the midnight cult movie circuit in New York, where, in times when the counterculture challenged social norms and values, its underdog message struck a chord. The maligned film that had effectively ended Browning's career had become the critical darling that the eternally bitter director always thought it was, though he never lived long enough to taste the victory in its reappraisal.

Halloween

dir **John Carpenter, 1978, US, 91m**

cast **Donald Pleasence, Jamie Lee Curtis, Nancy Loomis, P. J. Soles, Charles Cyphers** *cin* **Dean Cundey** *m* **John Carpenter**

One of the most successful films of all time in terms of its ratio of cost ($300,000) to takings on first release ($50 million), *Halloween* is the father of the modern slasher movie. But although director **John Carpenter** unleashed an endless wave of calendar maniacs-on-the-loose in its wake, he generated its constant menace by building up the suspense and not the gore.

The portrayal of the violence, which initiated many horror clichés, is brief and virtually bloodless; Carpenter deliberately went back to the tradition of suggestion rather than showing, albeit in the most grandstanding ways possible. In wide-screen, rarely used for horror, Carpenter accented subjective camerawork (the new gyroscopic Panaglide adding marvellous fluidity), quick editing, driving music (which he composed) and the creative use of light and shadow.

In a modern retelling of the cautionary urban legend *The Tale Of The Hook*, on Halloween 1963, six-year-old Michael Myers dons a mask and stabs his teenage sister to death; fifteen years later, Michael escapes from a lunatic asylum and is tracked down to Haddonfield, Illinois, by his doctor Sam Loomis (**Donald Pleasence**). Will he locate Michael before he stalks and kills college friends Annie (**Nancy Loomis**), Lynda (**P. J. Soles**) and Laurie Strode (**Jamie Lee Curtis**), on babysitting duty with the bogeyman-phobic Tommy?

Carpenter combined the dark, spooky atmosphere essential to Val Lewton, the humour and tension that go hand and hand in Alfred Hitchcock's oeuvre – Pleasence's character has the same name as John Gavin's in *Psycho* – and the fun shocks found in William Castle potboilers to phenomenally scary effect. But what made it such a massive crossover hit was the believability of its teenage characters and their easy-going interaction. Laurie is smart, feels her intelligence is the reason she doesn't get dates and is slightly jealous of her sex-mad friends. That was something every girl in the world under-

Jamie Lee Curtis

Capable, assured and attractive, the daughter of Janet Leigh and Tony Curtis briefly became a fixture in slasher shockers after her appearance as the engaging and resourceful heroine of *Halloween* (1978). Immediately afterwards came *Prom Night*, *Terror Train*, *The Fog* (all 1980), *Road Games* and *Halloween II* (both 1981), before she did the virtually impossible and escaped the typecasting trap, carving out a reputation as a first-class comedienne in the aftermath of *Trading Places* (1983). It was her suggestion that led to *Halloween H20* (1998) and to her reprisal of the iconic role of Laurie Strode. Ironically horror films have always terrified Curtis and she prefers not to watch them – even her own.

Urban legends

Essentially modern-day folk-tales, appearing mysteriously and spreading like wildfire, these stories of the misfortunes of a friend's friend's girlfriend's father are a means of expressing our often irrational fears about the dangers just beneath the surface of our seemingly calm world. The macabre apocryphal stories often have a basis in truth, but it's their ever-changing lives after the events that makes them intriguing.

Jamie Blanks' *Urban Legend* (1998) and John Ottman's *Urban Legends: Final Cut* (2000) both failed because they included *too many* urban legends, but all horror movies have effectively used elements of *The Tale Of The Hook*, the legend that Stephen King has described as "the most basic horror story I know", in which a young couple on the verge of "the sin of fornication" are saved from the clutches of a mad stalker by the timely deflation of the sexual urge. Other urban legends to appear in films include the ones about a maniac on the top of the car (*Halloween*, 1978), a maniac calling a babysitter from inside the same house (*When A Stranger Calls*, 1979) and the alligators living in the New York sewers (*Alligator*, 1980).

stood and the impressive debut by Curtis – who as the daughter of *Psycho* star Janet Leigh was part of another Hitchcock in-joke – led to her being temporarily typecast as the scream queen *du jour*.

Her particular plot strand also led to the popular cliché of promiscuous teenagers being marked for horrific death. Carpenter had this to say about the connection that was made between sexual activity and dead-cert doom: "They completely missed the point there. The one girl who is the most sexually uptight just keeps stabbing this guy with a long knife. She's the most sexually frustrated. She's the one that's killed him. Not because she's a virgin but because all that sexually repressed energy starts coming out. She uses all those phallic symbols on the guy."

Of the seven *Halloween* sequels, *Halloween III: Season Of The Witch* (1983) is the quirkiest because Nigel Kneale, who wrote the television series *The Quatermass Experiment* (1953), deliberately avoided anything to do with the Michael Myers backstory. Instead it focused on a mad toy-maker intending to restore the holiday to its witch cult origins.

The Haunting

dir Robert Wise, 1963, UK, 112m, b/w
cast Julie Harris, Claire Bloom, Richard Johnson, Russ Tamblyn, Lois Maxwell *cin* Davis Boulton *m* Humphrey Searle

While Hammer were continuing during the early Sixties with their colourful excesses, it took **Robert Wise**, an apprentice of producer Val Lewton, to take horror back to its less-is-more, atmospheric roots. *The Haunting,* which fed into the trend of renewed public interest in extrasensory perception and psychic phenomena, marked a triumphant return to the genre in which Wise had made his name but hadn't worked since Boris Karloff's *The Body Snatcher* in 1945; using the **Shirley Jackson** novel *The Haunting Of Hill House*, he turned a fairly conventional haunted house potboiler into one of the most effectively frightening chillers of all time.

Hill House is a Victorian mansion in New England with a reputation for being eerie. Legend has it that the wife of the eccentric

Eleanor (Julie Harris) and Theodora (Claire Bloom), both of whom are seeking ghosts

architect who built it, Hugh Crain, was killed when her carriage crashed into a tree on the grounds, and that since then the house has been the cause of many mysterious deaths. Eager to learn if the dwelling is as ghost-filled as the locals believe, psychic investigators arrive to put the place through its poltergeist paces. Led by Dr John Markway (**Richard Johnson**), the team includes Eleanor (**Julie Harris**), a girl who has experience of the supernatural, Theodora (**Claire Bloom**), a woman with a history of extrasensory perception and Luke Sanderson (**Russ Tamblyn**), sceptical nephew of the current property owner.

The spiritual manifestations begin with an icy caress from nowhere brushing Eleanor's cheek and her name written in dust, pinpointing her as the target of the house's paranormal powers. By

Haunted and old dark houses

A group of strangers with dark secrets are brought together by a will being read, a dinner party, a dare or by accidents on a stormy night; but whatever gets them into the chilly interior, you can be sure that, because of crazed relatives or something more supernatural, they'll be lucky to get out alive. And you can be sure of massive rooms with giant fireplaces; endless stairways and dark passageways; sliding panels in walls and portraits with spy-holes; statues of armoured knights along creepy corridors; and flickering lights. The locations are clearly advertised in *Terror In The Haunted House* (1958), *House On Haunted Hill* (1959) and *The Haunted House Of Horror* (1969) but *The Uninvited* (1944), *13 Ghosts* (1960) and *The Haunting* have a similar share of poltergeist activity. The most famous old dark house of them all, however, is the Bates's home in *Psycho*.

the time Markway's cynical wife Grace (**Lois Maxwell**) shows up, the house has become a roaring dynamo of invisible psychic energy that is trying to penetrate her bedroom. To booming sound effects and over-emphatic music, and through subtle anamorphic camera lens use and infra-red (or false colour) technical trickery, walls melt and doors buckle while furniture flies and all manner of black souls from the beyond torment the highly-strung Eleanor. In a chilling conclusion echoing past events, the house of hell makes one last attempt to make Eleanor part of its ethereal realm for ever.

Without showing anything overtly, Wise creates superb scares and projects an atmosphere of palpable evil and menace in the claustrophobic locales. Indeed, one of the neatest explanations for the possession is the idea that because Crain deliberately avoided using any right angles in the house construction, all the wrong angles added up to a massive distortion, allowing the spirit to find a home.

Notable for its fine-tuned characterizations and for its ability to shatter the nerves via suggestion, *The Haunting* belongs to acclaimed stage actress Julie Harris, who gives one of the finest performances that the genre has ever seen. As the neurotic virgin medium haunted by her feelings of other-worldliness and possible attraction to lesbian Theo, her frightened mouse literally has a special effect in a film devoid of SFX. Wise's intention was for the audience of *The Haunting* to take it seriously – hence the lack of explicitness that doubled its power to horrify – and **Jan de Bont**'s terrible remake in 1999, in over-emphasizing the computer generated imagery to catastrophic effect, only proved how right Wise's approach was.

The Innocents

dir **Jack Clayton, 1961, UK, 99m, b/w**
cast **Deborah Kerr, Martin Stephens, Pamela Franklin, Megs Jenkins, Michael Redgrave** *cin* **Freddie Francis** *m* **Georges Auric**

Oozing class and academic distinction, director **Jack Clayton**'s stunning version of **Henry James**'s *The Turn Of The Screw*, one of literature's most famous ghost stories, was a prestige picture from the first frame. The psychosexuality barely hinted at in the 1897 novella was leapt upon by screenwriters **Truman Capote** and **William Archibald** (one of the writers of Hitchcock's 1953 thriller *I Confess*), who had no problem translating James's signature theme of the corruption of innocence into the post-Freudian analytical idiom so popular at the dawn of the Sixties. It was becoming more accepted then that traumatic childhood events could have devastating effects upon the adult personality.

Adding enormous resonance to the well-bred shivers, shudders and spine-tingling ambiguity is the ethereally beautiful black-and-white-photography of **Freddie Francis**, who went on to become a prolific horror director. And the remarkably shaded performance by **Deborah Kerr**, at the top of her game during this period, is the frosting on the multi-layered cake. She plays the repressed governess Miss Giddens, who is employed to look after the orphaned Flora (**Pamela Franklin**) and Miles (**Martin Stephens**), niece and nephew of a selfish uncle (**Michael Redgrave**).

The first clue to the theme of this sophisticated shocker comes when he asks the new nanny if she has an imagination – something he thinks will prove an asset in dealing with his wards. In fact she has an increasing belief that the two children in her care are possessed by evil spirits, possibly the product of her own sick fantasies and spinster suppressions.

Why else do the ghosts of sadist gardener Peter Quint (**Peter Wyngarde**) and masochist Miss Jessel (**Clytie Jessop**), the children's former governess, only become visible after Miss Giddens has seen their portraits and housekeeper Mrs Grose (**Megs Jenkins**) has informed her of their odd deaths? Whatever the truth – and Clayton's masterstroke is that he stages most of the uncertain imagery during daylight – Miss Giddens is determined to drive the spirits out, and embarks on a tragic path of exorcism.

Very much a product of its unspoken times – the only way for Clayton to capture the taboo sexuality of the piece was through suggestion – its proper

Deborah Kerr as the repressed governess Miss Giddens, with Martin Stephens as Miles

approach is precisely what heightens the inexplicable terror. A brilliant double-edged example is when nine-year-old Miles kisses Miss Giddens on the mouth and her reaction is one of breathless shock, as if the ravished heroine of a bodice-ripping romance. Is it merely a display of innocent affection? Or is he playing up to the stand-in romantic illusions that she is imposing on him because of her attraction to Quint?

While critics still argue over the justice done to James's subtleties, the stature of *The Innocents* as a rare breed of delicate horror continues to grow, not least because of the cinematography. "It was one of the very few films ever to be designed for Cinemascope," said Freddie Francis. "It was an intimate story so I had some large sideways graduated filters made up. That way we could move in and out of shots but leave the frame edges dark and dirty. So viewer interest was kept centre frame and they could never really see what was going on beyond it. Therefore something could conceivably happen at any time. It was that sort of suspense that made *The Innocents* so creepily effective. It's the best work I've ever done."

I Walked With A Zombie

dir **Jacques Tourneur, 1943, US, 69m, b/w**
cast **Frances Dee, Christine Gordon, Tom Conway, James Ellison, Edith Barrett** *cin* **J. Roy Hunt** *m* **Roy Webb**

By the time *Cat People* defied all odds and began to rack up the money, RKO production head **Charles Koerner** had already decided what producer **Val Lewton**'s follow-up was going to be. He had bought the rights to an article published in *American Weekly* magazine by columnist Inez Wallace entitled "I Walked With A Zombie". Lewton was mortified and was convinced that no one would go to see a psychological horror study with such a catchpenny label. So he wisely made the diversion more classy by jettisoning everything in Wallace's feature and, in the guise of a zombie chiller, freely adapting the dark romance *Jane Eyre*, a personal favourite of the Charlotte Brontë scholar, in the tropical setting of the West Indies. The final result is Lewton and director **Jacques Tourneur**'s greatest achievement in the genre; it's a rare piece of visual poetry, constructed as a haunting symphony of elegant nightmare imagery.

Canadian nurse Betsy (**Frances Dee**) goes to Haiti to look after the catatonic Jessica (**Christine Gordon**), the wife of the rich American plantation owner Paul Holland (**Tom Conway**). The St Sebastian island natives believe that Jessica's mindless state is the result of a voodoo curse placed on her by Holland's mother Mrs Rand (**Edith Barrett**) for having had an affair with Wesley (**James Ellison**), his half-brother. But Holland refuses to listen to local superstition and is convinced that Jessica is mentally ill. Then further troubles develop: Betsy and Paul start to fall in love with each other. Betsy seeks to solve the various problems, however, by curing Jessica, through taking her to a voodoo ceremony. She hopes that this will help her return to her normal self.

Betsy (Frances Dee) and Jessica (Christine Gordon) on their nocturnal walk

It's this nocturnal walk that is Tourneur's supreme tour de force. After a servant draws a map in cornmeal showing how to get to Houmfort, the island's voodoo nerve centre, Betsy leads Jessica through the eerie sugar cane fields, past various talismans – a tree-hung goat carcass, a horse's skull garlanded with faded flowers – as approaching drums drown out the sound of the rustling wind. This hypnotic, wordless and completely stage-managed sequence of gliding tracking shots and twinkling dissolves ends when Betsy's flashlight hits the imposing Carre-Four (**Darby Jones**), the giant zombie guard. Constituting the chilling core of the tone poem, this gorgeous gala of shadows, light, music and exotica represents a high watermark in screen terror.

Remarkably respectful of the customs of the voodoo culture used as an atmospheric backdrop, Tourneur brings to the fore Lewton's most common thematic thread – the powers of reason struggling against the powers of the unknown. Complete with a one-man Greek chorus, calypso singer **Sir Lancelot**, to fill in the plot gaps – "Shame And Scandal In The Family" is adapted to explain the underlying infidelities, sibling rivalry and meddling in-laws – *I Walked With A Zombie* blends beauty and beastliness to perfection.

Jaws

dir Steven Spielberg, 1975, US, 125m

cast Roy Scheider, Robert Shaw, Richard Dreyfuss, Lorraine Gary, Murray Hamilton *cin* Bill Butler, *m* John Williams

Jaws minted the sea suspense formula

Shark sightings rose at an extraordinary rate during the summer of 1975 while **Steven Spielberg**'s rampaging Great White ripped

apart American box-office records – it was the first film to reach the coveted $100 million mark – and redefined the blockbuster. An unprecedented and expensive marketing campaign shot the exciting horror adventure based on **Peter Benchley**'s bestseller to the top of the charts around the world too. It became not only the most profitable Hollywood film that had ever been made but also a benchmark for every future event movie.

Police chief Martin Brody (**Roy Scheider**) fears that a large man-eating shark has been picking off swimmers at his sleepy New England seaside town of Amity Island. Mayor Vaughn (**Murray Hamilton**) won't let him go public with his suspicions because of the lucrative July 4 tourism that is approaching. But when the shark causes wholesale beach panic the cover-up is over. So Brody, ichthyologist Matt Hooper (**Richard Dreyfuss**) and grizzled shark-hunter Quint (**Robert Shaw**) take a small boat out to sea to track down the eating-machine. Is it also searching for them?

There is constant fun, tension and horror, with Spielberg brilliantly mining the primal fear of being in the ocean and not knowing what could be swimming below, about to bite. Just as Alfred Hitchcock minted the shower scare with *Psycho*, the 27-year-old Young Turk, who despite being recognized as an emerging talent had only one feature film behind him, set in stone the sea suspense formula: water lapping unsettlingly over the camera lens, the shark appearing out of left field (when Brody casually dispenses chum into the ocean) and sly direction (the head of a shark victim appearing in a hole in a sunken shipwreck). Solid performances from the three leads, and their convincingly volatile dialogue, added to the shrewd package of terror, humour and – trendy in the aftermath of Watergate – authority-figure conspiracy.

Spielberg insisted on filming in the Atlantic Ocean rather than a studio backlot water tank because he maintained that "it just wouldn't look real". But the nightmare logistics and variable weather on location at Martha's Vineyard meant endless waiting around for the three mechanical sharks – named Bruce after Spielberg's lawyer – to operate properly in the salt water. Each cost $150,000 and malfunctioned, dragging out the shooting schedule and doubling the original budget. But, knowing that the success of the film rested entirely on the shark being believable, everyone stuck to their guns and crafted the best nature-retribution fable

Horror soundtracks

Nowadays every movie soundtrack is available for purchase – and often there is also the "music inspired by the movie". But it wasn't always like that. The first soundtracks released to wide acclaim that recorded sales to match were obvious Rodgers and Hammerstein musical spin-offs and *West Side Story* (1961); and **Bernard Herrmann** was already well known when he scored *Psycho*, so it was understandable that his music would have a large market.

It was the success of Ennio Morricone's scores for spaghetti Westerns such as *A Fistful Of Dollars* (1964) that put soundtracks in the charts that were not from musicals or written by eminent composers. In the horror world the soundtrack for *The Exorcist* was the first to be bought by the masses; none of the famous Hammer movie soundtracks was available until decades after the films were released, after the composer-as-celebrity vogue really took off in the Seventies. Soundtracks from before then are, however, among the ten greatest in the history of horror, listed here in descending order:

• *Psycho* (1960). Bernard Herrmann forced Alfred Hitchcock to use the seminal strings-only nerve-shredding score. Hitch wanted a jazz soundtrack and no music in the shower scene! Happily for horror history, Herrmann had enough clout to insist.

• *The Bride Of Frankenstein* (1935). In one of the first movie scores to use leitmotifs for the characters, Franz Waxman wittily incorporated wedding bells into the bride's first steps towards her intended monster mate, and to build tension expertly employed timpani to suggest her beating heart.

• *Suspiria* (1977). Goblin's pounding progressive rock fusion of lead guitar, discordant contrapuntal melody, breathy whispers and amplified sighs proved revolutionary in the way that music is used in horror movies.

• *Jaws* (1975). Steven Spielberg's composer of choice **John Williams** used brilliantly a deceptively simple low string motif in his classic theme.

since Hitchcock's *The Birds* (1963). Here the shark represents the force of nature determined to reclaim its home.

There were further Hitchcock analogies. **John Williams**'s pounding shark music became the most celebrated and talked-about score since Bernard Herrmann's score for *Psycho,* winning an Oscar, a

It symbolizes the great white shark's hunting mode: slow at first, and then getting faster and faster, louder and louder as it circles its prey and suddenly strikes without warning.

• *Halloween* (1978). On one of the most well-known and re-used of all horror soundtracks, director **John Carpenter** exploited the limitations of early synthesizers when creating a jolting mix of piano, rattle and pounding for his effectively repetitive stalking theme.

• *The Wicker Man* (1973). "Corn Rigs", "Gentle Johnny", "Willow's Song" and Christopher Lee singing "The Tinker Of Rye" are a few of the haunting melodies on a chillingly authentic pagan folk song compendium by Paul Giovanni, played by Magnet, that is laced with sinister eroticism and bawdy darkness.

• *The Exorcist* (1973). When Lalo Schifrin had his entire score axed by director William Friedkin on went Mike Oldfield's dreamy "Tubular Bells", alongside original work by Jack Nitzsche and previous compositions, to make horror soundtrack history. **Krzysztof Penderecki**'s "Polymorphia" track also featured in *The Shining* (1980).

• *The Haunted Palace* (1963). Big, bold and full of shimmering strings, growling brass and clashing cymbals, this is the most memorable and ambitious score by the musical director of American International Pictures, Ronald Stein. It's laden with creepy dissonance to artfully raise the tension.

• *Hellbound: Hellraiser II* (1988). The score for *Hellraiser* was incredibly powerful, but Christopher Young surpassed himself for the sequel, with his awesome orchestral soundtrack rapidly gaining ground as one of the most unsung horror gems.

• *Frankenstein Meets The Wolf Man* (1943). The ability of Vienna-born Hans J. Salter, who brought harmony to countless Universal horrors, to convey dark mystery behind the most ordinary of events reached its melodious zenith in director Roy William Neill's sequel to *The Wolf Man* (1941). Even the lilting song "Faro-La, Faro-Li" has a descending tonality that evokes brutal inevitability.

Bafta and a Golden Globe. And the poster featuring one of the most famous film logos ever – a woman swimming above a giant open-mouthed shark – showed up constantly in popular culture. None of the three sequels that followed – *Jaws 2* (1978), *Jaws 3-D* (1983) and *Jaws – The Revenge* (1987) – matched the power of the first.

Near Dark

dir **Kathryn Bigelow, 1987, US, 94m**
cast **Adrian Pasdar, Jenny Wright, Lance Henriksen, Bill Paxton, Jenette Goldstein** *cin* **Adam Greenberg** *m* **Tangerine Dream**

In 1987 two vampire movies were released that had virtually the same story. One was Joel Schumacher's *The Lost Boys*, a flashy piece of entertaining fluff. The other, perhaps the only essential horror movie to be directed by a woman, ingeniously revamped the genre with a dose of erotic symbolism, influenced by Anne Rice, that was tempered with AIDS awareness. **Kathryn Bigelow**, who soon afterwards was briefly married to director James Cameron, had only co-directed the biker movie *The Loveless* (1981) before this cult vampire Western, scripted with writer of *The Hitcher* (1986) **Eric Red**, which put her firmly on the map when it came to the macabre.

In their effort to modernize the creaky neck-biting genre, the duo got rid of all the gothic aspects of the mythology – the fangs, the bats, the holy water, the crucifixes and the mirrors – and kept only the most salient: the undead are burnt by sunshine, aren't killed by bullets, are incredibly strong and live forever. "I wanted a hybrid of genres," explained Bigelow. "At heart, it's a road movie with modern-day gunslingers, and because we set it in the Midwest, it was shadows at High Noon."

Texas farm boy Caleb Colton (**Adrian Pasdar**) picks up Mae (**Jenny Wright**) one hot summer night and lives to regret it. After a passionate kiss turns into something more than a love bite, Caleb finds himself uncomfortable in the daylight. And when he's kidnapped by a pack of marauding punks, whose camper van's windows are covered in tinfoil, his destiny becomes clear – he must learn to kill and drink his victims' blood in order to survive. But that's an act Caleb can do only by proxy.

In a brilliantly conceived shake-up of vampire lore, Pasdar gives a wonderfully nervous performance as the adjusting would-be nightwalker. He's backed by precision characterizations from **Lance Henriksen** (Jesse, the wise Civil War veteran who was turned into a vampire then and is resigned to his fate) and **Bill Paxton** (Severen, who makes a dangerously manic ritual out of every conquest). After a slow-burning start, Bigelow's precise direction locks in when the murderous nomads lay siege to a local bar. The power of this sequence – unified by an orgy of violence and psychological torture – is so strong that it takes the rest of the movie to get over the shock.

Yet for all Bigelow's purging of Hammer hokiness, one of the story's seemingly less logical premises – that a vampire can be saved if given a transfusion of mortal blood – comes straight from the original authority on the undead, Bram Stoker. "It was called 'blood-letting' in Stoker's *Dracula*," remarked Bigelow. "The whole notion of being able to reclaim a victim that way interested me." Even so, the word "vampire" is not mentioned once during her movie, as she did not want it to be easily categorized. Vampirism is merely her metaphor for the restlessness of youth: the constant search for new thrills and the inevitable fateful consequences.

With a driving score by **Tangerine Dream**, pertinent in-jokes such as the bullet that remains in the flesh before being coughed out, and the sublimely visual motel-room police raid, *Near Dark* is a neon-washed nightmare from a director who sadly never returned to the genre in which she made her name. Although she said at the time that women are interested in violence, she found that the cinema was a male-dominated industry, also observing: "Within the codes of who does what material, women are more associated with emotional material and men with the apparatus, the technology, the hardware." Indeed, she said: "I don't think of *Near Dark* as a violent horror movie, but an emotional, moral one."

A Nightmare On Elm Street

dir Wes Craven, 1984, US, 91m

cast John Saxon, Ronee Blakley, Heather Langenkamp, Amanda Wyss, Nick Corri, Johnny Depp, Robert Englund

cin Jacques Haitkin *m* Charles Bernstein

After dabbling with the "Is it a dream, or is it real?" concept in *The Last House On The Left* (1972) and *Deadly Blessing* (1981), **Wes**

Craven concocted a whole surreal shocker based on that conceit and re-energized the moribund teens-in-terror cycle. In the process he invented one of the most recognizable of modern horror villains in the grotesquely scarred Freddy Krueger, a vicious sadist with one-liners as razor-sharp as his steel fingernails.

In Craven's fresh nerve-rattler, getting a good night's sleep can severely damage your mental health. Four teenagers led by Nancy Thompson (**Heather Langenkamp**) share an identical nightmare about a dead child-molester who has returned from Hell to haunt their dreams. Nancy's best friend Tina (**Amanda Wyss**) is thrown around her bedroom – a bravura sequence based on a similar revolving-set trick as the 1950 Fred Astaire musical *Royal Wedding*. Then Tina's boyfriend Rod (**Nick Corri**) is strangled by a sheet and Nancy's boyfriend Glen (**Johnny Depp**, in his feature film debut) is sucked into his mattress and spat out as blood.

The reason why all this is happening is eventually explained by Nancy's perpetually drunk mother Marge (**Ronee Blakley**). When local child-killer Freddy Krueger escaped justice on a technicality, the townspeople, including Nancy's police chief father Donald (**John Saxon**), turned vigilante and burnt him to death in the basement furnace. So Freddy is tormenting the children of his old enemies through their nightmares. Soon Nancy realizes that the only way to stop the vengeance-crazed dream demon is to draw him into her reality and confront him on her own terms with a little help from her booby-trapped house.

What elevates Craven's warped twister above its mundane stalk-and-slash contemporaries is that the plot invites intellectual involvement – and this is why it was such a critical and commercial hit. While offering the visceral thrills, inventive jolts and sequel hook necessary for a mid-Eighties horror, Craven also wanted viewers to think – about the multi-layered divisions between nightmare worlds and dreamscapes, illusion and delusion, and, ultimately, closed parental attitudes and their children seeing that Freddy has no power in the cold light of day.

Investing Craven's wild ghost train ride with major teen appeal is all-American girl-next-door Heather Langenkamp. Aided by witty dialogue – "God, I look 20 years old!" she sighs after one sleepless night – her virtuoso performance remains credible throughout, whether being pulled under bathwater into a pitch-black pool or chased down a shadow-strewn back alley, while Craven blurs all distinctions relating to fantasy and reality. "It worked because it was one from the heart," he said about its success. "It had a good, solid story, it was totally original and Freddy did not use any cliché weapons." It also epitomized all that was great about Eighties horror.

Night Of The Demon
(aka Curse Of The Demon)

dir Jacques Tourneur, 1957, UK, 82m, b/w
cast Dana Andrews, Peggy Cummins, Niall MacGinniss, Maurice Denham, Athene Seyler *cin* Ted Scaife *m* Clifton Parke

One of the finest horror movies produced in the Fifties had nothing to do with the contemporary Hammer horror trend sweeping all before it. Instead it had everything to do with the summoning of the ominous in understated and suggested forms that had been the signature of **Jacques Tourneur**, in partnership with producer Val Lewton, a decade earlier. Tourneur's forte was to create mood and atmosphere to chilling effect, and using M. R. James's famous Edwardian ghost story *Casting The Runes* he excelled with a masterful essay on the realm of the supernatural.

Establishing the film's tenseness right from the start, a frenzied chase sequence has crusading demonology debunker Professor Harrington (**Maurice Denham**) hounded to his death by an unworldly ball of light that gradually comes to resemble a demon. Cut to Dr Holden (**Dana Andrews**), arriving in London intending to help Harrington, now deceased, to expose the supposedly fake devil cult operated by Dr Karswell (**Niall MacGinnis**). Befriending Harrington's daughter (**Peggy Cummins**), the sceptic Holden takes up the baton, aiming to prove the other doctor a fraud and connect him to the Professor's bizarre death.

But as Holden researches witchcraft at the British Museum, Karswell, the real satanic deal, passes him a parchment inscribed with runic symbols. This slip of paper has the power to summon primeval ghouls from places outside time and space, and unless Holden can

The influence of monster movies was occasionally clear in a film that was also very subtle

pass the runes back to Karswell within three days, he'll face a similar fate to Harrington.

With well-constructed precision and his trademark use of shadow-filled dark corners, Tourneur leads the viewer along the same path as his hero, from disbelief to uncertainty to sheer terror. Each commonplace situation turns implacably into a nightmare: the corridor at the Savoy that stretches into infinity, the party for orphaned children thrown by clown-dressed Karswell that turns into a demonstration of his formidable powers, the picturesque farm that Holden discovers is run by a coven, and the cat that suddenly turns into a diabolical panther when Holden breaks into Karswell's house. Every visual flourish is geared to putting the viewer on alert: horror could be only a nanosecond away.

The script by **Charles Bennett**, who wrote many early Alfred Hitchcock screenplays, retained the literary grace and sinister mystery elements of James's short story, and it's the accent on elaborated suspense here that makes the horror so potent. Much of it is generated by the charmed parchment trying to escape of its own accord from Holden before he and Harrington's daughter realize how to relocate its curse; there's also the startling appearance of light splinters forming a fireball in the distant forest signalling that Holden hasn't got much time left. Although producer **Hal E. Chester** added demonic shots against Tourneur's wishes that go against the grain of the subtly wrought atmosphere – for reasons that were commercially understandable given the popularity of monster movies at the time – it is a tribute to Tourneur's directorial skill that these never compromise the film's dread and the presence of the supernatural.

Night Of The Living Dead

dir George A. Romero, 1968, US, 96m, b/w

cast Judith O'Dea, Duane Jones, Karl Hardman, Marilyn Eastman, Kyra Schon *cin* George A. Romero

From the moment that director **George A. Romero**'s flesh-eating zombies lumbered across the screen, they left an indelible mark on the history of horror cinema and spawned countless imitations. Before abject terror was struck in the hearts of mortified audiences by Romero's assured debut, horror had mainly been about rubber monsters, cardboard gravestones or hands groping in the shadows.

Suddenly naked ghouls were visibly eating human meat, an adolescent girl viciously killed her own mother with a garden trowel and, worst of all, no one got out alive; even the hero was slaughtered. And having a black man as the lead was as radical as setting the terror firmly in the present day. Romero revolutionized the genre and finally made the horror picture something to contend with graphically and socio-politically.

Barbara (**Judith O'Dea**) and her brother Johnny (**Russ Streiner**) are making their annual trek to a cemetery in Pennsylvania to lay a wreath on their father's grave. "They're coming to get you," taunts Johnny wickedly as an unnoticed figure clumsily staggering in the background suddenly attacks and kills him and chases Barbara to an isolated farmhouse. This galvanizing and unexpected shock serves notice that what follows will continue in an unsentimental and pessimistic vein.

Realizing that her only companion is a mutilated corpse, Barbara rushes back outside, into the blinding glare of headlights. The truck driver Ben (**Duane Jones**) pulls her back inside and proceeds to board the place up against the unstoppable gathering of the undead. This zombie plague is explained perfunctorily as being casued by high radiation from a disintegrating space probe returning from Venus. But this old Fifties standby is the only cliché used by Romero; in another landmark departure from horror heroine

Graveyards

From the Allegheny Cemetery on Butler Street, Pittsburgh, the famous location for *Night Of The Living Dead*, to the dry-ice covered soundstages of the Titanus Studios, Rome, for Mario Bava's *Black Sunday*, the graveyard is a classic backdrop for horror movies. Cemeteries are places where vampires congregate and zombies emerge, where detectives nose around for clues and the disturbed hang out, and where demonic rituals take place and teens spend nights alone for a dare. Bodies are either buried alive, exhumed, snatched or displayed for gruesome laughs; and when coffins are unearthed and their lids wrenched open they reveal either nothing inside or steps leading down to somewhere mysterious. Two of the most interesting graveyard movies are from Italy: Massimo Pupillo's *Terror Creatures From The Grave* (1965) and Lucio Fulci's *The House By The Cemetery* (1981).

convention, Barbara slips from hysterical confusion into a state of catatonia where she remains immobilized, never to bounce back.

After the house has been securely barricaded, a group of fugitives hiding in the cellar reveal themselves. These include the annoying pain Harry Cooper (producer **Karl Hardman**), his wife Helen (**Marilyn Eastman**) and their daughter Karen (Hardman's daughter **Kyra Schon**), who has become sick after being bitten. Stupid survival squabbles within the farmhouse start to outweigh the threat from the zombies with Ben and Harry continually arguing over what to do for the best. In the downbeat end, it doesn't really matter.

Night Of The Living Dead was shot on 35mm black-and-white film, using natural lighting and hand-held camerawork for a documentary realism that helps to emphasize the ruthless logic, the subtle irony, and the claustrophobia and primal fears of hopelessness and the dark. And although Romero has repeatedly said there was no racial implication in casting Jones – he simply gave the best audition – it can't be denied that his ghastly and grisly opus reflects the social upheavals of the turbulent time. "It was 1968, man," Romero said, "Everybody had a 'message'. The anger and attitude and all that's there is just because it was the Sixties. We lived at the farmhouse, so we were always into raps about the implication and the meaning, so some of that crept in."

Nosferatu - eine Symphonie des Grauens
(Nosferatu - A Symphony Of Terror)

dir **F. W. Murnau, 1922, Ger, 95m, b/w**
cast **Max Schreck, Alexander Granach, Gustav von Wangenheim, Greta Schröder. G. H. Schnell** *cin* **Fritz Arno Wagner**

Alongside *The Cabinet Of Dr Caligari*, few films have had a more profound and lasting impact on horror movies than **F. W. Murnau**'s prime example of German Expressionism. But while *Caligari*'s influence was mainly a result of its distorted design, it was Murnau's determination to evoke unsettling chills with a strong visceral appeal that would lead to *Nosferatu*'s indelible stamp on the genre. His symphonic lighting, rhythmic editing and symbolic mise en scene were unparalleled and the horror imagery that he minted has been copied endlessly and probably will be forever. Werner Herzog attempted an often shot-by-shot remake in 1979; Francis Ford Coppola lifted chunks for his *Bram Stoker's Dracula* in 1992; and E. Elias Merhige was so entranced by the whole inception of the seminal shocker that he wrote and directed *Shadow Of The Vampire* (2000) to communicate the importance of Murnau's genius creation.

The vampire myth had been almost ignored in cinema's early days, until **Henrik Galeen**, who wrote two versions of *The Golem* (1915 and 1920) for director Paul Wegener, adapted an unofficial version of Bram Stoker's novel *Dracula*. Stoker's widow and estate

Max Schreck as F. W. Murnau's stunning creation Count Orlok, who is fading away

were not pleased, and sued the German producers, and eventually an English court ordered that the negatives be burnt. Despite the resulting mad scramble to destroy all copies, with historians attempting to save what they knew was a milestone cinematic achievement, numerous versions were available around the world, including in the United States, where it was shown in its most butchered form.

Nosferatu is a pretty straightforward Stoker rip-off, even though Galeen changed all character names, moved locations from London to Bremen and virtually excised the Irish writer's lore of the undead; the vampire here does cast shadows and reflections in mirrors. But while such deletions might remove the genuine horror of Stoker's original story, it's obvious why they were made. Shadows and reflections were crucial components of the Expressionist palette, and Murnau intended to use them as substitutions for shock to help create an eerie and disturbing atmosphere.

At the time of the Bremen plague in 1838, young estate agent Hutter (**Gustav Von Wangenheim**) is sent to the Carpathian mountains to arrange a property sale for the mysterious Count Orlok (**Max Schreck**). Disregarding local peasant warnings about the Count's blood-drinking habits, Hutter falls under his thrall and goes half-mad when his master leaves with several coffins and boards a ship to Bremen. While Hutter's wife Ellen (**Greta Schröder**) has ominous dreams about her husband's safety, and his boss Knock (**Alexander Granach**), a student of the occult, is sent raving to an asylum, Hutter escapes from the castle and heads home. As Orlok's boat docks, the plague breaks out – victims have scars on their necks – and after reading a vital book that explains what she must do Ellen devises a plan to lure him to her bedroom and keep him there until the cock crows, so that he will evaporate into thin air.

Using negative (for Hutter's passenger ride in Orlok's hearse-like coach through the land of phantoms) and fast motion (for Orlok piling up coffins in his cart), Murnau calls into duty sophisticated narrative patterning, dramatic lighting and editing tricks to lend his masterpiece an uncanny atmosphere that remains true to the intimidating, illogical nature of nightmares. The most famous sequence features Orlok climbing the stairs to Ellen's boudoir, the shadows highlighting his menacing outline and elongated claw-like fingers; and then the focus is on her eyes, which show pure fear.

Count Orlok is the film's most stunning creation. As portrayed by Max Schreck (whose name translates as "Maximum Terror"), he's a walking corpse, with the stiffest of gaits, pointed ears and teeth that resemble those of the rats that are one of the film's leitmotifs. (His skinned-bat look was copied by Tobe Hooper for Reggie Nalder's Kurt Barlow in his 1979 TV adaptation of Stephen King's *Salem's Lot*, and by Neil Marshall in 2005 for the cannibal creatures in *The Descent*). But although, unlike many villains, the vile Orlok is highly unsightly, *Nosferatu* still has an erotic side to it, with hints of sexual repression, necrophilia, sadomasochism and homosexuality – and the vampire horror would continue throughout its life to trade on that unusual aspect of attraction.

The Old Dark House

dir **James Whale, 1932, US, 71m, b/w**

cast **Boris Karloff, Melvyn Douglas, Charles Laughton, Gloria Stuart, Raymond Massey, Lilian Bond** *cin* **Arthur Edeson** *m* **Heinz Roemheld**

Deformity and disfigurement

Usually character deformity, from birth, or disfigurement denote villainy or latent homicidal tendencies: plot motors have been communicated cynically through facial scars (Boris Karloff's in *The Old Dark House*, 1932), birth defects (the dwarf in *Don't Look Now*, 1973) or amputees (Lon Chaney in numerous mutilated performances). *The Hunchback Of Notre Dame* in its many screen versions (including 1923, 1939 and 1956) is one of the few instances where a physically repulsive character is treated sympathetically.

Deformity and disfigurement are usually the work of talented make-up specialists, but real circus acts have been used for potent dramatic effect in *Freaks* (1932), *House Of The Damned* (1963), *The Mutations* (1973) and *The Sentinel* (1977). Rondo Hatton, who suffered from acromegaly, a progressive deforming of bones, portrayed murderers and specifically "The Creeper" in *The Pearl Of Death* (1944), *House Of Horrors* (1946) and *The Brute Man* (1946).

In the same year that Tod Browning made "freaks" appear more human than humans, **James Whale** reversed the idea by putting on a dazzling display of caricature grotesqueness. In the process he gave **Boris Karloff** his first top billing and provided **Charles Laughton** and **Raymond Massey** with their American film debuts.

After the phenomenon that *Frankenstein* became in 1931, Whale was crowned Universal's master of horror, and making this deceptively sly, melodramatic chiller honed his penchant for wit and elegance into a skilful style, which confounded viewers at a time when most other directors were still struggling to adjust to the addition of sound to the medium. Distilling the best features of *The Cat And The Canary*, and filtering them through Whale's own sardonic twistedness, *The Old Dark House* is the definitive film about a group of lost travellers trapped overnight in a spooky mansion. Every *Rocky Horror Picture Show* cultist knows that.

Whale blackened J. B. Priestley's story *Benighted*, an allegory about disillusionment in postwar England, into a study in darkly eccentric extremes. Lost in the Welsh mountains, Philip Waverton (Massey), his wife Margaret (future *Titanic* star **Gloria Stuart**) and Roger Penderel (**Melvyn Douglas**) seek refuge from a raging storm causing road landslides in a remote mansion owned by the Femm family. Whale's wicked parody of the upper classes has the unwelcoming house serve as the home to the aged bedridden patriarch (named John Dudgeon in the credits but really **Elspeth Dudgeon**), his prissy atheist pensioner son Horace (**Ernest Thesiger**), Horace's extremely religious sister Rebecca (**Eva Moore**) and their hulking mute butler Morgan (Karloff), who cannot be trusted near alcohol or pretty girls. The dynamic changes when two bedraggled travellers arrive, Sir William Porterhouse (Laughton) and chorus girl Gladys DuCane (**Lilian Bond**); as they all try to get some rest, Roger falls for Gladys, and a jealous Morgan frees the Femm's secret shame from his attic prison – older brother Saul (**Brember Wills**), who is a mad pyromaniac.

Creating a thick gothic atmosphere, Whale brings out the goose bumps even though the whimsical terrors arise from nothing more than the human foibles of insanity, decrepitude, sibling hatred and infirmity. With the safe haven proving to be just an illusion, the acting ensemble leave no stone unturned in highlighting the perversity of each character cipher. Whale brought in Ernest Thesiger from England specifically to play Horace, and his waspishly haughty personification is another outrageously demented delight. Thesiger comes into his own when sarcastically berating his sister for wanting to say grace at dinner and then, in menacing and miserly fashion, offering his unwanted guests a potato in turn.

Whale alternates between humour and horror, lulling viewers into a false sense of security until building up the sinister suspense in the madman-on-the-loose finale. In a tongue-in-cheek nod to *Frankenstein*, he introduces Karloff as the dangerously drunk brute Morgan with three jump cuts, each moving closer to his scarred face. As is the case with all Whale films, every camera angle, every use of lighting and every character is there for a reason, and here the elaborate camera movements are clearly designed to get the best three-dimensional effect out of the limited sets, to detract from any possible staginess. William Castle's dreadful Hammer remake in 1963 completely failed to do this.

Onibaba (The Hole)

dir **Kaneto Shindo, 1964, Jap, 105m, b/w**
cast **Nobuko Otowa, Jitsuko Yoshimura, Kei Sato, Taiji Tonoyama, Jukichi Uno** *cin* **Kiyomi Kuroda** *m* **Hikaru Hayashi**

For too long the image of Japanese cinema in the West was somewhere between the arthouse sobriety of Akira Kurosawa's *Seven Samurai* (1954) and a man in a rubber suit stomping on a miniature model of Tokyo in *Godzilla* (1954). Even though Kenji Mizoguchi's thriller *Ugetsu monogatari* (*Tale Of The Pale And Mysterious Moon After The Rain*, 1953)

Jitsuko Yoshimura, Nobuko Otowa and Taiji Tonoyama in Kaneto Shindo's period melodrama

had attracted wide critical acclaim outside the Orient and Nobuo Nakagawa was hard at work perfecting the *kaidan eiga* ("ghost story") genre on home shores, to scant international attention, very few people had ever seen a Japanese horror movie. **Kaneto Shindo**'s *Onibaba* was the first to attract a substantial release worldwide.

And for all the wrong reasons. Audiences flocked to see this absolute peak of atmospheric black-and-white horror in the crisp Val Lewton tradition largely because of its topless actresses and frank sexuality, Western cinema at the time facing heavy censorship. These were the days when people travelled hundreds of miles for a soft-core Scandinavian sex flick. Shindo's sexy period melodrama opened at most inner-city grind houses, and horror aficionados could finally experience the terrors which had shaken the supposed Japanese reserve.

The cruelty of war-ravaged feudal sixteenth-century Japan snaps into harsh focus in Shindo's comfortless, rebarbative screenplay that is fraught with an atavistic eroticism. An elderly woman (**Nobuko Otowa**) and her daughter-in-law (**Jitsuko Yoshimura**) live hand-to-mouth by killing battle-weary samurai, dumping their bodies in a deep black pit and selling their stolen armour for food. Bad news arrives with Hachi (**Kei Sato**), who returns from the war and informs the old woman that Kichi, her son, is dead. When the daughter and Hachi become lovers, the old woman grows increasingly desperate, fearful that the young girl will leave her, and is powerless when she goes off on her nightly trysts.

One night a lost soldier (**Jukichi Uno**) wearing a horrific demon mask (to protect his handsome face in combat, or so he claims) surprises the old woman and orders her to show him the way out of the grass forest. She kills him by leading him into the hole, and a plan forms in her mind. The next time her daughter-in-law heads for Hachi's hut, she dons the mask, pretends to be a devil, and scares her into running home. Each night she repeats the trick, and her plan appears to work – her daughter-in-law is too fearful to visit Hachi, believing the advent of this "devil" to be retribution for her sin. But the feudal mask of superstition ultimately proves to be a curse that will have terrifying effects.

Surprisingly slanted away from the traditional Japanese cinema theme of the haunted samurai (as seen in Hideo Gosha's *Goyokin*, from 1969), *Onibaba* focuses on the destitute peasant trying to make ends meet in near sub-human conditions. It has startling imagery, with slender spears of pampas grass stabbing the darkness in high-contrast black and white. It has poetic symbolism: the hole itself is the fulcrum of the movie, an omnipresent menace around which all the characters must take care, and is a symbol that could represent death, moral consciousness or even the oppressiveness of the superego. And, ultimately, the film has a harsh, moralistic twist when the supernatural intervenes to punish the two women's greed. *Onibaba* is full of pent-up emotions, and is fuelled by a slow-burning tension that eventually builds to abrupt violent horror, all borne of desperate material need.

Peeping Tom

dir **Michael Powell, 1960, UK, 109m**

cast **Carl Böhm, Anna Massey, Maxine Audley, Moira Shearer, Esmond Knight** *cin* **Otto Heller** *m* **Brian Easdale**

"The only really satisfactory way to dispose of *Peeping Tom* is to shovel it up and flush it swiftly down the nearest sewer," read a not unrepresentative review. "Even then the stench would remain." The heavily censored, authentically Sadeian and prescient psychological thriller about a scoptophiliac – a term coined by Freud for a person sexually stimulated by looking or being looked at – ruined the glittering career of its director overnight. **Michael Powell** had already indulged

Carl Böhm as Mark Lewis in Michael Powell's sophisticated study of watching and being watched

his passion for the bizarre in such outré excursions as *The Red Shoes* (1948) and *Tales Of Hoffmann* (1951), but no one was expecting him to cross the line so fearlessly with a complex intellectual discourse on voyeurism, disguised as a sleazy horror movie, from the cheap outfit behind such lurid exploiters as *Horrors Of The Black Museum* (1958).

Peeping Tom was a sophisticated study exploring the links between watching and being watched, and between being horrified but too fascinated to look away. Powell's brilliantly analytical approach to horror, so misunderstood at the time, is now seen for what it always was: daring exploration of the correlation between acts of violence and sexual gratification and their wide philosophical implications. Sex, pain, fear and filmmaking are related to each other endlessly in Powell's open acknowledgement that voyeurism has a horrifying price.

The four powerful forces are all interconnected in the life of the lonely Mark Lewis (**Carl Böhm**), who works as a focus-puller in a London film studio, as a sideline takes pornographic pictures, and is obsessed with the effects of abject fear and how it registers on the face and in the behaviour of the frightened. As a result of his childhood, when his callous scientist father used him as a guinea pig in his psychology experiments, he has turned into a compulsive murderer killing women with a knife concealed in his camera tripod leg that also has a mirror attached. That way he can film their dying gasps and contorted features as they watch their own reflections of terror, for private snuff movie projection.

Peeping Tom brims with mordant wit (Mark pretending to be a news photographer from *The Observer*, bad actress **Shirley Anne Field** playing a bad actress), overt symbolism (the phallic presence of the erect tripod leg, the literal and metaphorical blindness of his wholesome girlfriend's mother) and hidden allegory (all three of Mark's victims – prostitute, starlet, pin-up – rely on being gazed at for their trade). Powell's masterstroke is that he plays Mark's coldblooded father in the grainy black-and-white home movies that show how he induced his son's psychosis just as, directing, he induces not only terror but also a mortified reaction to it.

From the opening murder, shot subjectively through Mark's camera so that we watch a film within a film, to its richly saturated Technicolor filtered look, Powell uses elaborate techniques to infuse *Peeping Tom* with multi-layered meaning about the experience of watching a true horror movie. It may be drenched in the pale imagery of Fifties pornography – the pin-up was played by **Pamela Green**, the era's nude icon – but Powell's controversial shocker, eternally creepy and uniquely perverse, has never gone out of style.

The Phantom Of The Opera

dir **Rupert Julian, 1925, US, 94m**
cast **Lon Chaney, Mary Philbin, Norman Kerry, Snitz Edwards, Arthur Edmund Carewe** *cin* **Charles van Enger, Virgil Miller, Milton Bridenbecker**

The first filming of **Gaston Leroux**'s novel from 1908 is one of the great horror classics of the silent era, and is **Lon Chaney**'s crowning achievement as an actor/make-up artist, in a role that would immortalize him. It also established a formula that Universal studio head **Carl Laemmle** would rigorously rework well into the Thirties and Forties, introducing the significant idea for horror that those who are monstrous-looking will inevitably act monstrously. A pinnacle of the Hollywood fantastic – "Wild, Weird, Wonderful, the Picture Sensation of the Age" boasted the poster – it is memorable for three moments: the falling chandelier, the masked ball and, most famous of all, Chaney's image-shaping unmasking.

Dogged by persistent director problems – Chaney hated the credited **Rupert Julian**, had him replaced with Edward Sedgwick, and then directed many scenes himself - and extensively re-edited before release, Leroux's Gothic romance spirals into nightmare horror as the hero, Vicomte Raoul de Chagny (**Norman Kerry**), undergoes a series of booby-trapped ordeals to rescue beauty from the beast.

The beast here is disfigured composer Erik (Chaney), who haunts the backstage of, and the maze of tunnels under, the Opéra in Paris. (All the sets were built on the Universal backlot by production designer Ben Carré, who had worked in the place.) Smitten with ingénue soprano Christine Daae (**Mary Philbin**), he trains her to sing his composition "Don Juan Triumphant"

Erik (Lon Chaney) entering the masked ball dressed as if Poe's Red Death

and informs the Opéra's directors of the dire consequences that will befall the company if she does not perform it. But Christine betrays her mentor by seeing suitor Raoul again, and as Erik's evil side takes control of his tortured mind he imprisons her in the macabre bridal suite of his cellar lair. She is eventually saved, but Erik meets a grisly death.

From the moment the Phantom summons Christine into his catacomb domain through a mirror on the wall, this celebrated classic becomes a perfect evocation of Grand Guignol elegance and powerful nightmare imagery, which culminates in the quintessential unmasking scene. The intrigued Christine sneaks up behind Erik, who is playing the organ manically, and removes his mask, and there's a double shock: his skull-like face opens its distorted mouth in a silent scream before Christine shrieks, and her terrified delayed reaction adds another layer of fright.

Although the film has been remade several times, the chills have never been bettered, because of Chaney's self-imposed suffering, through his make-up, for his art. And while the story found new popularity as a musical, composer Andrew Lloyd Webber paid tribute to the Chaney version by re-creating exactly Erik's entry at the masked ball down a sweeping staircase dressed as if Edgar Allan Poe's Red Death – a chilling moment heightened by being presented in the tints of early two-strip Technicolor. With its epic playing of light and shadow and its creepy cobwebby secret passageways that hold hidden dangers, and with Chaney's awesome performance creating the most accurately portrayed of Leroux's figures of mystery, the film has a reputation that is fully deserved. There have been remakes by directors ranging from Dario Argento to Joel Schumacher, but none can match it.

The Pit And The Pendulum

dir **Roger Corman, 1961, US, 85m**

cast **Vincent Price, Barbara Steele, John Kerr, Luana Anders, Antony Carbone** *cin* **Floyd Crosby** *m* **Les Baxter**

After the box-office success of their inaugural Edgar Allan Poe adaptation *The Fall Of The House of Usher* (1960), which gained all-important acceptance from snobby critics who rarely reviewed low-budget horrors, American International Pictures immediately asked director **Roger Corman** for another. *The Pit And The Pendulum* set the Corman house style – even if it was considered ersatz Hammer – that would serve him well during the following non-stop Poe years. "It determined the way we did the rest of the

Poe films," said Corman. "Most of the short stories were only two or three pages long. They were really wonderful fragments. The method we adopted was to use the Poe short stories as the climax for a third act. We then constructed the first two acts in what we hoped was a manner faithful to Poe."

This quintessential Corman/Poe production might not owe much to the Boston-born author beyond its chilling torture apparatus, but the ambience created is completely faithful, intertwining habitual Poe ciphers (submissive male, dominant female) in a foreboding atmosphere of gloom, doom and death.

The only film to pair **Vincent Price**, the king of American horror, with **Barbara Steele**, the Italian queen, finds Francis Barnard (**John Kerr**) travelling to coastal Castle Medina in Spain, where he discovers his sister Elizabeth (Steele) has died and her husband Nicholas (Price) on the brink of madness. Given assurance that his sister died of natural causes, Francis is taken to the burial chamber and shown where her wall-interred coffin lies. But Elizabeth's physician Dr Charles Leon (**Antony Carbone**) tells him that she was frightened to death by a husband who seems to have inherited the family penchant for torture.

Soon the ghost of Elizabeth is haunting the castle grounds, and to satisfy Francis's mounting suspicions and Nicholas's gnawing guilt her crypt is opened. The agonizing posture of the decaying corpse suggests that she was buried alive. But the whole charade has been planned by the scheming Elizabeth to drive her husband crazy so that she can inherit his fortune.

Marvellously fusing sustained horror suspense, rich colours, Les Baxter's creepy music and production designer Daniel Haller's torture implement, the completely demented Nicholas chains Francis below a razor-sharp swinging pendulum and shuts Elizabeth in the spiked iron maiden in which his father killed his mother. Although many of the costumes, props, furniture and special effects would be reused (and easily recognized) in every future Corman/Poe production, here they all combined to create genuinely nerve-wracking accumulative horror.

In this lusty and gloriously Grand Guignol sideshow, Price gives a suitably rococo performance as the manipulated aristocrat rather than the villain. "Am I not the spawn of depraved blood?" he moans, racked with remorse. Steele uses her dark, fiery femme fatale looks to great effect yet again and the final shot through the iron maiden's eye slit, of her face contorted in horror, creates the finest frisson in the Poe series.

The Plague Of The Zombies

dir John Gilling, 1966, UK, 91m
cast Andre Morell, Diane Clare, Brook Williams,
Jacqueline Pearce, John Carson *cin* Arthur Grant *m*
James Bernard

By the mid-Sixties Hammer horrors had become a staple of the British film industry, and after producing nearly a hundred movies a certain conveyor belt mentality had crept into the studio's ethos. But occasionally they released a left-field entry that made critics and audiences sit up and take more note than usual. Don Sharp's fairytale *Kiss Of The Vampire* (1964) was one, and the superhero-infused *Captain Kronos – Vampire Hunter* (1974) another.

But the quirkiest was **John Gilling**'s *The Plague Of The Zombies*, which was not only one of the most pessimistic Hammers, but also contains one of their most imitated clips. It's a nightmare sequence suffused with green that sums up the film's darkest concerns – rotting graveyard corpses with dead fingers churning their way up through the earth to encircle the shocked dreamer in a clutching, crawling mass. Copied by filmmakers ever since – it caused a whole horror generation to have bad dreams – it may also have been one of the subconscious inspirations behind George A. Romero's *Night Of The Living Dead*.

Hammer had run out of old Universal films to remake by the time the Sixties were really swinging. So they were forced to find inspiration in other sub-genres, and they found it in the voodoo ceremonies of Haiti that had served well both *White Zombie* (1932) and *I Walked With A Zombie*. Shot back-to-back in 1965 at Bray Studios with Gilling's other oddball slice of nineteenth-century Cornish gothicism, *The Reptile*, *The Plague Of The Zombies*, originally titled *The Zombie*, has village folk falling victim to a fatal illness. When his wife Alice (**Jacqueline Pearce**) falls strangely sick, distraught doctor Peter Tompson (**Brook Williams**) calls on his former tutor Sir James Forbes (**Andre Morell**) for help. After he arrives with his daughter Sylvia (**Diane Clare**), an old school friend of Alice's, they uncover a macabre plot by Squire Hamilton (**John Carson**) to keep his tin mine productive after a work accident legally enforced its closure. He has been using ancient voodoo rites to raise the dead "plague" victims – though, in a typical Hammer come-on, it's not a plague – who serve at night as slave labour.

Scripted by the writer of Terence Fisher's *The Hound Of The Baskervilles* (1958), **Peter Bryan**, the visually captivating piece does not have a hard-hitting moral and political tone; but for Hammer horror in the second half of the Sixties, it struck, even if not deliberately, an untypical political note with its premise of the corrupt, arrogant aristocrat at the decadent manor being responsible for "infecting" his community. Those sharp enough to be on Gilling's wavelength would have guessed immediately that Hamilton was the villain: as Forbes arrives in the stricken village, the foxhunting nobility ride through a funeral procession and knock the coffin to the ground, positioning Hamilton as a callous landowner with no respect for the working class.

There's no sense of relief once the mystery has been solved. The most attractive character, Alice, meets the worst fate – she's decapitated with a spade – and although fire purges the community of foul Godforsaken wickedness in typical Hammer style, the ending is unusually downbeat.

Psycho

dir Alfred Hitchcock, 1960, US, 109m, b/w
cast Anthony Perkins, Janet Leigh, Vera Miles, John Gavin, Martin Balsam, John McIntire *cin* John L. Russell
m Bernard Herrmann

All modern horror starts here. **Alfred Hitchcock**'s landmark psychological thriller is undoubtedly the boldest, most innovative and most influential horror film of all time. Hitchcock was the master

The shower scene was terrifying but showed less than is often thought

of audience manipulation and suspense, and *Psycho* is the most frightening film ever produced because he made a murderer the nice boy next door, meticulously laced his sleekly modern chiller with subtle wit and repeatedly had the violence happen when least expected.

Psycho is a manual for any would-be horror director: the shower scene, which seemed to show everything – blood, stabbing, naked flesh – but actually showed very little; the cascading death on the stairs, seen from above until **Bernard Herrmann**'s seminal shrieking strings shatter the silence and our nerves; Lila finding the corpse of Norman's mother in the cellar basement and hitting a lightbulb as she recoils that accents every frightful eye-socket detail and mummified wrinkle.

Based on **Robert Bloch**'s grisly pulp novel, itself based on the life of Wisconsin necrophile Ed Gein, the story, and its surprise ending, is now part of the fabric of popular culture. Marion Crane (**Janet Leigh**) and her lover Sam Loomis (**John Gavin**) can't marry because of his heavy debts. So Marion steals $40,000 from her real estate employer and leaves Phoenix, Arizona, to start a new life with him in California. A heavy storm and fatigue cause her to spend the night off the beaten track at the Bates Motel, where shy owner Norman (**Anthony Perkins**) seems to live with his elderly, cranky mother.

After Marion is murdered in the shower, her sister Lila (**Vera Miles**) joins Sam and insurance detective Milton Arbogast (**Martin Balsam**) to investigate her sudden disappearance. It's only when Sam and Lila learn from the local sheriff (**John McIntire**) that Mrs Bates has been dead for years and search the Bates home to solve the mystery that they discover the terrifying truth. Norman is a schizophrenic homicidal lunatic who has kept his mother's rotting corpse in the house and takes on her domineering personality in the effort to deny his crime of matricide.

Psycho was revolutionary in many ways. It was the first movie in which a character who had been cleverly positioned as the main protagonist was killed off early on (after forty minutes), to make the initial murder even more disturbing, and that was the reason Hitchcock chose Janet Leigh at the height of her celebrity: no one would guess that he would dare dispense with Tony Curtis's wife so viciously and arbitrarily. Hitchcock also broke new ground by filming a toilet bowl; by putting a star (Leigh) on screen in a brassiere in a movie that wasn't sexploitation; and by casting a popular teen idol, and Top Forty hit-maker, as a murdering transvestite. Anthony Perkins knew he was making the career move of his life: he was right, but he didn't know how typecast he would be because of the film's astonishing success.

Psycho was also the first English-language movie to be promoted with the "No one … BUT NO ONE … will be admitted to the theatre after the start of each performance" gimmick. Audiences of the day thought nothing of arriving in the middle of movie and leaving during the next showing; Hitchcock knew that his shock ending would never work in that environment and he instigated a permanent change in viewing habits.

Most significantly, though, *Psycho* was the first horror movie to scare audiences senseless and leave them rigid with terror.

Re-Animator

dir Stuart Gordon, 1985, US, 86m

cast Jeffrey Combs, Bruce Abbott, Barbara Crampton, David Gale, Robert Sampson *cin* Mac Ahlberg *m* Richard Band

Rhode Island recluse H. P. Lovecraft's *Herbert West – Reanimator* short stories were going to be the basis of a play at Chicago's Organic Theatre and a pilot for a television series, but innovative stage director **Stuart Gordon** was persuaded by first-time producer **Brian Yuzna** that film would be the best medium. The horror world will always remain eternally grateful, for *Re-Animator* is a witty excess-all-areas horror gem capturing perfectly the sick humour of Lovecraft's pulp pastiches, written purely for the money, which were first published in the magazine *Home Brew* (1922) and were reprinted twenty years later in the magazine *Weird Tales*.

"It was deliberately re-written as a horror feature that wouldn't pull any punches," recalled Yuzna. "Since Stuart and I were both novices, I reasoned that not stinting on the horror would at least win over the hardcore audience, however deficient it might be in other areas. I did not want to be in debt for the next decade. It was the perfect example of beginner's luck."

Shot in sixteen days at an old studio in East Hollywood, Gordon's demented comedy horror is different in its use of Lovecraft's material from Roger Corman's *The Haunted Palace* (1963), David Greene's *The Shuttered Room* (1967) and Daniel Haller's *Die, Monster, Die!* (aka *Monster Of Terror*, 1965) and *The Dunwich Horror* (1970). "We stayed close to the original," as Gordon put it. "All the main routines are Lovecraft's, and I made sure we used his recurrent signature line 'I guess it wasn't fresh enough' because I believe he intended it to be funny."

After a gory mishap in a college in Switzerland where his professor literally explodes (accompanied by composer **Richard Band**'s disco remix of Bernard Herrmann's *Psycho* score), intense student Herbert West (**Jeffrey Combs**) arrives at the Miskatonic Medical School of Arkham, Massachusetts, determined to make a scientific breakthrough and bring the dead back to life. Creating a luminous green serum that reanimates dead tissue, he involves roommate Dan Cain (**Bruce Abbott**) and Dan's fiancée Megan Halsey (**Barbara Crampton**) in his dubious research by experimenting on their deceased cat. The next stop is the hospital laboratory of West's egotistical tutor Dr Carl Hill (**David Gale**), where the unstable reagent causes the death of Megan's father, the Dean (**Robert Sampson**) of the school. Because he wants to claim the formula as his own, Hill is turned into a megalomaniac head on a platter plotting with his severed body to bring West down and move in on Megan.

The outrageously over-the-top finale is twenty minutes of gory morgue mayhem, where drooling lobotomized zombies fight each other and, in the movie's most censored sequence, Hill's severed head performs oral sex on a screaming Megan. *Re-Animator* is a major-league splatter spectacular with an accent on grisly, ludicrous humour; and the film is made more macabre by its deadpan direction. It was followed by Brian Yuzna's *Bride Of Re-Animator* (1990) rehash and his Spanish-shot *Beyond Re-Animator* (2003).

Repulsion

dir **Roman Polanski, 1965, UK, 104m, b/w**

cast **Catherine Deneuve, Yvonne Furneaux, John Fraser, Ian Hendry, Patrick Wymark, Helen Fraser** *cin* **Gilbert Taylor** *m* **Chico Hamilton**

Still blood-freezing after all these years, Polish arthouse director **Roman Polanski**'s first English-language movie is a compelling study in homicidal psychosexual mania. The intelligence with which it explores the symbolic language of Freudian fantasies, desires and anxieties within the context of commercial horror cinema lingers in the mind long after the final image has disappeared. With this classic work, Polanski allied himself with horror pioneers Alfred Hitchcock, Michael Powell and Fritz Lang in his understanding that cinema as voyeuristic spectacle involves a complex balancing act of informing, engaging and entertaining.

Carol (Catherine Deneuve) with suitor Colin (John Fraser)

In *Psycho* Hitchcock made the viewer identify with the victims. In *Repulsion* Polanski cleverly inverts this and the viewer identifies with the sexually repressed psychotic Carol Ledoux (**Catherine Deneuve**) while being slowly and seductively taken into her deranged private world. The Belgian beautician lives in South Kensington, London, with older sister Helen (**Yvonne Furneaux**, star of 1959 Hammer movie *The Mummy*) and her lover Michael (**Ian Hendry**). All day long Carol hears from her ageing clientele how men are crude beasts and is whistled at by vulgar construction workers. All night long she's kept awake by Helen and Michael's noisy lovemaking.

Romance looks on the cards when she meets young suitor Colin (**John Fraser**) but he mistakes her paranoid shyness for erotic acquiescence, and his brush-off leads her to withdraw completely from reality. With her sister and boyfriend away on holiday, she starts to imagine that men are breaking into the apartment and raping her. And when Colin tries to apologize for his actions, her murderous fantasy becomes reality when she pounds him to death with a candlestick.

Sleazy landlord (**Patrick Wymark**) arrives to investigate the infestation of flies around Colin's corpse, stored in the bathroom, and in the film's most unforgettable and gasp-inducing scene, is slashed to death with a razor. Her sister returns home to find two dead bodies, the apartment a shambles and Carol out of her mind. In the famous Rosebud-style ending, which influenced Stanley Kubrick's last shot in *The Shining*, the camera moves in on an early photo of an unsmiling and self-conscious Carol, revealing that she was "different" even then.

Carol's deterioration into madness is shown in stark hallucinogenic horror form, with rooms becoming distorted, solid plaster turning mushy and hands shooting out of it to claw and caress her frigid body. Her unrelieved alienation, sexual frustration that she both repulses and attracts, and loneliness gain further artful resonance by being depicted in searing black-and-white.

Played with utter haunted conviction by the exquisite Deneuve, Carol becomes a predecessor of the "bunny boiler", because of the thematic density of frequent Polanski collaborator **Gérard Brach**'s script; for her slide into ever more frantic and disturbed behaviour is linked to leaving out a skinned rabbit that she hadn't yet cooked to rot for days on end. A truly harrowing descent into murderous claustrophobia, this masterpiece of personality disintegration was revisited by Polanski for his bleak black comedy *The Tenant* (1976).

Ringu (The Ring)

dir **Hideo Nakata, 1998, Jap, 95m**
cast **Nanako Matsushima, Miki Nakatani, Hiroyuki Sanada, Yuko Takeuchi, Hitomi Sato** *cin* **Ichiro Hayashi** *m* **Kenji Kawai**

Accept no substitute – especially the ridiculously overblown 2002 Hollywood remake directed by Gore Verbinski. (What were those horses doing?) Before its festival showcasing and eventual worldwide release in 2001, the West had completely missed out on the massive Asian horror phenomenon kick-started by **Hideo Nakata**'s *Ringu*. Japan's highest-grossing horror movie rivalled the global Pokemon craze in terms of tie-in merchandise and quick-fire copycat clones, which made its central evil spirit, Sadako, the new Freddy Krueger.

Based on the young adult novel of 1991 by **Koji Suzuki**, the Japanese Stephen King, Nakata's breath of fresh scare has a deceptively simple premise, which combines the conventions of New Wave American urban legend with the classic *kaidan eiga* tradition of long-haired, pale-faced lady spooks: a videotape curse. Anyone who watches the strange VHS cassette, and sees the fractured grainy visual of a woman combing her hair in a mirror, receives an ominous telephone call immediately afterwards saying that they have only seven days left to live.

Following many unexplained deaths linked to the video, television reporter Reiko Asakawa (**Nanako Matsushima**) investigates. Finding a copy, and blinded by naive curiosity, she watches it. Sure enough, the phone rings, she's told that her days are numbered, and in a panic she calls her ex-husband Ryuji (**Hiroyuki Sanada**) for help. He too can't resist the impulse to watch the video and both realize that they must decipher its weird arcane images and, more importantly, learn everything about Sadako (**Orie Izuno**), the terrifying demon girl at the root of each demise. Together they discover that forty years earlier, a psychic woman who could predict volcanic eruptions had an affair with a married researcher, and bore him a daughter who is responsible for the killing curse.

With its intelligent script, nerve-wracking gradual pace, disturbing atmosphere that is carefully contrived and often left-field twists, *Ringu* exerts a steely grip from the restrained opening onwards

Mirrors

Who would have thought that an ordinary household object could reveal a vampire who casts no reflection, act as a gateway to strange worlds, display an evil alter ego or be possessed by the evil deeds committed in front of it? But these are respective scenarios in *Dance Of The Vampires* (1967) and many more, *House* (1986), *Snow White: A Tale Of Terror* (1997), and both *The Haunted Mirror* segment of *Dead Of Night* (1945) and *Mirror, Mirror* (1990). You can conjure up the hook-handed villain in *Candyman* (1992) if you say his name five times while looking in a mirror, and breaking one brings particularly bad luck in *The Boogeyman* (1980), in which a malevolent supernatural force is contained in a glowing shard.

and delivers a conveyor belt of delectable shocks and unsettling surprises. The need to watch the unwatchable, a key feature of the horror tradition, is neatly encapsulated in modern form using video technology and the primeval spiritual thrust of the piece is rooted in such classic iconography as the water-well imagery from Kaneto Shindo's *Onibaba*. Matsushima, cool as ice, gives a paranoid edge to her demure role and is brilliantly choreographed by Nakata (direct-ing only his second film, following *Ghost Actress* in 1996), within his well-calculated and tightly constructed terror frame.

Ringu is highbrow horror that packs sneaky multiplex punches. The spine-tingling tension created when Sadako slowly crawls out of a television screen that is rewinding the angst-ridden video memories she has is a landmark moment in contemporary horror and must be seen by any fan of the genre. The film was followed by *Ringu 2* (1999) and the prequel *Ringu 0* (2000); *Ring 2: Spiral* (1998) and *The Ring Virus* (1999), two unofficial cash-ins; and every variation possible on the theme of the ancient curse meeting mod-ern technology, including *Phone* (2002), *One Missed Call* (2003) and *Shutter* (2004).

Rosemary's Baby

dir **Roman Polanski, 1968, US, 137m**
cast **Mia Farrow, John Cassavetes, Ruth Gordon, Sidney Blackmer, Ralph Bellamy** *cin* **William A. Fraker** *m* **Krzysztof Komeda**

Although produced by king of gimmick horror **William Castle**, starring headline-grabber **Mia Farrow** – Mrs Frank Sinatra at the time – and based on a Gothic coffee-table bestseller by **Ira Levin**, *Rosemary's Baby* wasn't burdened by the weight of expectation. But no one had banked on **Roman Polanski** taking a fresh look at the American Dream turned Nightmare or credibly placing such ancient biblical evil slap-bang in the centre of modern Manhattan.

Rosemary and Guy Woodhouse (Farrow and **John Cassavetes**), young and in love, move into an apartment and find themselves embraced by the very friendly neighbours, and in particular

Mia Farrow in Roman Polanski's vision of evil in modern Manhattan

elderly Minnie and Roman Castevet (**Ruth Gordon** and **Sidney Blackmer**). Soon Minnie is handing out lucky charms and chocolate mousse with a chalky under-taste on the same evening that the young couple have planned a romantic baby-making session.

After a weird dream in which she is surrounded by naked chanters, and Guy changing demonic shape before her eyes, Rosemary learns that she is indeed pregnant. But as her husband's acting career soars, her health and mental stability plummet. And her paranoia and concern for her child grow, especially when the Castevets' own doctor, Abraham Sapirstein (**Ralph Bellamy**), delivers her baby and says that it was born dead. However, searching the house after hearing a baby crying, she discovers that everyone in her new life is a witch, that Guy betrayed her for fame and fortune, and that her baby is Satan's son. The issue is whether she will accept the child as her own.

In his first Hollywood film Polanski successfully turned Levin's somewhat old-fashioned page-turner into an absorbingly tense study with mounting terror. The suspense comes from the empathy felt for Rosemary as she struggles to retain her sanity in the completely alien situation she finds herself dealing with. The pregnancy anxiety was the reason that the film also became one of the first horrors to appeal directly to women.

The Devil

The Devil is the main force behind every supernatural horror film, but is rarely shown in red-skinned, horned and cloven-hoofed glory. Exceptions include *Witchcraft Through The Ages* (1922), *The Devil Rides Out* (1968), *Fear No Evil* (1981) and *Legend* (1985). Most often he's depicted as a suave, well-dressed gentlemen with a keen wit. Actors who have played Lucifer's human persona include Adolphe Menjou (*The Sorrows Of Satan*, 1925), Telly Savalas (*Lisa And The Devil*, 1972), Jack Nicholson (*The Witches Of Eastwick*, 1987), Robert De Niro (*Angel Heart*, 1987) and Peter Stormare (*Constantine*, 2005).

The malevolent atmosphere grows through the sheer narrative momentum provided by Polanski's script (which discarded the novel's interior monologue), his restraint with visual images when horrific occurrences are taking place and his use of naturalistic settings, including the later even more infamous Dakota apartment building. Even though many people who saw the film swore that they actually saw the devil's spawn in the black crib, they imagined it. And that was Polanski's overall triumph.

God is absent in the world of the acclaimed Polish director, professionally and personally. He watched his mother die in a Nazi concentration camp and he escaped after being used by German soldiers as target practice. So a victory for the coven with their omnipotent dark powers isn't a surprise in an adult-themed masterpiece that replaces the usual terror thrills associated with the genre with tightly-wound unease.

An overnight sensation when released, *Rosemary's Baby* became one of the few horror movies to win an Oscar – for 71-year-old **Ruth Gordon**. She was one of the Hollywood veterans who Polanski had deliberately cast around Farrow to further accent her gamine, youthful, callow confusion. Polanski commented, "When I made *Rosemary's Baby* I was severely attacked by Catholic groups. Never by witches as some people said. Witches told me they liked the film."

Scream

dir Wes Craven, 1996, US, 111m

cast Drew Barrymore, Neve Campbell, David Arquette, Courteney Cox, Henry Winkler *cin* Mark Irwin *m* Marco Beltrami

Self-reflexivity became an art form in **Wes Craven**'s teen blockbuster *Scream*. The first horror movie to pay tribute to stalk-and-slashers and to explore sardonically the relationship between gore movies and their hardcore audience, it was a scream in both senses. Just as he breathed fresh life into his *A Nightmare On Elm Street* series with *Wes Craven's New Nightmare* (1994), the veteran director reinvents the slice-and-dice genre while also paying homage to it, thanks to fan Kevin Williamson's elaborate script, which manages to chill and thrill subversively even when sinister events are at their funniest. Williamson's screenplay was originally called "Scary Movie" – the reason why every character says it at least once – and the title was cheekily commandeered by producers at Miramax for their lampoon series, which started in 2000.

The sick maniac is on the loose in the small town of Woodsboro. First this phone freak pretends he's got a wrong number; then he asks his prey questions about her favourite horror movies before moving in, as in *When A Stranger Calls* (1979), for the sudden kill. Casey Becker (**Drew Barrymore**) gets her facts wrong on *Friday The 13th* (1980) and her disembowelled body is found hanging from a tree because of her sore lack of terror flick trivia.

Now the tightly knit community is living in fear again because Sidney Prescott (**Neve Campbell**) is being threatened, a year after her mother was found brutally murdered. As the news media gathers disbelievingly in the troubled town again – most notably TV reporter Gale Weathers (**Courteney Cox**), who always thought Sidney identified the wrong person as her mother's assassin – bumbling deputy sheriff Dewey Riley (**David Arquette**) tries to sift facts to make sense of the movie-driven stalkings and slashings. Events shift into jolting top gear when principal Arthur Himbry (**Henry Winkler**) is horrifically mutilated and news of his death reaches a house party being thrown by Stuart (**Matthew Lillard**), where the nervous students are watching a video of *Halloween* for tips on dealing with a masked assailant.

In this typical haunted house setting the completely atypical Grand Guignol finale is staged expertly by Craven to maximize tense bloodletting while indulging in hilariously smart theatrics. As video store worker Randy (**Jamie Kennedy**) advises everyone not to lose their virginity, a sure way to attract death, and wishes he'd watched *Prom Night* (1980) for extra security, the real psychopath creeps up on him from behind the sofa just as Michael Myers does the same to Jamie Lee Curtis on the television screen. How Craven manages to combine the two in his film is a devious delight among many that together altered the shape of Nineties horror.

In less skilful hands the fast and furious self-referencing might have tripped itself up. Here it only heightens the suspense, because Craven exposes the genre's devices while deftly using them for his own ends. And he doesn't cheat when it comes to the final unmasking. After slyly pointing a finger at each character in turn, Craven bucks convention yet again by delivering a perverse denouement that comes as a genuine surprise. "*Scream* confirmed my belief that horror films are essentially great character pieces," he said. "They get in deep under the skin of human psychology. Kids today have fears and need a way to process their terror in a positive and funny manner. *Scream* accomplished that with scenarios of intense anxiety and playfulness."

Scream has it all: engaging performances; inventive deaths (the garage door cat-flap crushing is pure genius); cameos from Priscilla Pointer (*Carrie*), Linda Blair (*The Exorcist*) and Craven himself dressed as Freddy Krueger; and great dialogue – "Life is a movie, only you can't pick your genre." There's also a trademark Craven message, with one character telling Sidney: "Don't blame the movies. Movies don't create psychos. Movies make psychos more creative." The sequels, *Scream 2* (1997) and *Scream 3* (2000), mocked the shock with diminishing returns.

The Shining

dir **Stanley Kubrick, 1980, UK, 146m**
cast **Jack Nicholson, Shelley Duvall, Danny Lloyd, Scatman Crothers, Barry Nelson** *cin* **John Alcott** *m* **Wendy Carlos**

Celebrated directors – and you couldn't ask for a bigger name than *A Clockwork Orange* maestro **Stanley Kubrick** – all make the same blunders when it comes to horror. They arrogantly think the rules don't apply to them when they deign to tackle the idiom, and/or they are so unfamiliar with the genre that the most moribund cliché images are called upon in the mistaken belief that viewers have never been shocked by them before. Many have come a cropper with both problems – Richard Donner with *The Omen* (1976) and Peter Hyams with *End Of Days* (1999) are only the tip of the iceberg. And Kubrick fell into this trap too with his carefully nurtured ghost story based on the bestseller by Stephen King.

The author wasn't very impressed with the finished result. "Kubrick knew exactly where all the scares should go and where all the pay-offs should come," he said. "It seems as though he simply said, 'This is too easy, I'm not going to do it that way.' So he didn't, and what he got was very little." But King changed his mind when the critical dust had settled. "Could it have been done better? Over the years I've come to believe that it probably could not." It's a sentiment echoed by many and now *The Shining* regularly tops lists of masterpieces of modern horror.

Kubrick may have minted the visual lexicon for science fiction with *2001: A Space Odyssey* (1968), but he did nothing remotely similar when focusing on a son's primal fear that his father will murderously turn on him and his defenceless mother. The only exceptions were the outdoor maze shots and his pioneering use of the Steadicam, a stabilized hand-held camera brace allowing the operator to achieve seamless fluidity in difficult locations.

Heavily influenced, as King admitted, by Shirley Jackson's book *The Haunting Of Hill House* (which was turned into the classic 1963 chiller *The Haunting*), the movie finds failed schoolteacher and would-be writer Jack Torrance (**Jack Nicholson**) offered the winter caretaker job at the luxurious Overlook Hotel in the Colorado mountains. Seeing it as an opportunity to work on his novel in an isolated environment, and despite its grisly past – the previous care-taker, Mr Grady, went insane and murdered his family – he accepts the position and moves into the imposing snow-bound edifice with his wife Wendy (**Shelley Duvall**) and son Danny (**Danny Lloyd**). Danny has a special mental power, "the shining", to see things that no one else can and has visions of the previous slaughters and premonitions of his father's homicidal tendencies.

Rejecting King's screenplay, Kubrick wrote his own version (with **Diane Johnson**) and changed the hotel from the embodiment of pure evil, affecting the inhabitants' personalities, to a place that merely

Stanley Kubrick put Shelley Duvall through 127 takes of the infamous "Here's Johnny" bathroom scene

houses the evil entity that Torrance, suffering from writer's block, has become. Not for nothing did many reviews comment that it wasn't King's vision that appeared on screen but "the house that Jack built" – a reference to the Torrance character and to Nicholson's overly crazed playing of the psychotic axe-wielder, complete with the Joker smile that he reprised in *Batman* (1989). By far the best performance comes from Duvall, who attributed her woman on the constant verge of hysterics to Kubrick's exhaustingly endless takes – 127 for the infamous "Here's Johnny" bathroom scene.

There are scary moments - the appearances of the mysterious twin girls, the never-explained vision of an elevator unleashing a river of blood and Wendy reading her husband's lengthy manuscript and realizing that it simply repeats "All work and no play makes Jack a dull boy". Yet Kubrick struggles to maintain a sense of unease as absurdities and Nicholson's tedious muggings pile up. But if it's borne in mind that this is a Kubrick film first and a horror film second, this mannered, big-budget version of *The Amityville Horror* (1979) could be the celebration of the perverse beauty of horror that some of its defenders proclaim it to be.

Shivers (aka The Parasite Murders/They Came From Within)

dir **David Cronenberg, 1974, Can, 87m**
cast **Paul Hampton, Joe Silver, Lynn Lowry, Allan Migicovsky, Barbara Steele, Fred Doederlein** *cin* **Robert Saad**

David Cronenberg has the uncanny ability to produce cautionary horrors that with hindsight are prophetic. And it all began with *Shivers* (originally released in Canada as *The Parasite Murders* and in the United States as *They Came From Within*, before being given the name by which it is best known), which chillingly seemed to forecast the onset of the AIDS virus. Cronenberg's take on *Invasion Of The Body Snatchers* (1955), with a sexual slant, was the most financially successful Canadian movie of the decade and it has only improved with age in the light of the devastating events that followed it.

Starliner Island seems the ideal suburban development. Only minutes from Montréal, it offers a self-contained community away from the hustle and bustle of the big city. Amenities include shops, a Laundromat and resident doctor Roger St Luc (**Paul Hampton**). But as a real estate agent drones on about the advantages of the luxury apartments, one of them is the scene of a brutal suicide and murder. Dr Emil Hobbes (**Fred Doederlein**) has cut open his teenage mistress,

Shivers seemed to forecast the onset of AIDS and won David Cronenberg a cult following

poured acid into her stomach and then slashed his own throat.

The reason? Experimenting with venereal diseases and aphrodisiacs, Hobbes has accidentally invented a parasite that causes rampant and wanton sexual behaviour while it gestates inside the body. And because his Lolita-like lover was far from faithful, she has infected quite a few other residents with the turd-like creature that crawls into any orifice available. St Luc and his girlfriend Forsythe (**Lynn Lowry**) – the wooden Ken and gorgeous Barbie of Cronenberg's sexual fantasy – are the last to succumb to the high-rise orgy and they join the promiscuous convoy heading for the mainland to start infecting the rest of the world with their deadly brand of permissiveness.

Owing equally to Don Siegel's *Invasion Of The Body Snatchers* and George A. Romero's *Night Of The Living Dead*, the first of Cronenberg's seminal "body horrors" travels through a nightmare world of our own making where the grotesque and bizarre make the flesh creep. The parasites of special effects make-up artist Joe Blasco are terrifically sleazy-looking and phallic and are disgusting when flying out of washing machines, crawling from bath plugholes, vomited out of windows, wriggling in the stomach, or prised off screaming faces with pliers. Striking slow motion is used when a parasite is passed via a lesbian kiss, involving scream queen **Barbara Steele**.

It was the sexual pastimes portrayed in Cronenberg's catalogue of excess that meant that *Shivers* not only was a gut-churner but also broke into the arthouse and soft-core porn enclaves. There is incest, bestiality and a notable scene of a young girl raping the apartment doorman, though no sense of exploitation. That was why world censors were unusually kind to Cronenberg's cutting-edge work: they saw the intelligent subtext amid the nudity and explicit bloodletting. And the director's attitude won him a die-hard cult following; he felt that the ending of *Shivers* was a happy one and that the pansexual shenanigans were a response to uptight society regarding imagination in the bedroom as a disease.

The Silence Of The Lambs

dir Jonathan Demme, 1990, US, 118m
cast Jodie Foster, Anthony Hopkins, Scott Glenn, Ted Levine, Anthony Heald, Roger Corman *cin* Tak Fujimoto
m Howard Shore

Michael Mann's adaptation of Thomas Harris's book *Red Dragon* into *Manhunter* (1986) gave movie audiences the first glimpse of Hannibal Lecter, played by Brian Cox. But it was **Anthony Hopkins** who, doing the seemingly impossible, made the cannibal viewer-friendly and won an Oscar for playing the smiling face of erudite evil to perfection. It was a clean sweep, as the film won the best movie Oscar, and there were also Academy Awards for director **Jonathan Demme**, actress **Jodie Foster** and screenwriter **Ted Tally**.

Demme's must-see of the 1991 summer season was an awesome shudder masterpiece and the leanest, meanest psycho-chiller for a long time. The protégé of Roger Corman – who cameos as the director of the FBI – delivered the sensationally scary goods with one of the finest ever adaptations of a bestseller. Thanks to Ted Tally's faithful tuning of Harris's perverse companion piece to *Red Dragon*, for once a gripping novel arrived on screen with every ounce of brutality and menace intact. Eschewing Mann's *Manhunter* designer splatter, Demme focuses on tight close-up performances and hard-hitting adult themes to generate maximum edge-of-the-seat suspense, and the intelligent result evokes a visceral response without relying on hackneyed visual clichés.

Tenacious FBI recruit Clarice Starling (Foster) is in hot pursuit of the transsexual serial killer known as Buffalo Bill (**Ted Levine**) who is kidnapping, murdering and skinning young girls across America's Midwest. For behavioural pointers and clues to his identity, she enlists the reticent aid of an imprisoned psychopath, Lecter. But in exchange for possible leads, the cool, calculating cannibal gleefully forces the troubled Starling to confront her own haunted past. In some of the most chilling scenes committed to film, the intellectual worming of the brilliant Lecter into Starling's vulnerable psyche, to uncover her innermost secrets and fears, is unforgettably potent.

Anthony Hopkins played the cannibal perfectly

It's their relationship and the developing dynamics of their cat-and-mouse battles of nerves that drive Demme's dance of derangement, and, frank imagery aside, the scalp-freezing core comes from the dialogue; and only a top-flight director like Demme would have the confidence and courage to let such shivers occur without flashy embellishment. A hypnotic Hopkins reinvents the warped genius Lecter, making the role unequivocally his own with a numbing effectiveness; like Boris Karloff in *Frankenstein*, he recognized the importance of the iconic part and rose to the challenge, etching the character indelibly into popular culture even though he later joked that he based the voice on "a combination of Truman Capote and Katharine Hepburn". Hopkins returned to this signature role in Ridley Scott's *Hannibal* (2001) and Brett Ratner's *Red Dragon* (2002).

There's not a single false note in Demme's masterwork, and beautifully designed touches leave the fingers hovering over a panic button: the huge hall where Lecter is eerily caged before making his gruesomely clever escape; his arrival at an airport in a metal straight-jacket with barred mouthpiece; the dingy cellar where "Buffalo Bill" keeps his terrified quarry. It's guaranteed to electrify.

The Sixth Sense

dir M. Night Shyamalan, 1999, US, 107m
cast Bruce Willis, Toni Collette, Olivia Williams, Haley Joel Osment, Donnie Wahlberg *cin* Tak Fujimoto *m* James Newton Howard

It put the phrase "I see dead people" in the vernacular and in every spoof; but the real importance of writer/director **M. Night Shyamalan**'s supernatural brainteaser is that it made the clever script leading to the big surprise ending, thanks to sleight-of-hand clues and sly misdirection, a winning formula again, as was clear from films such as *Switchblade Romance*. "Can you keep the Secret?" was one of the many taglines employed to scare up record-breaking business in this psychological meditation on the afterlife, which was designed by Indian-born Shyamalan to be "a cross between *The Exorcist* and *Ordinary People*". Even though its famous sucker punch tends to distract from its hidden qualities – "Aren't all endings a surprise?" asked

Shyamalan – *The Sixth Sense* remains a revered paranormal chiller and is uncommonly intelligent.

The champion bamboozler, unfolding at an effective measured pace, opens with Philadelphia-based child psychologist Malcolm Crowe (**Bruce Willis**) and loving wife Anna (**Olivia Williams**) celebrating his latest prize-winning achievement. Suddenly, a patient, Vincent Gray (**Donnie Wahlberg**) breaks into their bedroom, accuses Crowe of having failed him years before, and shoots the doctor before committing suicide. The following autumn, the slowly recovering Crowe is at a professional and personal crossroads: he's torturing himself over Gray's accusations and his self-obsession is making his medicated wife consider an affair.

Then Crowe takes an interest in the case of eight-year-old Cole Sear (**Haley Joel Osment**), whose problematic psyche seems to resemble that of Gray's aberrant schizophrenia. Cole's single mother Lynn (**Toni Collette**) is at her wit's end trying to understand why her loner son walks around in a perpetual state of anguish, covered in inexplicable cuts and bruises. The truth is that Cole can see the ghosts of victims of murder, accidents and suicide, who need his assistance to resolve issues in the real world so that they can cross over to the other side. Sceptical at first of Cole's powers, Crowe soon helps him to come to terms with his abnormal capability and in doing so takes his own shattered existence towards a genuinely touching and gasp-worthy revelation.

Tapping effortlessly into the ethereal vibe of *Ghost* (1990) and the carefully constructed jolts first seen in the gimmick-ridden catalogue of William Castle, Shyamalan carefully builds an eerie mood through confidently stylish direction, and the potent synergy of disarming shocks and intense acting makes for an unsettling and painfully believable experience. If Willis overdoes the cuteness, it doesn't matter, because Osment is riveting as the moppet spirit intermediary bemused by his strange gift. Shyamalan builds his whole harrowing house of cards around the young actor (who had previously played Forrest Gump Jr), which pays dividends that are intimate and tear-jerking – so much so that he and Collette, and Shyamalan for his writing, were all nominated for Oscars. In many ways, however, *The Sixth Sense* was a curse for Shyamalan; he felt compelled to increase the power of his conclusions, and often veered into silliness, as his next three mysteries, all withholding information – *Unbreakable* (2000), *Signs* (2002), *The Village* (2004) – revealed.

Poster taglines

Nothing that has gone before can compare with this! They couldn't escape the horror – and neither will you! It's the year's shock suspense sensation, the most terrifying story ever told and you'll grip your seat in sweat-inducing excitement!

If the taglines of many horror films were true we'd have been frightened by now into early graves, but we fall for exaggerated taglines because they describe exactly what we want to see – and this is more so for horror than for any other genre. But in horror, where marketing materials have more impact than critics, few movies have lived up to the outrageous campaigns created by press agents and copywriters.

The cheapest trick is comparison: "First *Rosemary's Baby*, then *The Omen* and now …". And never believe reviews from magazines you've never heard of because they probably don't exist. As a rule of thumb, the further over-the-top the claim, the worse the movie. Here are ten of the best, ending with two that are plain daft:

The Abominable Snowman (1957): "We dare you to see it alone! Each chilling moment a shock-test for your scare-endurance!"

Blood And Black Lace (1964): "Guaranteed! The 8 greatest shocks ever filmed!"

Blood Beach (1981): "Just when you thought it was safe to go back in the water – you can't get to it!"

The Curse of Frankenstein (1957) "will haunt you forever!"

Dr Jekyll And Sister Hyde (1971): "The sexual transformation of a man into a woman will actually take place before your very eyes!"

Pieces (1982): "You don't have to go to Texas for a chainsaw massacre. Pieces … It's exactly what you think it is!"

Suspiria

dir **Dario Argento, 1976, It, 97m**
cast **Jessica Harper, Stefania Casini, Flavio Bucci, Miguel Bosé, Udo Kier, Joan Bennett** *cin* **Luciano Tovoli** *m* **Dario Argento**

Dario Argento, "The Italian Hitchcock", turned his back on the

Schlock (1973): "Due to the horrifying nature of this film, NO ONE will be admitted to the theatre."

Spider Baby (1968): "So shocking we can't advertise what's in it. So shocking – it will Sliver Your Liver!"

The Abominable Dr Phibes (1971), in a spoof on *Love Story*: "Love means never having to say you're ugly."

Taste The Blood Of Dracula (1970): "Drink a pint of blood a day."

A poster for Mario Bava's *Blood And Black Lace* (1964), which combined classic elements of horror with an exaggerated tagline

stylish cosmopolitan thrillers with which he made his name (such as *The Bird With The Crystal Plumage* in 1970) to direct *Suspiria,* his first fully fledged horror fantasy. It remains his biggest international success and one that has influenced everyone from John Carpenter to Quentin Tarantino.

Written by Argento and his partner at the time, **Daria Nicolodi**, the three-ring Grand Guignol circus pushed the furthest boundaries of vicarious shock, visual flair and vicious violence, through ultra-gory special effects, lush decor and dazzling lighting, achieved by filming with outmoded Technicolor stock that gave the effect of being 3-D. In tandem with Argento's extraordinary contrapuntal use of a pounding progressive rock soundtrack by Italian super-group Goblin (he discovered them for *Deep Red* in 1975), this made for a breakthrough into new levels of cinematic sensation. Argento stated, "Fear is a 370 degree centigrade body temperature. With *Suspiria* I wanted 400 degrees!"

Suspiria was based in part on Thomas De Quincey's semi-autobiographical classic from 1822 *Confessions Of An Opium Eater* – and in particular the section on the "Three Mothers of Sighs, Darkness and Tears" – and also on the Walt Disney cartoon *Snow White And The Seven Dwarfs* (1937) and the true story of Nicolodi's grandmother attending a Swiss school with witchcraft on the curriculum.

Aspiring ballerina Suzy Banyon (**Jessica Harper**) enrols as a dance student at the Tanz Akademie in the Black Forest. But her arrival in Germany on a stormy night concludes with two female students being savagely murdered in the most acclaimed Argento set piece of them all. Beginning with one victim having her heart exposed and repeatedly stabbed, before hanging from an ornate ceiling, and ending on another girl's face sliced through by falling skylight glass as blood drips on her from the dangling corpse, *Suspiria*'s opening salvo is the most electrifying in the history of horror. The point was to start the film in the way that a normal horror would usually finish; that kept the audience on edge wondering what could possibly come next.

After further stunning occult deaths (by steel coils, possessed dog, nailed eyes), and a clue mouthed during gale force winds by one of the mutilated students, Suzy realizes that the school is held in a grip of terror by "the Black Queen" Elena Markos, reincarnated as headmistress Madame Blanc (**Joan Bennett**). And Suzy must fight the rotting witch's zombie alter ego if she is to escape from the cursed Akademie alive.

"Don't think, panic," read one contemporary review, and this is the best way to view Argento's treatise on the magical chaos lurking beneath everyday reality that still exerts a spellbinding allure. Argento said, "All the sets were built to scale, the higher than normal door handles for example, because I wanted to reduce the actresses down in size and have them seem like adolescents. *Suspiria* is told from the child's point of view – the reason it remains so primal and frightening." It was followed by the commercially unsuccessful sequel *Inferno* (1980), focusing on the Mother of Darkness.

Switchblade Romance
(Haute tension)

dir Alexandre Aja, 2003, Fr, 91m
cast Cécile De France, Maïwenn Le Besco, Philippe Nahon, Franck Khalfoun, Andrei Finti, Oana Pellea *cin* Maxime Alexandre *m* François Eudes

Switchblade Romance was the first influential horror film of the new millennium to terrify, disturb and shock. French director **Alexandre Aja**'s sophisticated slasher conforms to the trend of young devotee filmmakers recreating their favourite morbid memories, as crafted by the older generation of merchants of menace. "It's **Gregory Levasseur** [co-writer and art director] and my self-confessed homage to such survival exploiters as Wes Craven's *Last House On The Left*, Bill Lustig's *Maniac* and William Fruet's *Death Weekend*," explained Aja. "Those were the movies we enjoyed most because the violence was excruciatingly real." Hence the neo-nasty atmosphere, courtesy of wincing make-up effects by *Zombie Flesh-Eaters* veteran Giannetto de Rossi. The contemporary touches of **Maxime Alexandre**'s crisply cool photography and **François Eudes**'s nerve-jangling score – composed for instruments that he created for bodily and aural sensation – take the suspense to new heights in this grisly charnel house of horror.

Students Marie (**Cécile De France**) and Alex (**Maïwenn Le Besco**, the blue diva in the 1997 fantasy *The Fifth Element*, which was directed by *Switchblade Romance* co-producer **Luc Besson**) arrive at Alex's family's house in the French countryside to cram for exams. As soon as they have settled in for the night a mysterious trucker (**Philippe Nahon**) appears at the door, decapitates Alex's father, cuts her mother's throat, and ties Alex up and puts her in the back of his rusty vehicle after raping her. Having witnessed everything in mute distress, Marie – "my take-charge Jamie Lee Curtis, Linda Hamilton and Sigourney Weaver all rolled into one", said Aja – hides alongside Alex, and when their assailant stops for petrol she tries to get the garage cashier to call the police. But the suspicious trucker axes him through the heart and drives off with Alex, whom

Aja's film is made more powerful by its cool photography

he tortures during the rest of the journey into the dark backwoods and into a major plot twist.

In a highly controversial sudden climactic shift to gruesome reality, Aja (son of French director **Alexandre Arcady**) gleefully sets up an instant rewind of all that has happened to take on board new psychosexual implications and redefine what's initially considered glaring slice-and-dice cliché. It's a daring and outrageous move (and yet its politically incorrect sordidness dovetails with the film's tone of nostalgia). "The violence has to over-convince the audience into averting their eyes so they might miss that vital piece of crucial information," revealed Aja.

From start to finish, all the blood-soaked ultraviolence carries a forceful impact. Underlined by layers of ironic wit in the style of Brian De Palma (the bravura slow slitting of Alex's mother's throat and death rattle), the relentlessly involving action is bookended by scenes in a lunatic asylum. Watch out for the torch, the string, the plastic bag and the barbed wire in this artfully deranged, horrifically flinch-inducing bloodbath.

The Texas Chainsaw Massacre

dir Tobe Hooper, 1974, US, 83m
cast Marilyn Burns, Gunnar Hansen, Allen Danziger, Edwin Neal, Paul A. Partain, William Vail, Teri McMinn *cin* Daniel Pearl *m* Tobe Hooper, Wayne Bell

"Who will survive and what will be left of them?" was one of the greatest ever horror poster taglines. It belongs to this landmark classic that started the power tool cult and is the recognized ancestor of splatter mania, even though it doesn't contain the geysers of blood that everyone imagines it does. What's really astounding is that the scalp-freezing value of **Tobe Hooper**'s ferociously terrifying horror has never diminished, because of the razor-sharp skill with which it was made.

Hooper's trump card in this grungy marvel – the micro-budget only adds to its harshly gritty, creepy tone – is his reliance on grainy *cinéma vérité* realism coupled with the true horror of anticipation and suggestion. It was the three sequels – *The Texas Chainsaw Massacre 2* (1986), which Hooper directed, *Leatherface: Texas Chainsaw Massacre III* (1989) and *The Return Of The Texas Chainsaw Massacre* (1994) – that were more violent and exploitative, but they were nowhere near as uncompromisingly scary.

Based on the same story of Ed Gein that provided the inspiration for *Psycho* and *Deranged: Confessions Of A Necrophile* (also 1974), Hooper's scream-filled suspense masterpiece has five young hippie Texans, Sally Hardesty (**Marilyn Burns**), her wheelchair-ridden brother Franklin (**Paul A. Partain**), her boyfriend Jerry (**Allen Danziger**) and friends Kirk (**William Vail**) and Pam (**Teri McMinn**), visiting a graveyard

Gunnar Hansen as Leatherface

desecrated by vandals where Sally's grandfather is buried. After picking up slimy hitchhiker (**Edwin Neal**), who cuts himself and slashes Franklin, they stop for petrol and encounter a demented family of murderous cannibals who kill passers-by and use the human meat in their special-recipe sausages.

Cleverly making his audience identify vicariously with the plight of animals in a slaughterhouse, Hooper has the innocent victims hung on meat hooks, put in freezers and sliced into chunks. If these murders don't stun you into shocked silence, the toe-curling climax set around a ramshackle dinner table will finish you off. Sally is tied up, tortured and held over a bucket by the crazed inbred family as their corpse-like grandfather attempts to hit her over the head with a too-heavy hammer. This grotesque tableau is the film's most prolonged and unpleasant scene and owes itself to Hooper's intent to have each family member embody one of Gein's personality traits; from mumbling shyness to sudden barbarity, there is a Geinocological side to each diner, such as the skin mask of Leatherface.

Although filled with quirky humour and bizarre characters (the prime example being Leatherface, played by **Gunnar Hansen**), it's the brutal accumulative effect of Hooper's disturbingly matter-of-fact direction that sears the brain and puts the alarmed imagination on exhausting overdrive. The revulsion that the film engenders is the result of the senselessness and cruelness of the murders rather than gruesome special effects.

Hooper said, "It's a film about meat, about people who have gone beyond dealing with animal meat and rats and dogs and cats. Crazy retarded people going beyond the line between animal and human. The single most important influence on *Chainsaw* was the old EC Comic collections which I loved reading as a seven–year–

That's exploitation

Dictionary definitions of the verb "to exploit" give the meanings of using, especially for profit, and using selfishly for one's own ends. "Exploitation" films can be tied to both definitions.

The movie industry is a business and the bottom line is that, as in every other industry, the products have to make money, and exploitation films are made solely for this purpose and have few redeeming features. They are usually made by canny businessman filling a gap in the market, as the director Herschell Gordon Lewis did in *Blood Feast* (1963), when he drenched mannequins in more gore than had been used before.

Exploitation movies are also the price that society pays for living a lie: no one wants to admit they enjoy watching the misfortunes of others, but that enjoyment is what horror exploitation promotes. Although the ideal of the cinema is of life-enhancement, for many people, there is a secret thrill in witnessing the misfortunes of others, and exploitation films can provide that without the guilt attached to situations when the victims are real.

While exploitation films have been around since the dawn of cinema, and came into their own in the grind houses of the Thirties and Forties, with the accent more on nude titillation, horror exploitation began in 1947 with the publication of the notorious EC Comics. Their graphic depictions of wronged victims taking inventive bloody revenge soon had the Establishment banning them, but not before exploiters saw a way to tap an eager audience. The inexpensive gruesome binges featured graphic detail that inadvertently led to the rise of Hammer.

Later developments showed that films could be exploitative in other ways. The term can refer to movies where unscrupulous producers promise perverse chills on the poster that are not delivered, and indeed much of American International Pictures' drive-in fodder started with a poster first – such as *Creature From The Haunted Sea* (1960) – that then had to be vaguely adhered to on a shoestring budget by the unfortunate director. Also coming under the banner of exploitation are the films by hungry wannabes who deliberately court controversy solely to get noticed – *The Last House On The Left* (1972) by Wes Craven being a textbook example.

Whatever category the filmmakers fall into, they are all totally shameless (and in some cases talent-less), but precisely because of that they often create bone-chilling reactions that are unparalleled; Tobe Hooper showed that he could do this in the twisted cheapie *The Texas Chainsaw Massacre*. Always seen as the lowest, sickest and most shocking of sub-genres, the exploitation film finally became respectable when Paramount picked up the distribution rights to *Friday The 13th* in 1980 and forever changed the way the once derided product was viewed by the industry and by the public.

old." When remade reasonably in 2003, director **Marcus Nispel** merely piled on the gore and filtered the retooled story through thirty intervening years of slasher cliché.

The Uninvited

dir Lewis Allen, 1944, US, 98m, b/w
cast Ray Milland, Gail Russell, Ruth Hussey, Donald Crisp, Cornelia Otis Skinner *cin* Charles Lang Jr *m* Victor Young

Advertised as "The story of a love that is out of this world", director **Lewis Allen**'s polite tale of the supernatural was the cinema's first really good and unapologetic ghost story. With Universal interested only in the classic franchise monsters, anything of a phantom or spectral nature was conspicuously absent from most studios' agendas during the first golden age of horror. Or if they crept in they were used for comic effect, as in René Clair's *The Ghost Goes West* (1936), its huge popularity based on sidelining eeriness in favour of side-splitting fantasy, putting anything mildly scary on the back-burner. Even haunted houses, such as those featured in *The Cat And The Canary* and its remakes, were revealed to be dull, ordinary and usually just full of bogus bogeymen and jokers dressed in white sheets. But *The Uninvited* was different.

Made by Paramount Pictures as a big-budget riposte to the cheap RKO chillers produced by Val Lewton that were frequently attracting critical acclaim, the film is almost a forerunner of *The Haunting*. Based on Dorothy Macardle's female-friendly 1941 novel *Uneasy Freehold*, it follows composer and music critic Roderick Fitzgerald (**Ray Milland**), on holiday in Cornwall with his sister Pamela (**Ruth Hussey**). Coming across the charming Wentwood House overlooking the sea and finding it up for sale at a (suspiciously) low price, they buy it. But the moment they move in, strange things start to happen; their pet dog refuses to go upstairs, some places feel decidedly chilly, flowers wilt almost instantly, one room is impregnated with the scent of mimosa and a romantic piano piece suddenly turns sombre as the ghostly chords waft through the house.

Conducting a séance, they learn that the house is haunted by two female apparitions: one friendly and mournful, the other evil and

Ray Milland and
Ruth Hussey in Lewis Allen's
Lewton-influenced classic

hostile. Matters soon become clearer when Roderick falls in love with neighbour Stella Meredith (**Gail Russell**), who lived in the house as a child and believes that her dead mother's ghost is trying to tell her something important. The other spirit is determined to stop this, being implicated in the tragically haunting secret.

Very much a product of its Lewton-influenced time, and similar to Alfred Hitchcock's *Rebecca* (1940) in being a popular mystery romance featuring an eerie house, Allen's disquieting melodrama has a chilling touch when dosing out its well-calculated shivers, and is greatly aided by Charles Lang's stylish cinematography. The eerie séance still has simple shock value through exploiting a natural fear of the unseen – the well-timed moment when a window flies open remains an effective jolt – and the menacing mysteriousness is well maintained until the movie finishes with a wholly satisfying climax and a witty last line.

Yet Paramount felt that the film would perplex audiences with its wilful obscurity, so they added some shots of Stella's mother's ghost to spell out the supernatural explanation. But in the United Kingdom the censor removed them and, as a result, *The Uninvited* pleased British critics for relying on mood rather than tacky visualization.

Witchfinder General (aka The Conqueror Worm)

dir **Michael Reeves, 1968, UK, 87m**
cast **Vincent Price, Ian Ogilvy, Hilary Dwyer, Rupert Davies, Robert Russell, Nicky Henson, Wilfrid Brambell**
cin **John Coquillon** *m* **Paul Ferris**

Vincent Price gave a performance that was more restrained than usual as the Puritan angel of death Matthew Hopkins in wunderkind director **Michael Reeves**'s final masterpiece before he committed suicide at the age of 25. A work of classic horror that is brutal, despairing and thematically fascinating, this nihilistic chiller based on the vaguely factual book by **Ronald Bassett** carries the message that evil begets evil and violence begets violence. It was condemned on all sides when released for its extreme savagery; but it crystallized Reeve's reputation, after he died, as a stylish filmmaker of serious intent.

Hopkins is appointed by Parliament during the English Civil War to root out sorcery and witchcraft across the land. Richard Marshall (**Ian Ogilvy**), a young soldier on leave from Cromwell's army, heads home to Brandiston, Norfolk, where his girlfriend Sara (**Hilary Dwyer**) lives under the watchful eye of her priest uncle John Lowes (**Rupert Davies**). Having promised to marry Sara so that she'll come to no harm in such Godforsaken times, Marshall passes Hopkins and his sadistic apprentice John Stearne (**Robert Russell**) on the journey back to join his regiment.

But Hopkins has gone to Brandiston to brand Lowes an idolater, and takes up Sara's desperate offer of her body for her uncle's life. After Stearne rapes her, has Lowes killed anyway and scythes through the rest of the village, Marshall returns to uncomprehending mayhem. Learning of what Sara has gone through, he swears to bring Hopkins and his assistant before God's divine judgement. Yet as Hopkins' reign of terror spreads, and Marshall's bloodlust grows, it becomes clear that his intention is to bring the witchfinder not to society's justice, but his own.

Although Reeves does focus on the ludicrously loaded witch tests that always resulted in death – the pricking to find the Devil's mark, the ducking stool, hanging, burning on a pyre – it's his brilliant staging of the horrifying climax that pulls together all the elements of the Jacobean revenge tragedy. As Sara undergoes further torture by Stearne pricking her and Hopkins moving in to brand her with a cross, Marshall knocks Stearne to the floor, gouges out his eye with his spur and hacks Hopkins repeatedly with an axe. It's then trooper Swallow (**Nicky Henson**) who shoots Hopkins to put him out of his misery – the last thing Marshall wanted. "You've taken him from me," he screams, deranged, as audiences retreated behind their seats in stunned shock at such a powerful and meaningful conclusion.

For if *Witchfinder General* effectively depicted how men in authority can exploit their positions to satisfy their own debauched and depraved tastes, it also showed the perversion of a once innocent man being driven to become exactly what he despises. Marshall's desire for vengeance comes not from the harm done to his beloved – he is oblivious to Sara's final torment – but from the realization that Hopkins caused him to break his oath to protect her. Yet ultimately he relishes the torture that he metes out to Hopkins as much as the witchfinder enjoyed his. The circle of corruption is complete.

Michael Reeves's film showed how evil begets evil

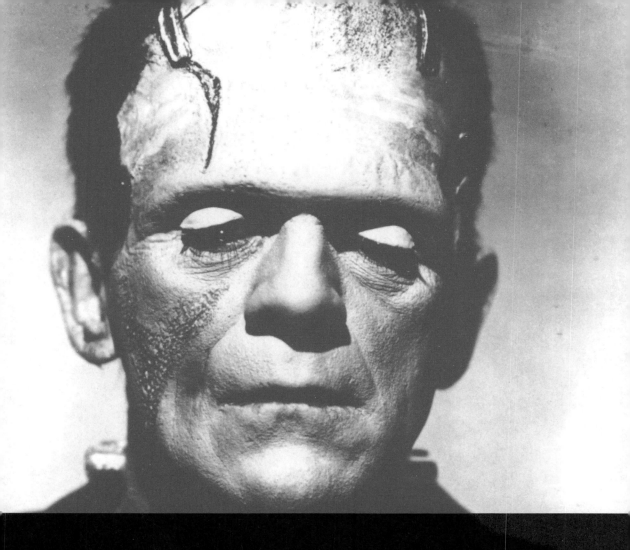

The Icons: the faces of horror

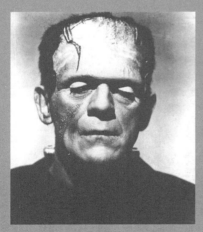

Boris Karloff as Frankenstein, the part
that made him a household name, in
James Whale's film of 1931

The Icons:
the faces of horror

Horror can be analyzed not only through its key films, but also through the influential actors and directors whose careers are spent entirely or predominantly in the genre, and the characters who have been re-created constantly or popular enough to have their own franchise. This alphabetically arranged chapter tells you about all those who in this way are crucial to the genre of horror: the icons.

Dario Argento
Director, 1940-

Dario Argento was born in Rome to a family already immersed in the visual arts; during the 1950s his father, Salvatore, was crucial to the introduction and popularization of Italian films around the world, thanks to his job as a public relations executive at Unitalia, the government-funded organization for promoting cinema exports, and his Brazilian mother, Elda Luxardo, was a famous celebrity photographer. Starting his career as a film critic for the newspaper *Paese Sera*, Argento was lured into directing after his collaboration with **Bernardo Bertolucci** on

the script for Sergio Leone's *Once Upon A Time In The West* (1968).

His first directorial effort, *The Bird With The Crystal Plumage* (1970), was a chilling thriller that appropriated the basics of Mario Bava's *gialli* but made the murder of key stylistic importance rather than the plot, and thus marked a sea change for the Italian film industry. Its massive critical and box-office success led him to be dubbed "the Italian Hitchcock". More sexually graphic and violently bloody shockers followed in its wake, all filmed with his signature overwrought flair – *The Cat O'Nine Tails, Four Flies On Grey Velvet* (both 1971) and *Deep Red* (1975). The latter, showcasing a score by Goblin, set an international benchmark for use in a soundtrack of high decibel progressive rock music.

It was the visually ornate, shocking horror *Suspiria* (1977, see Canon) that brought Argento cult status, recognition around the world and credit for influencing the modern splatter sub-genre. His imagery, striking technique and startling use of camera moves added lustre to disturbing visions that pushed the boundaries of epic violence and that few dared follow – *Inferno* (1980), *Tenebrae* (1982), *Phenomena* (1985) and *Opera* (1987). This last grisly opus contains his most enduring and upsetting sequence – a girl forced to keep her eyes open because of needles taped under her eyelids so that she has to watch

scenes of abject horror. Argento never bettered this image, which reflected the experience of watching his own oeuvre.

In 1978 Argento turned to producing horror, overseeing **George A. Romero**'s zombie classic *Dawn Of The Dead* (see Canon), and then films that included *Demons* (1985) and *Demons 2: The Nightmare Returns* (1986), by Mario Bava's son Lamberto; Michele Soavi's *The Church* (1989) and *The Sect* (1991), which starred Kelly Curtis, Jamie Lee's sister; and the debut of his veteran special effects man Sergio Stivaletti, *Wax Mask* (1997). He teamed up again with Romero for the Edgar Allan Poe tribute *Two Evil Eyes* (1990), before embarking on a trilogy of terror with his

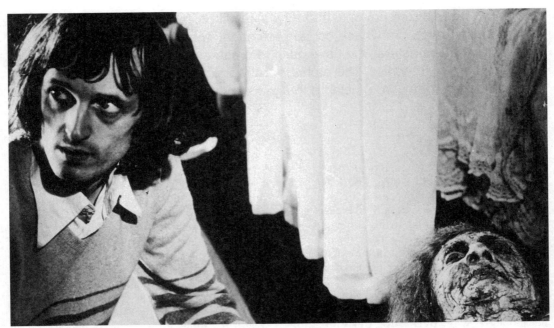

Argento, who led where few dared to follow, with "the Black Queen" from *Suspiria* (1976)

actress daughter Asia: *Trauma* (1993), *The Stendhal Syndrome* (1995) and *The Phantom Of The Opera* (1998), a very Italian remake.

After that European hit, Argento returned to the *gialli* – the fear formula he has made well and truly his own – with *Sleepless* (2001), *The Card Player* (2003) and the TV movie *Do You Like Hitchcock?* (2005). His other TV work includes producing, hosting and directing two of the four parts of the series *The Door Into Darkness* (1973), and producing the 1987 game show *Giallo*. His devotees are still waiting for him to direct the last part of the trilogy begun by *Suspiria* and continued in *Inferno, The Third Mother.*

Inferno
dir Dario Argento, 1980, It, 107m

The sequel to *Suspiria* is a gothic masterpiece; an alchemic tapestry that, like the music world it's set in, provides variations on the themes of surrealistic magic. Mark Elliot (Leigh McCloskey) searches for "the Mother of Darkness" in Manhattan and uncovers a dream-like landscape of hallucinogenic horror, all of which is orchestrated to Keith Emerson's hard rock music.

Mario Bava
Director, 1914-1980

One of the horror world's most important directors, Mario Bava, during a glittering career, played a part in every influential development of twentieth-century Italian cinema. He became a cameraman for director **Roberto Rossellini** in 1939 just as the neo-realist movement took hold. He photographed and directed segments of the sand-and-sandal progenitor *Hercules* (1958). His comic-strip fantasy *Danger: Diabolik* (1968) preceded *Barbarella*. And **Ridley Scott** paid homage to the visuals of *Planet Of The Vampires* (1965) in *Alien* (1979).

Bava's ability to conjure up weird and wonderful, spectral and sadistic worlds in bizarre tales of warped terror became his signature talent and remains unparalleled. Having learnt everything from his cameraman father Eugenio (*Quo Vadis?*, 1913), a special effects expert, he created chilling atmospheres simply through deft lighting, vivid colour schemes, unsettling sound effects and clever camera tricks.

It was teaming up with director **Riccardo Freda** for *I Vampiri* (*Lust Of The Vampire*, aka *The Devil's Commandment*, 1956) that was crucial to Bava's subsequent career, for Freda walked off the movie in a huff over the twelve-day schedule and Bava, his cameraman, completed the tale. Freda did the same again on *Caltiki, The Immortal Monster* (1959), leaving Bava to direct 70 percent of the rip-off of *The Quatermass Xperiment* (1955). Grateful producer Lionello Santi then offered him the chance to make his official directorial debut – and *Black Sunday* (1960, see Canon) was an instant classic and international success.

Bava made his stunning Technicolor debut with *Hercules In The Haunted World* (1961), starring **Christopher Lee** as the king of the underworld. His next effort was *The Evil Eye* (1962), a Hitchcockian parody, which, along with his *Telephone* segment from *Black Sabbath* (1963), was important for being the first move towards *gialli*, stylish shockers that focused on murders rather than mystery; the works upon which they were based had covers that were yellow – in Italian, *giallo*. Bava would develop this genre with the influential body counter *Blood And Black Lace* (1964), in which a masked psychopath brutally kills fashion models.

One of Bava's most censored Freudian nightmares was *The Whip And The Body* (1963), a beautiful work of pure Gothic art – inevitably different from the *gialli*, always set in the present

– that featured Christopher Lee in a sadomasochistic romance from beyond the grave. The three-part anthology *Black Sabbath* the same year gave **Boris Karloff** the chance to shine in a vampire tale. Three years later came Bava's worst film, the spy spoof *Dr Goldfoot And The Girl Bombs* (1966), which inspired the *Austin Powers* movies.

Other important works from Bava include the masterpiece of suggestive horror *Kill, Baby, Kill* (1966), in which a Transylvanian town is haunted by the ghost of a young girl, and *Twitch Of The Death Nerve* (1971), which is now seen as the blueprint for the splatter wave that started with *Friday The 13th* (1980). Bava's most subtle and personal movie was *Lisa And The Devil*, which put into focus his own obsessions and fears; only recently has the original cut been seen, on DVD, but it was re-edited, re-filmed and released everywhere as the jumbled concoction *The House Of*

Fog

The quintessential horror movie weather condition, fog is perfect for Sherlock Holmes to lurk in, the Wolf Man to emerge from and Jack the Ripper to cover his murderous exploits with, and Bava used fog in everything. The ability of fog to produce an eerie atmosphere is obvious, but less so is the fact that in shoestring budget shockers the dry ice was used as a necessity to mask tatty sets. In *Planet Of The Vampires* (1965) Bava used it throughout the picture to hide the fact that the only set dressing was a car that had been cannibalized to look like spaceship portholes.

Exorcism (1973) in the post-*Exorcist* exploitation frenzy. His later films included the sneaky kidnap thriller *Wild Dogs* (1974), which was unreleased for 25 years, and his last, un-credited, project was working on the special effects for Dario Argento's *Inferno* (1980).

Bava's treasure trove of horrors has stood the test of time: they are among the finest achievements the genre has to offer. His son Lamberto is a director (*Demons*, 1985) and his grandson Roy a technician (*The Card Player*, 2003).

 I Vampiri (Lust Of The Vampire, aka The Devil's Commandment)
dir Riccardo Freda, 1956, It, 81m

It was Bava who completed this retelling of the Countess Báthory legend, the first Italian horror film of the sound era – Mussolini having banned them. It beat Hammer's *The Curse Of Frankenstein* (1957) to the horror renaissance punch and minted the look of all Italian gothica to follow, but it flopped at the Italian box office, and Freda, believing that Italians didn't take Italian-made horror seriously, took on the nom de plume Robert Hampton. For the same reason, Bava's pseudonyms included John Foam, John Old and Mickey Lion.

Bava, whose work ranged from *gialli* to gothic art

Tod Browning
Director, 1882-1962

The first American director to fully understand the fascination of the audience with the macabre as well as ways in which it could be illuminated on screen, Charles Albert Browning was born in Louisville, Kentucky, and nicknamed Tod. As a teenager he courted a dancer in a travelling fair that sparked his interest in a life in the circus, and he went on to tour with several companies, as a clown, a barker, a contortionist, an escape artist and a man buried alive in a "hypnotic living corpse" sideshow.

Without question, it was this period of showmanship, and attendant hype in the highlighting the reaction to the bogus miracles and fantastic illusions, that shaped Browning's destiny and his genius for creating spectacles that were macabre and crowd-pleasing. His enduring fascination with carnival life informed his work and was a motif throughout his career, though it ended

Browning (left) with Lon Chaney on the set of *Where East Is East* (1929)

with his most penetrating look at big-top culture, the outrageous shocker *Freaks* (1932, see Canon).

A complicated, troubled, alcoholic and fiercely private man, his rapid climb to wealth and fame in the burgeoning silent film industry began after he met **D. W. Griffith**, then a rising director. Like Browning, the fellow Kentuckian had worked his way up through the circus hierarchy to managing the early slide shows that would segue into cinema; the link forged between the two led Griffith to hire the vaudevillian to star in two comedies, *Scenting A Terrible Crime* and *A Fallen Hero* (both 1913), and he found Browning a reliable actor who was eager to gain experience in all aspects of the fledgling movie industry. They moved to Hollywood together when Griffith embarked on his innovative epic *The Birth Of A Nation* (1915), and Browning then directed the one-reel *The Lucky Transfer* (1915) and his feature-length debut, *Jim Bludso* (1917).

It was *The Unholy Three* (1925), about a sideshow trio turning to jewel theft, starring **Lon Chaney**, that shot Browning into the front ranks of horror. In all of his mutilation melodramas featuring Chaney – whose roles ranged from a crook with a broken back in *The Blackbird* (1926) to a scarred animal trapper in *Where East Is East* (1929) – Browning served as either scriptwriter or co-writer, sometimes basing the finished product on one of his own ideas. His ability to give any literary work a surreal sense of nightmarish horror meant that all his films had an uneasy and menacing air.

Browning effortlessly got to grips with the new era of sound and put himself firmly in the horror vanguard when he made the cinematic landmark *Dracula* (1931, see Canon). With this vampire classic, starring **Bela Lugosi**, Browning launched the international horror movie and established Universal's tight hold on the genre that lasted for the next two decades. After the debacle of his terrifying trip into the twilight world of *Freaks*, he directed a musty remake of *London After Midnight* (1927), under the title *Mark Of The Vampire* (1935), and his genre swansong, before retiring to become a script doctor, was the bizarrely engaging *The Devil-Doll* (1936), which starred **Lionel Barrymore** in drag selling miniaturized humans as dolls in Paris. In 1962, like Chaney, his artistic muse, Browning died of throat cancer, just as the re-released *Freaks* was attracting interest. There are numerous film tributes: Tod Browning is the name of the hero, for example, in Hammer's *Blood From The Mummy's Tomb* (1971).

 The Unknown
dir Tod Browning, 1927, US, 65m, b/w

Alonzo the Armless Wonder (Lon Chaney), who performs a knife-throwing act with his feet but is actually a strangler, falls in love with the circus-owner's daughter (Joan Crawford), who fears touch, so he decides to have his arms amputated, just as she torments him by dating Malabar the Strongman (Norman Kerry). Elaborate deception and twisted psychosexual horror are the essential elements of Browning's pairings with Chaney, and this morbid carnival of the bizarre and the brutal features both.

John Carpenter
Director, 1948-

In 1953, when he was five years old, John Carpenter's mother took him to see Jack Arnold's *It Came From Outer Space*. As the meteor hurtled towards him in 3-D, exploding in his face, the boy from Carthage, New York, knew where his destiny lay. His enthusiasm for **Fifties B-movies** was reflected in all his work, as a director, producer, writer, actor and composer, and in his favourite theme – a group of people pulling together while struggling against unexplained outside forces.

While continuing within the horror genre, and making assets out of minimal budgets, Carpenter's later efforts haven't matched the energetic inventiveness of his three unqualified masterpieces – *Assault On Precinct 13* (1976), *Halloween* (1978, see Canon) and *The Thing* (1982). Yet he remains a powerful force in the horror industry and an eloquent spokesman for the positive qualities of the genre. He is also one of the few directors to have his name included in the title of his work, as in *John Carpenter's Vampires* (1998) and *John Carpenter's Ghosts Of Mars* (2001).

Carpenter studied film at the University of Southern California, where he wrote *The Resurrection Of Bronco Billy* (1970), which won the Oscar for best live-action short. His feature debut was the *2001* homage *Dark Star* (1974), which was written with and starred **Dan O'Bannon**, future *Alien* (1979) co-writer. And after directing the cult *Assault On Precinct 13*, drawing heavily on *Night Of The Living Dead* (1968, see Canon) for its inner-city police siege structure, Carpenter's breakthrough came with the landmark chiller *Halloween*.

His creative involvement with the series continues, and meanwhile his films have included *The Fog* (1980), in which the ghosts of shipwrecked sailors threaten a seaside town, and the futuristic thriller *Escape From New York* (1981), which sneaked in more social comment and featured his favourite actor, **Kurt Russell**; Carpenter used him in *The Thing*, the Hong Kong inspired supernatural action failure *Big Trouble In Little China* (1986) and *Escape From L.A.* (1996). *Memoirs Of An Invisible Man* (1992), starring Chevy Chase, seemed to halt Carpenter's spiral into mediocrity, though still

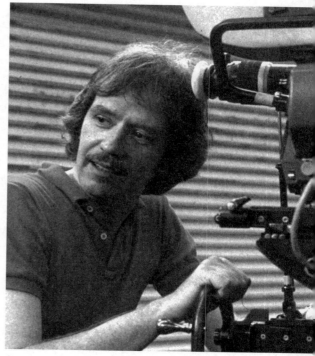

Carpenter on the set of *Christine* (1983), for which he also served as composer

to come was the dud H. P. Lovecraft adaptation *In The Mouth Of Madness* (1995) and *Village Of The Damned* (1995), based on the John Wyndham novel that Wolf Rilla made into a classic in 1960.

Carpenter also appeared as The Coroner in the *Body Bags* (1993) TV series, for which he composed the music and directed two of the three segments, and other writing credits include *The Philadelphia Experiment* (1984) and *El Diablo* (1990). He plays keyboard in the rock band The Coup de Villes, which also features *Halloween III* director Tommy Lee Wallace and Nick Castle, who plays The Shape in *Halloween*; the band can be heard on the soundtrack to *Big Trouble In Little China* and *The Boy Who Could Fly* (both 1986).

Christine
dir John Carpenter, 1983, US, 110m

Misfit student Arnie Cunningham (Keith Gordon) buys a killer car in this assembly line adaptation of the Stephen King best-seller that went into production before the book was even published. The possessed 1958 Plymouth Fury – which was seen to transform itself thanks to footage played backwards of the car being compressed – makes him trendy, trashes his enemies and plays vintage pop hits on the radio, but in other respects the film is clapped out.

Lon Chaney

Actor, 1883-1930

Born in Colorado Springs on April Fool's Day 1883, Leonidas Frank Chaney was the consummate silent film actor, a mime artist of immense talent who could easily summon feelings in an audience of horror, compassion and mirth, often at the same time. Because his parents were deaf mutes, Chaney became an expert visual communicator at an early age, and when his stagehand oldest brother John asked him to join a theatre group, his talent shone, and he flourished on the early-twentieth-century vaudeville circuit.

Chaney joined Universal in 1912, as an actor in dozens of comedy and action shorts and as a director (*The Stool Pigeon* and *For Cash*, both 1915). It was here that, playing the pickpocket "Stoop" Connors in *The Wicked Darling* (1919), he met director **Tod Browning** for the first time. But shortly afterwards Chaney left Universal for Paramount to take on a role that transformed his career, in *The Miracle Man* (1919). His portrayal of Frog, a charlatan

contortionist with corkscrew limbs and rolling eyes, drew critical praise and was the kind of pantomime grotesque performance – another came when playing Blizzard in *The Penalty* (1920) – that would propel him to stardom and the title "the Man of a Thousand Faces".

The two most famous Chaney characterizations are *The Hunchback Of Notre Dame* (1923) and *The Phantom Of The Opera* (1925, see Canon). The part of Quasimodo required Chaney to don a fifty-pound plaster hump, a breastplate, shoulder pads, a tight-fitting skin of hair-lined latex, a prosthetic eye, a dental device that held his mouth partially open and a harness that meant he could not stand up straight; and his painful dedication to his craft and to new make-up techniques made him an innovator. The masochism was necessary, according to Chaney, because he wanted "picture-goers to be bewildered and stirred by what they see", and he continued to refine his art through portrayals that included truncated criminals, Chinese fiends and ape-men. These roles gave rise to the joke: "Don't step on it, it may be Lon Chaney."

In terms of cinema that shocked, Chaney's collaborations with Browning were his best films, and their pairing resulted in some of the most deranged gems of the silent era. He featured in *The Unholy Three* (1925) as ventriloquist Professor Echo, in *London After Midnight* (1927) as Mooney, the hideous vampire man, and in *West Of Zanzibar* (1928) as "Dead Legs" Flint, a paralyzed magician. Acquitting himself well in the talkie remake of *The Unholy Three* (1930), he seemed destined to emerge as the first sound horror star, especially as Browning wanted him to star in *Dracula* (1931), but he died of throat cancer. He was played by **James Cagney** in a 1957 biopic, *The Man Of A Thousand Faces*, that focused more on his private life than his art.

The Unholy Three
dir Jack Conway, 1930, US, 72m, b/w

Chaney's first sound film replicated exactly Tod Browning's version from 1925, with the star playing Professor Echo, a drag ventriloquist whose identity is blurred with that of his dummy and who teams up with Tweedledee (midget Henry Earles) and Herman (strongman Ivan Linow) for ingenious criminal activities that lead to murder. Chaney died soon after filming, making this the only movie in the era of sound that he appeared in.

Chaney in *The Penalty* (1920) as double amputee Blizzard, who is mutilated by an evil surgeon

Roger Corman

Director, 1926-

Producer, director, writer, studio head, distributor, entrepreneur and talent scout: there isn't a

Corman with a prop from the stageshow of *The Little Shop Of Horrors*

job description in the movie industry that Roger Corman hasn't had. One of the most successful names in the history of the genre, he began as a runner for 20th Century Fox and became one of the main suppliers for American International Pictures, the distribution outfit begun by **Samuel Z. Arkoff** and **James H. Nicholson** in the mid-Fifties to cash in on the new teenage market. Corman's head for business, ruthless efficiency, eye for trends in pop culture and immaculate timing meant that he rarely lost money. Only when he veered from the drive-in date movie double-bill with a "message picture" – with *The Intruder* (1962), for example – did he come unstuck.

After producing and writing *The Monster From The Ocean Floor* (1954), which was shot in six days for $12,000, Corman rose swiftly; the film's director, **Wyott Ordung**, introduced him to Arkoff and Nicholson, who released his second production, *The Fast And The Furious* (1954), and a long and very fruitful relationship began. In his various roles Corman churned out multi-genre products that had liberal doses of sex, drugs and rock'n'roll, as well as violence and cheap monster menaces, and he made his directorial debut with *Five Guns West* (1955). The bravado, resourcefulness and wicked humour that Corman put into his high grade B-movies meant that a house style emerged that made him not only a popular favourite but also the darling of foreign critics, film school graduates and festival fans.

Key horror titles from this early period include *Attack Of The Crab Monsters* (1956), *A Bucket Of Blood* (1959), *The Creature From The Haunted Sea* and *The Little Shop Of Horrors* (both 1960). Then came Corman's most popular films, commercially and critically: the series of sumptuous Edgar Allan Poe adaptations that he made for AIP, beginning with *The Fall Of The House of Usher* (1960) and including *The Pit And The*

Pendulum (1961, see Canon). Outside the Poe arena he worked with **Vincent Price** on *The Tower Of London* (1962) and with Boris Karloff on the incomprehensible *The Terror* (1962), footage from which one of his many discoveries, **Peter Bogdanovich**, reused for *Targets* (1968).

Animal horror

After the horrifying attacks for no apparent reason in *The Birds* (1963), based on the novel by Daphne du Maurier and one of thriller director Alfred Hitchcock's rare ventures into horror, it was only a matter of time before other creatures freaked out against man's inhumanity towards nature. Usually the animals took a stand over the ecological damage being done to the planet (*Frogs*, 1972), but some went on the rampage because of laboratory experiments (giant rabbits in *Night Of The Lepus*, 1972); others just wanted to mete out to mankind a bit of revenge (rats in *Willard*, 1971). Whatever the reason for the protest, the sub-genre of nature's revenge has been around for a long time and can be relied upon for a good laugh (*Anaconda*, 1997) and a good scare (*Arachnophobia*, 1990).

Spiders have been the main stars in this field (*Kingdom Of The Spiders*, 1977, *Spiders II: Breeding Ground*, 2001), but watch out too for cats (*Night Of 1000 Cats*, 1972), ants (*Phase IV*, 1974), cockroaches (*Bug*, 1975), sharks (*Jaws*, 1975, see Canon; and *Devouring Waves*, 1984), worms (*Squirm*, 1976), bears (*Grizzly*, 1976), octopuses (*Tentacles*, 1977), bees (*The Swarm*, 1978), piranhas (**Roger Corman**'s *Piranha*, 1978) wild boars (*Razorback*, 1984) slugs (*Slugs: The Movie*, 1988), crocodiles (*Killer Crocodile*, 1989), ticks (*Infested*, 1993), mosquitoes (*Skeeter*, 1993) and komodo dragons (*Komodo*, 1999). A whole menagerie goes on the rampage in *Wild Beasts* (1984), when a disease mysteriously finds its way into the water supply at Hamburg Zoo, and because of damage to the ozone layer there is furry menace awaiting campers in the High Sierra in *Day Of The Animals* (1977).

Famous for being able to spot the best, and hungriest, young talent in Hollywood, Corman also kicked off the careers of Francis Ford Coppola, Martin Scorsese, Peter Fonda, Jonathan Demme and Jack Nicholson.

Tired of studio politics, Corman stopped directing in 1970 and formed New World Pictures. For more than a decade it produced and released an eclectic mix of foreign arthouse (Fellini's *Amarcord*, 1973, Ingmar Bergman's *Cries And Whispers*, 1972) and exploitation (*The Velvet Vampire*, *Lady Frankenstein*, both 1971, *Piranha*, 1978). Corman sold New World in 1982, created Millennium Pictures and then in 1985 formed Concorde/New Horizons exclusively for the video, cable TV and DVD markets. Since then he's overseen the production of hundreds of budget features, including many remakes of his own famous back catalogue.

Corman made an inauspicious directing comeback in 1990 with *Frankenstein Unbound* and that same year wrote his entertaining autobiography with Jim Jerome, *How I Made A Hundred Movies In Hollywood And Never Lost A Dime*. Innovative, versatile and indefatigable – the drug and motorcycle sub-genres didn't exist until he created them with *The Wild Angels* (1966) and *The Trip* (1967) – Corman's talent for making money and making movies, however uneven in quality, has carved him a special niche in Hollywood horror history.

The Little Shop Of Horrors
dir Roger Corman, 1960, US, 70m, b/w

Famous for being shot in two days and one night, using the set for a production that was about to finish and that was redressed, this camp cult classic has dim-witted florist Seymour Krelboin (Jonathan Haze) breeding a blood-hungry carnivorous plant named Audrey. Equally famous for Jack Nicholson's riotous masochistic dental patient reading *Pain* magazine in the waiting room, it was remade in 1986 as a big-budget musical.

Wes Craven

Director, 1939-

"To avoid fainting, keep repeating: It's only a movie … only a movie …" One of the most famous advertising campaigns in horror history was for Wes Craven's still controversial rape revenge drama *Last House On The Left* (1972). Based on **Ingmar Bergman**'s *The Virgin Spring* (1960), the hard-hitting shocker illustrated the malaise that existed in a country that had been battered and desensitized by nightly images of the Vietnam War. Many found Craven's frenzied stabbing, prolonged torture and intestine evisceration scenes too powerful to bear and his crude, brutal, barrier-breaking debut has been vilified, censored and banned.

Yet *Last House On The Left* – produced by future *Friday The 13th* director **Sean S. Cunningham**, and the first horror movie to feature a chain saw – established Craven's perennial themes: the undermining and destruction of the American middle-class family and the tensions of class, ethnicity and religion. Even when he showed a greater fascination for dreams, nightmares, the subconscious and self-reflexivity in *A Nightmare On Elm Street* (1984, see Canon) and *Scream* (1996, see Canon), Craven adhered to an analytical thoughtfulness that is rare among serious American horror directors.

With a masters degree from Johns Hopkins University, and a previous career teaching humanities in the university sector, Craven has had a harder time than other directors justifying his horror career to himself, and he often comes across as pretentious and self-important because of that. But no one can deny the social complexity than underpins even inane affairs such as *Swamp Thing* (1982), *Shocker* (1989) and *Vampire In Brooklyn* (1995).

Craven on the set of *Vampire In Brooklyn* (1995)

Craven's outrageous *Last House* follow-up, based on the "Sawney" Bean legend and tinged with black comedy, was the savage *The Hills Have Eyes* (1977), in which a degenerate cannibal family ruin the desert vacation of some innocent campers. The lousy *The Hills Have Eyes II* (1985) featured every surviving character, including Beast, the dog, having flashbacks to the superior original. Captive cannibals were *The People Under The Stairs* (1991) in Craven's political gore comedy. And just when it looked like his career was running on empty, along came *Wes Craven's New Nightmare* (1994), a reworking of his Freddy Krueger myth that had waned during five variable sequels. That conjuring trick led to three lashings of *Scream* (1996, see Canon, 1997, 2000), and *Cursed* (2004), the werewolf shocker famous for being filmed once and then virtually re-filmed from scratch.

Along the way Craven has been a producer for films including *Wishmaster* (1997), *Carnival Of Souls* (1998) and *Dracula 2000*. Films for television that he's directed include *Stranger in Our House* (1978), theatrically released in Europe as *Summer Of Fear*, *Invitation to Hell* (1984), *Chiller* (1984) and *Night Visions* (1990), and TV series he's worked on include *The Twilight Zone* (1985-86), *The People Next Door* (1989) and *Hollyweird* (1998).

Wes Craven's New Nightmare
dir Wes Craven, 1994, US, 112m

"He isn't you," says Heather Langenkamp to Robert Englund, the stars of *Nightmare On Elm Street* playing themselves in Craven's innovative and sophisticated revamp of his dream demon myth. "He's scarier." And he is too! The adept glimpse into the Hollywood horror industry, with a potent exploration of the need for dark fairy tales and a send-up of Craven conventions from prior Freddy films, is pulled off with magical aplomb.

David Cronenberg
Director, 1943-

"The King of Venereal Horror", "the Baron of Blood" and "the Canadian Prince of Body Horror": David Cronenberg has been dubbed all of these and more. But while his cinema is always sensationally visceral, visually unafraid and full of startling images aiming to disturb, the exploding heads, breathing television sets and phallic armpit growths are just one part of the terrible beauty he is keen to underline in his unique catalogue.

Go beneath the grotesque gore provocatively on show and the force of his dazzling visions becomes apparent. For Cronenberg has developed his own bizarre genre, incorporating philosophical dimensions, rare emotional intensity and richly complex seriousness. It isn't enough for Cronenberg to jolt his audience on an easy boos cruise. He wants to make the flesh creep even more, by relentlessly challenging our sensibilities and passions, and by breaking barriers with profound statements on the progress of humanity and on an ever-changing society. With his finger on the pulse, Cronenberg has often been eerily prophetic: *Shivers* (1975, see Canon) anticipated AIDS, and *Videodrome* (1983) foreshadowed the cheap sexual images of early satellite TV.

After starting by studying biochemistry, in Toronto, Cronenberg switched to English literature and wrote unpublished sci-fi fantasy stories. He made his first short film in 1966, *Transfer*, and followed it with the futuristic underground horrors *Stereo* and *Crimes Of The Future* (both 1969), both of which presented in rudimentary form the themes of telepathy, mutation and sexual disease that he would later expand upon. *Shivers*, *Rabid* (1977) and *The Brood* (1979) all focused

Cronenberg on the set of *Dead Ringers* (1988)

on a society that was under threat from moral decay and newly discovered neuroses, while his mainstream breakthrough *Scanners* (1981) and the masterpiece *Videodrome* took confrontational views on dark, corrupted futures.

In the same year he made *The Dead Zone*, which, though one of the best Stephen King adaptations, is conventional by Cronenberg's standards. The more technology-inspired *The Fly* (1986), a remake of Kurt Neumann's movie from 1958, was his biggest box-office success, though *Dead Ringers* (1988), featuring an amazing dual performance by **Jeremy Irons**, as identical twin gynaecologists in love with a woman with a deformed womb, was another sophisticated, offbeat and harrowing masterpiece. After a brave

attempt at filming William Burroughs's surrealistic drug trip *Naked Lunch* (1991), his adaptation of J. G. Ballard's *Crash* (1996) was far better and far more controversial, causing tabloid headlines because of its depraved automobile eroticism. The virtual reality essay *eXistenZ* (1999) was followed by a moving portrayal of mental illness in *Spider* (2002), with Ralph Fiennes, and the vigilante comic-book adaptation *A History Of Violence* (2005). *Painkillers* is scheduled for 2006.

"I want to show the unshowable, to speak the unspeakable," he once said. "All my films have to do with physical existence and what happens when that breaks down in some radical way." He's also played bit parts in his own films, and had significant cameos in *Into The Night*

(1985), *To Die For* (1995) and *Jason X* (2001), though his real acting debut came when he played a serial killer in Clive Barker's *Nightbreed* (1990).

Videodrome
dir David Cronenberg, 1983, Can, 89m

A multi-dimensional masterpiece fusing satire with shock as cable TV executive Max Renn (James Woods) monitors pirated "snuff" telecasts and learns too late that the signal causes brain tumours, bizarre hallucinations and bodily transformations. A surrealistic wonderland of grisly torture, perverse sex and archetypal Cronenberg chills with a philosophical kick, like many of the director's films it showed prescience, predicting that satellite television would rule the world.

Peter Cushing
Actor, 1913-1994

The true gentle man of horror, Peter Cushing never railed against the superstardom that his portrayals brought him. Realizing that his "serious" acting days were over once Hammer's *The Curse Of Frankenstein* (1957, see Canon) and *Dracula* (1958, see Canon) became global phenomena, Cushing remained philosophical about his instant typecasting and decided that the benefits far outweighed the disadvantages. He once lamented, "I suppose I'm only really a footnote to the kind of stage acting to which I once aspired. But I think that Baron Frankenstein – for which I know I'll be remembered – was a worthwhile creation." Cushing played the Baron six times, and Dracula's nemesis Van Helsing in five incarnations, all of these performances in Hammer productions.

Cushing, always an absolute professional, gave surprising depth to a range of villains who were usually driven, cool and cultured – a talent recog-

nized by **George Lucas** when the director cast him as Grand Moff Tarkin in *Star Wars* (1977), which brought him a whole new generation of admirers.

Taking every role deadly seriously, no matter how bad he thought the script was, Cushing put an enormous amount of preparation into each character. He never began any part without having every nuance worked on, his entire wardrobe

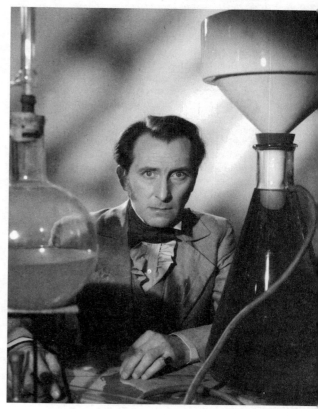

Cushing as Baron Frankenstein in *The Curse Of Frankenstein* (1957)

Hammer: The house of horror

The brand leader of the horror movie from the mid-Fifties until the late Seventies, Hammer still retains the affections of aficionados. Originally a production offshoot of Exclusive Films, a British distribution company formed in 1935 by **Enrique Carreras**, Hammer was named after entrepreneur founder **William Hinds**'s failed comedian alter ego, Will Hammer. He was half of the Hammer and Smith double act, so called because of the London district they lived in.

Hammer's first full-length feature was a sign of things to come, *The Mystery Of The Marie Celeste* (1935), starring **Bela Lugosi**, and during the late Forties and early Fifties they turned out a range of low-budget thrillers and comedies, which were mostly adaptations of BBC radio plays and serials. Their most successful was *Dick Barton: Special Agent* (1948), and that made Hammer think about licensing other BBC hits from the new medium of television. When they made *The Quatermass Xperiment* (1955), based on the series written by **Nigel Kneale** and dropping an E to cash in on the lure of the X certificate, they got a much-needed commercial boost.

The company's new prominence overseas rose further after the massive success of *The Curse Of Frankenstein*, and the access allowed to Universal's past monster glories led to films including *Dracula*, *The Mummy* (1959) and *The Phantom Of The Opera* (1962); meanwhile,

Hammer also built up an enviable repertory stable, including stars **Christopher Lee** and **Peter Cushing** and directors **Terence Fisher** and **Freddie Francis**. In the early Sixties the company launched a strand of thrillers in the *Psycho* vein, including *Taste Of Fear* (1960), *Paranoiac* (1962) and *The Nanny* (1965).

Keenly aware of market trends and the possibilities of exploiting well-known monsters and the relaxation in censorship laws, during the Sixties Hammer continued to satisfy audience demand for fantasy and horror. In 1968, the year after the company moved from Bray Studios in Berkshire to Pinewood in Buckinghamshire, the staff received the **Queen's Award for Industry** in recognition of their global success and their determination to make horror a respectable genre.

But after a rash of lesbian vampire flicks drenched in gore, including *The Vampire Lovers* (1970) and *Twins Of Evil* (1971), Hammer lost their grip on their core youth market by refusing to locate their monsters in the contemporary world. When they did try to follow this American trend, with *Dracula AD 1972* and *To The Devil A Daughter* (1976), they failed miserably. Hammer remained in the Carreras and Hinds families until cashflow problems put it in the hands of the Official Receiver in 1979. Despite many attempts at revivals, Hammer now remains a distant memory – but a glorious one.

sketched out and every prop he was going to use already selected. He considered that each of these elements was essential for conveying truth to an audience who always expected the best from him and always got it.

Although Cushing began his acting career in Hollywood, as Louis Hayward's stunt double in **James Whale**'s *The Man In The Iron Mask* (1939), it was the new medium of television that provided him with security, and he was named British TV Actor of the Year from the Guild of Television Producers and Directors for his performance as Winston Smith in **Nigel Kneale**'s BBC adaptation of George Orwell's *1984* (1955). Another BBC adaptation by Kneale was *The Creature* (1955), which Hammer transformed into Cushing's *Frankenstein* follow-up, *The Abominable Snowman* (1957), once they had tempted the award-winner into their fold.

Cushing's career then became studded with gems. He was a superb Sherlock Holmes in *The Hound Of The Baskervilles* (1959), a brilliant body-snatching Dr Robert Knox in *The Flesh And The Fiends* (1959) and a delicious Grim Reaper in *Dr Terror's House Of Horrors* (1965); and there were similar performances in *Dr Who And The Daleks* (1965), *Corruption* (1967), *Tales From The Crypt* (1972) – playing Arthur Grimsdyke in one of his favourite roles – *The Ghoul* (1975) and *Shock Waves* (1977).

After he had cancer diagnosed in 1982, Cushing made his last film, *Biggles*, in 1986. Appointed OBE in 1989, he occupied his final years writing two volumes of autobiography (*An Autobiography*, 1986, and *Past Forgetting: Memoirs Of The Hammer Years*, 1988). There he confessed to having many affairs with his glamorous leading ladies before the death of his wife, Helen, in 1971.

Corruption
dir Robert Hartford-Davis, 1967, UK, 91m

Cushing hated this energetically sleazy gem, scripted by Hartford-Davis's regular writers, brothers Donald and Derek Ford, in which he plays a brilliant surgeon decapitating prostitutes for pituitary gland fluid to repair the disfigured face of his model girlfriend. The depraved film, which advertised itself as "not a woman's picture", remains a benchmark in Cushing's Sixties golden period. Its ending – hippies sending a lethal laser beam out of control – is demented.

Brian De Palma

Director, 1940-

Part of the "Movie Brat" generation (with director friends Steven Spielberg, George Lucas, Martin Scorsese and Francis Ford Coppola), Brian De Palma is touted as "the American Hitchcock"; but while Alfred the Great was primarily a director of thrillers, De Palma earned this nickname because of his graphic re-workings of themes, artifices and images flagrantly lifted from him. Many critics have been unable to look beyond his predilection for successfully synthesizing updated "quotes" for modern audiences in his unapologetic assaults on the senses.

His technically polished manipulative style and accent on visceral shock has also made him a controversial figure in the debate about violence against women, and this has often overshadowed his sublimely suspenseful, visually stunning and blackly humorous work. "My view of the world is ironic, bitter, acid", he once stated. "But basically funny too. I'm a real gallows humorist. I see something funny in the grimmest of circumstances."

The son of a surgeon, De Palma made short films while studying physics at university. After seven independent productions, including *The Wedding Party* (filmed in 1964 and released in 1969) and *Greetings* (1968), both starring Robert De Niro, his first success came with *Sisters* (1973), a voyeuristic *Psycho* shocker complete with a score by **Bernard Herrmann**. Then *Phantom Of The Paradise* (1974) cleverly took the Gaston Leroux classic into the rock music idiom. *Obsession* (1975) was De Palma's riff on *Vertigo*, and featured another magnificent Herrmann score.

After his horror breakthrough with *Carrie* (1976, see Canon), there was more telekinetic action in his vastly underrated psychic phenomena chiller *The Fury* (1978). His next take on *Psycho*, *Dressed To Kill* (1980), which features **Michael Caine** as a transvestite stalker, recreates a part of De Palma's childhood that explains his obsession with voyeurism. When he was a child, his parents split up, his mother accusing his father of infidelity, and the young De Palma spent several days stalking his father with recording equipment, hoping to find evidence to confirm his mother's suspicions.

De Palma, who likes using updated "quotes"

Dressed To Kill
dir Brian De Palma, 1980, US, 104m

The best Eighties *Psycho* movie – it starts and ends with a shower scene – is this bloody suspense horror revealing psychiatrist Robert Elliott (Michael Caine) to be a transvestite killer who murders Kate Miller (Angie Dickinson). The wonderful splitting of the screen and lyrical camera choreography make this macabre black joke, which was criticized when released for its violence towards women, a real jolter – and especially the unforgettable razor murder in the elevator.

Dracula

The most famous vampire of them all is Dracula (an elongated form of the Romanian for devil), based on the novel by Anglo-Irish writer **Bram** (short for Abraham) **Stoker**, published in 1897. Inspired by a nightmare he had in 1890 about three predatory females, their fondness for kissing necks, their entranced male victim and an old Count who wants their prey for himself, no other single book has had a greater impact on the horror movie than this classic of English literature.

Like the vampire bat in nature and Vlad the Impaler, the infamous mid-fifteenth-century ruler of Wallachia, the southern half of Romania, Dracula feeds on human blood, and preferably that of beautiful women such as Lucy Westenra and Mina Harker, two of the novel's several narrators. From influences including the blood-and-thunder of **Shakespeare**'s *Macbeth*, anxieties about his sexual prowess (in 1912 Stoker died from syphilis), his favourite holiday destinations (Whitby is the scene of the arrival of Dracula's ship), the early psychoanalytical theory of **Freud** and the characteristics seen as degenerate at the time, Stoker created a story with a sexually alluring, much-imitated monster in a mystifying human shell.

Then came De Palma's grimmest ending, in *Blow Out* (1981), in which the sound technician, played by **John Travolta**, uses the death-scream recordings of his girlfriend for exploitation horror looping; the film turned **Michelangelo Antonioni**'s *Blow Up* (1966) into a paranoid conspiracy. In *Body Double* (1984), set inside the porn industry, there was a woman drilled to the floor, in *Raising Cain* (1992), a psycho with multiple homicidal personalities, and in *Femme Fatale* (2002), double-crossing doppelgangers.

De Palma's output has been extremely diverse, ranging from gangster movies such as *Scarface* (1983), *The Untouchables* (1987) and *Carlito's Way* (1993) to *The Bonfire Of The Vanities* (1990), *Mission: Impossible* (1996) and *Mission To Mars* (2000). But all his movies have been excessive displays of the mesmerizing nature of stylish visuals.

Tapping into the wish-fulfilment fascination with immortality and the inferred decadence of living by night, Stoker brought to life the "undead," allowing him to break all taboos without consequence. Moreover, Stoker's folkloric interpretation of the deployment of garlic, crucifixes and wooden stakes has powerfully shaped all cinematic depictions of his "filthy leech" from Transylvania who moves from the dark and sinister reaches of the Carpathian Mountains to fog-shrouded England. That's where vampire hunter Dr Abraham Van Helsing must use every arcane skill he can to defeat the attractively evil Prince of Darkness.

Stoker's rich combination of terror, mystery, romance and pulse-pounding adventure provided perfect material for filmmakers, and although the first notable but unofficial adaptation was *Nosferatu* (1922, see Canon), it was *Dracula* in 1931 (see Canon), based on Hamilton Deane's stage play and starring **Bela Lugosi**, that became the iconic foundation for the entire Dracula film industry, which is still in existence today. Aside from the Universal and Hammer films, the latter including **Terence Fisher**'s *Dracula* (1958, see Canon), there have been scores of foreign language interpretations, including the Hungarian *Drakula* (c.1920), the Turkish *Drakula Istanbul'da* (1953) and the Pakistani *Zinda laash* (*The Living Corpse*, 1967).

The long list of actors who have played the nefarious bloodsucker includes Lon Chaney Jr, Carlos Villarías (in the Spanish version of 1931), John Carradine, Christopher Lee, Howard Vernon, Udo Kier, Paul Naschy, Gary Oldman, Klaus Kinski, David Carradine, Leslie Nielsen and Jamie Gillis, in the 1978 porno version *Dracula Sucks*, which uses much of the script from the Lugosi classic.

Stoker revived his most famous creation in just one short story, published posthumously in 1914, *Dracula's Guest*, which became the basis for the first Universal sequel, *Dracula's Daughter* (1936), starring **Gloria Holden**. Since then hosts of Dracula's relatives and associates have arrived on the scene: *Son Of Dracula* (1943), *Countess Dracula* (1970), *Doctor Dracula* (1977), *Mamma Dracula* (1979), *Dracula's Widow* (1992) and even *Dracula's Dog* (1977).

 Dracula
dir George Melford, 1931, US, 85m, b/w

Based on the same script, using the same sets, and shot at night when Tod Browning's production had wrapped, the Spanish *Dracula* by Melford and his translator Enrique Tovar Ávalos is 30 minutes longer, while fast-paced, and more cine-literate. Carlos Villarías isn't bad, but Lugosi's performance in the Browning version is so unforgettable that Melford's lesser-known effort is inferior, despite being superior technically and aesthetically.

Terence Fisher
Director, 1904-1980

Terence Fisher could never be called daring: when it came to visuals and lighting, he was so measured and undemonstrative that he often verged on the pedestrian. But his consistently high standards of craftsmanship, and his laid-back techniques that accent the robustness of his solid dramatic narratives and their physical and emotional energy, redefined the moribund horror genre and defined the **Hammer** style. Fisher translated the classic Universal monster gallery into colour and as one of the originators of the modern vocabulary of horror, such as the use of gore and showing of nastiness, he left an indelible impression on a generation of filmmakers and filmgoers.

After serving an apprenticeship in the Merchant Navy and working as a window

Fisher: gave Hammer gore and gravitas

dresser, London-born Fisher joined **Shepherd's Bush Studios** in 1930 as "the oldest clapper boy in the business", as he put it. Within six years, he had become a film editor, and twelve years later, he directed his first feature, *Colonel Bogey* (1948). A variety of cheap fillers followed before he joined Hammer in 1952 and made the

Pygmalion-lite horror *A Stolen Face* (1952), and two science-fiction thrillers, *Four Sided Triangle* and *Spaceways* (both 1953).

Because he was always dependable and speedily efficient, Hammer entrusted Fisher with their first colour gothic retread, *The Curse Of Frankenstein* (1957, see Canon). Its meteoric global success meant that Fisher became Hammer's principal director of their choice product and forged a reputation as a prime purveyor of gore with gravitas. *Dracula* (1958, see Canon), *The Mummy*, *The Hound Of The Baskervilles* (both 1959), *The Two Faces Of Dr Jekyll* (1960), *The Curse Of The Werewolf* (1961) and *The Phantom Of The Opera* (1962) gave all the basic stories Technicolor trappings and Fisher even tried to add to the monster pantheon with the plodding *The Gorgon* (1964).

Sidelined by Hammer when his early Sixties output started to falter at the box office, and when younger talents were brought in to cut their teeth on the franchises, Fisher's work for other production companies – *Sherlock Holmes And The Deadly Necklace* (1962) and a sci-fi trio – was variable. He returned to the Hammer fold triumphantly with *Frankenstein Created Woman* (1967), *Frankenstein Must Be Destroyed* (1969) and their last in the series, *Frankenstein And The Monster From Hell* (1974). Easily his best Hammer film in this later period is *The Devil Rides Out* (1968).

If any terror theme was Fisher's it was the charisma of evil. Prior to his and Hammer's breakthrough in the mid-Fifties, it was an ugly force that was always depicted visually as repellent. But Fisher felt that the "great strength of evil" was that it could make itself attractive. "Evil always tempts you – the promise of something you'll get … That's [the Devil's] great power."

The Devil Rides Out (aka The Devil's Bride)

dir Terence Fisher, 1968, UK, 95m

Dennis Wheatley's classic black magic novel provided the basis for Fisher and Christopher Lee's best Hammer horror after *Dracula*. Lee, in a rare role as a good guy, is occult specialist Duc de Richleau, stopping a close friend from being initiated into a coven, and in a terrific supernatural showdown fights giant spider apparitions and the Angel of Death. Dignified, gripping and scary, the film, though a box-office flop, was loved by the critics.

The Frankenstein Monster

With a filmography that ranges from the one-reeler *Frankenstein* (1910), produced by **Thomas Edison** and directed by J. Searle Dawley, starring Charles Ogle as an ashen-faced, frizzy-haired hunchback, to Shuler Hensley's hi-tech creature in **Stephen Sommers'** *Van Helsing* (2004), the monster that **Mary Shelley** called her "hideous progeny" is reinvented by every movie generation and is still thriving.

Frankenstein; Or: The Modern Prometheus was written as part of a ghost story competition in June 1816, when Mary Wollstonecraft Godwin, her future poet husband Percy Bysshe Shelley and Dr John Polidori (who would introduce the word "vampire" into the English language in *The Vampyre: The Tale*, 1819) stayed at their friend Lord Byron's rented Villa Diodati on Lake Geneva. The parlour game creation of her gothic horror story, suggested by a dream but also reflecting public fascination with both the invention of electricity and evolutionary theory, was used as a dramatic prologue in *The Bride Of Frankenstein* (1935), *Gothic* (1986) and *Frankenstein Unbound* (1990).

Expanded during her 1817 stay in Bath and published anonymously in 1818, her novel was abridged by Shelley in 1831; the scientific and political polemic was cut to give more flesh-creeping action and adventure, and a prologue was added about the story's birth that worked its way into popular culture. Because it was published in three unwieldy volumes – Arctic explorer Robert Walton's letter about finding the frozen creature, Victor Frankenstein's reminiscences about making it, and the creature's own interior monologue – it has always been difficult to bring the complete story to the screen, but this has not prevented directors from trying, as **Kenneth Branagh** did with *Mary Shelley's Frankenstein* (1994).

Its original form also helps to explain why the story skeins have been plundered, realigned and expanded to create a bewildering range of titles. Yet what connects everything from *Frankenstein Meets The Wolfman* (1943) and *I Was A Teenage Frankenstein* (1957) to *Frankenstein's Great Aunt Tillie* (1983) and *Frankenhooker* (1990) is the basic theme of a scientist creating an unpredictable monster out of a load of body parts.

The quintessential Frankenstein monster was unequivocally **Boris Karloff**, aided by **Jack Pierce**'s make-up, in Universal's pioneering classic of 1931. Copyright on the Karloff look meant that many outré designs have been used, including the hairy Neanderthal in Hammer's *Frankenstein And The Monster From Hell* (1972) and the bulbous-headed, well-endowed lover of *Lady Frankenstein* (1971). The creature has been played by a wide range of actors, including Lon Chaney Jr, Bela Lugosi, Glenn Strange, Christopher Lee, wrestler Kiwi Kingston, Fred Gwynne (Herman Munster in TV's *The Munsters*), Peter Boyle (in *Young Frankenstein*, 1974), Paul Naschy, Robert De Niro and pop idol Luke Goss.

Mary Shelley's Frankenstein
dir Kenneth Branagh, 1994, US, 123m

Over-referential and overwrought, Branagh's take on Shelley's influential myth, starring himself, is not so much *The Modern Prometheus* as post-modern and problematic: it's an empty exercise in grandiose style full of luvvie acting. It's as haphazardly stitched together as the monster who Branagh's driven surgeon Victor Frankenstein is hell-bent on zapping to life in the only imaginative sequence, and Robert De Niro, playing the creature, barely registers at all.

Famous for 15 minutes

After producing Paul Morrissey's *Flesh* (1968) and *Trash* (1970), pop artist Andy Warhol used his Factory icon branding for two of the wildest and campiest decadent horrors, *Blood For Dracula* and *Flesh For Frankenstein*. Both were made in Italy in 1973, co-directed by Morrissey and Italian hack Antonio Margheriti, and German favourite Udo Kier starred in both title roles. The former is kept light by consistent humour – Kier's heavily accented utterance of the word "wirgin" helping enormously – and in the latter excellent 3-D meant that glossy guts on ends of poles jutted into the audience. *Flesh For Frankenstein* was the first gross-out horror to reach a wide audience, because of its stereoscopic shock.

Alfred Hitchcock

Director, 1899–1980

Although Sir Alfred Hitchcock's only horror movies are *Psycho* (1960, see Canon) and *The Birds* (1963), he is the genre's patron saint and has exerted a major influence on the genre and many of its key practitioners – not least **Dario Argento**, **Brian De Palma** and **John Carpenter**. *Psycho* became a crucial turning point in the development of the genre, after "the Master of Suspense",

determined to frighten audiences, used all the techniques that he had perfected over more than three decades in cinema.

The son of a greengrocer, he was born in Leytonstone, London, had a Jesuit education and became interested in the cinema as a teenager. After working for a telegraph company, in 1920 he joined the Lasky studio in London, designing the titles between the shots in silent films. His first film was *The Lodger* (1926), a re-telling of the story of Jack the Ripper, and like all of his films, the last of which was *Family Plot* (1976), it was imbued with paranoia, revelations and abnormal psychological states.

On constant guard of repeating himself, Hitchcock continually made daring experiments with cinema. He confined suspense to microcosms (*Lifeboat*, 1945; *Rear Window*, 1954), splashed it across famous public places (*The 39 Steps*, 1935; *North By Northwest*, 1959), made it part of a surreal Dali-esque dreamscape (*Spellbound*, 1945), used such gimmicks as the ten-minute take (*Rope*, 1948) and 3-D (*Dial M For Murder*, 1953), and played with harrowing emotional and intellectual metaphysics (*Vertigo*, 1958).

He made the low-budget, black-and-white *Psycho* which he saw as a radical departure from his Fifties rash of all-star colour epics, to "recharge the battery". But in doing so, in the process filming his much-copied scream-filled shower scene, he recharged the battery of the entire horror genre too, through the influence of his themes (such as voyeurism), techniques (lighting, camera angles) and methods of storytelling (the heroine, played by **Janet Leigh**, being killed off early in the film).

Hitchcock then changed tack again with his adaptation of Daphne du Maurier's novel *The Birds*, starring **Tippi Hedren**, which was an audacious new take on the monster-on-the-loose

Hitchcock, who inspired horror directors despite making only two films within the genre, *Psycho* (1960) and *The Birds* (1963)

format of the Fifties. The stunning example of construction and the use of the creatures was simply terrifying, not least because of the silences between attacks – there was no soundtrack but composer **Bernard Herrmann** was employed as a sound consultant – and the result influenced all subsequent revenge-of-nature films.

Famous for his portly figure and profile, thanks to the popularity of two TV series (*Alfred Hitchcock Presents*, 1955-62, and *The Alfred Hitchcock Hour*, 1962-65), he made a brief cameo appearance in every one of his movies. His use of MacGuffins – seemingly important objects that lead absolutely nowhere – was as frequent as his falling for blonde leading ladies (including **Grace Kelly** and **Kim Novak**), despite being notoriously dismissive of actors. He was never an Oscar winner for best director, despite being nominated five times, but in 1979, the year before he died, he was knighted and was the recipient of the American Film Institute Life Achievement Award.

Tobe Hooper

Director, 1943-

Until his remarkable 2003 comeback with the remake *The Toolbox Murders*, Tobe Hooper never properly capitalized on his astonishing horror debut, *The Texas Chainsaw Massacre* (1974, see Canon). Precisely because it was such a ferocious, unforgettable and one-off nightmare, it overshadowed everything that came afterwards. Even the success of *Poltergeist* (1982) was mainly laid at the feet of **Steven Spielberg**, who wrote and produced it.

Hooper started watching films at a very early age. "My memories from childhood are mostly memories of movies rather than my own life because I spent a lot of time in a movie theatre," he recalled. "My dad owned a movie house in San Angelo, Texas, so I stayed there when they went out to dinner." The first film he made himself was the little seen *Eggshells* (1969), about hippies in a haunted house, which was written with **Kim Henkel**, his *Chainsaw* collaborator.

Following their breakthrough in the mid-Seventies, Hooper directed *Death Trap* (aka *Eaten Alive*, 1977), which detailed the habit of a Bayou hotelier of scything his guests into alligator food before they checked out. Neville Brand's harrowing turn, the screaming from **Marilyn Burns** that echoed her performance in *Chainsaw*, and the same grim rural atmosphere, made it a cult favourite. The future Freddy Krueger, **Robert Englund**, appears as a cowboy uttering the immortal line "My name is Buck and I like to fuck."

After directing the television mini-series *Salem's Lot* (1979), adapted from Stephen King, which in some countries was cut down to feature length, furnished with extra gore and given a cinema release, Hopper administered a distinctive twist to his sleazy carnival-set stalk-and-slash *The Funhouse* (1981), in which thrill-seeking teens get murdered by a cleft-headed freak in a Frankenstein mask.

Post-*Poltergeist*, Hooper directed two disasters, *Lifeforce* (1985) and *Invaders From Mars* (1986), and then *The Texas Chainsaw Massacre 2* (1986). In the strikingly perverse sequel **Dennis Hopper** plays an obsessive, evangelical former Texas Ranger pursuing the Sawyer family, demented cannibals, after the disappearance of his nephew, the wheelchair

Hooper (left): came to light with an astonishing debut

victim of the first film. Bursting with style, energy and inventive satire – the poster was a wicked parody of *The Breakfast Club* – it also had a frighteningly epic scope that fleshed out powerfully the stark terror of his original. A rich slice of American Gothic, *Chainsaw 2* is Hooper's most underrated horror, solely because it remains in the shadow of its predecessor.

But he then hit rock bottom cinematically, with *Spontaneous Combustion* (1990), two Robert Englund vehicles – *Night Terrors* (1994) and the Stephen King story *The Mangler* (1995) – and *Crocodile* (2001). Meanwhile he had turned to the music video (Billy Idol's "Dancing with Myself") and television (*Freddy's Nightmares*, 1988, *Taken,* 2002).

Hooper's infamous script rewriting and post-production tinkering gets in the way of the actual process of directing, and his scattershot career is filled with more commercial ups and downs and fiascos – he was replaced as director on both *The Dark* (1979) and *Venom* (1982) – than actual achievements. But modern horror will always have *The Texas Chainsaw Massacre*, and that is more than enough to excuse everything else.

The Toolbox Murders
dir Tobe Hooper, 2003, US, 95m

In the same year that Marcus Nispel remade *The Texas Chainsaw Massacre* surprisingly well, Hooper did the same to this exploitation classic from 1978. His supernatural reinvention combined the original's sleazy derangement with gorier splatter, with the maniac cutting a swathe through apartment tenants now a deformed monster who has been kept alive by occult symbols. Hooper's strength has always been his realism and he executes this catalogue of carnage expertly for maximum shock value, while also echoing *Scream* in referencing genre B-movies.

Peter Jackson
Director, 1961-

"I never set out to become a horror director," said Peter Jackson. "My two major movie loves are James Bond and Ray Harryhausen stop-motion animation techniques." Once the bad-boy pariah of the New Zealand Film Commission, iconoclast Jackson is now their mascot thanks to his mammoth *Lord Of The Rings* trilogy, which has swelled local bank balances and created a new tourist trade.

How different it was back in 1983, when Jackson began a four-year period of shooting his debut feature at weekends, with friends playing the roles and an improvised script. Based on an idea from 1981 entitled "Roast Of The Day", *Bad Taste* (1987) was a homage to **George A. Romero**'s famous trilogy, zombies being cheap to employ as a plot focus. It lived up to its name with its Alien Investigation and Defence Service – the initials were one of the film's many outrageous jokes – who are surrounding a small town depopulated by cannibals from outer space. The creatures intend to use low-calorie human flesh as the main ingredient for their new intergalactic fast food chains. During the assault on the aliens' headquarters, the A.I.D.S. operatives are marinated, forced to eat Martian vomit and mutilated in all the gory ways that Jackson could think of when working with yoghurt, muesli and food colouring in his mother's kitchen sink.

Jackson funded most of the film himself, until the NZFC gave him money to finish it after being impressed with what he'd already made. It was when *Bad Taste* started riots at the Cannes Film Festival and attracted controversy in reviews, which called it everything from vile to vital, that the Council regretted their decision. Yet because

Jackson (left) with Ian Watkin on the set of *Braindead* (1992)

of the growing interest around the world they felt they had to support Jackson's next effort, *Meet The Feebles* (1989), a depraved puppet show. Much too extreme for most markets, it led the aghast NZFC to give the naughty filmmaker only half the budget for his next outing, the even sicker and more outrageous *Braindead* (1992, see Canon).

Having made the gore movie to end them all, what Jackson did for his surprising encore put him on the road to fame beyond his hardcore fan base, forgiveness from the NZFC and fortune from the *Lord Of The Rings* trilogy. His next film, *Heavenly Creatures* (1994), dissected chillingly a notorious 1954 murder case in which schoolgirls Juliet Hulme and Pauline Parker battered the latter's mother to death. In many ways his most shocking movie, and certainly his most dazzling technically, through use of stunning fantasy visuals to depict the girls' crumbling grip on reality, it won the Silver Lion Award at the Venice Film Festival and made a star out of **Kate Winslet**.

The film also won the attention of Universal, who grabbed him to direct an ironic script, written with his wife **Fran Walsh**, that took him back to his ghoulish roots. *The Frighteners* (1996) starred Michael J. Fox as a ghostbuster for hire who is actually in cahoots with the spooks he's paid to exterminate. After it flopped Jackson embarked on his epic Oscar-winning Tolkien voyage and a remake of his favourite movie, *King Kong* (2005).

Meet The Feebles
dir Peter Jackson, 1989, NZ, 97m

The all-singing, all-dancing puppet show, with less taste than *Bad Taste*, Jackson's previous film, is a deranged Sesame Street, where characters including Robert the Hedgehog and Barry the Bulldog, not too far removed from Miss Piggy and Kermit the Frog, indulge in every vice and sleazy perversion imaginable. An off-beat, clever marvel in which a hippo ends up firing a machine gun, it's continuously camp and shocking.

Boris Karloff
Actor, 1887-1969

Born William Henry Pratt in Camberwell, London, Boris Karloff was one of the few actors to be billed by his last name only and one of the first kings of horror. Brought up to follow his father into public service, Karloff rebelled and at the turn of the century moved to Canada, before turning to acting and joining a small theatre company there and then moving to California, lured by the movies. A heart murmur prevented him from fighting for Britain in World War I so he started playing bit parts in Hollywood films, and his big break came with *The Bells* (1926), in which he was a Caligari-like sideshow mesmerist who breaks down a murdering Alsatian innkeeper, played by **Lionel Barrymore**.

Karloff's murder scene in *The Criminal Code* (1931), which he had appeared in on stage, brought him to the attention of director **James Whale** and Universal after **Bela Lugosi** turned down the Monster role in *Frankenstein* (1931). It was Karloff's flawless ability to bring compassion and pity to a seemingly thankless part, and his gimmick billing as "?", that would ironically make him a household name.

Though Karloff made many mainstream films – *Scarface* (1932), *The Secret Life Of Walter Mitty*

(1947) – it was his monstrous portrayals that the public demanded. *The Mask Of Fu Manchu*, *The Mummy* (both 1932), *The Ghoul* (1933), *The Black Cat* (1934, with Lugosi), and *The Raven* (1935) all added to his evil repertoire, and the two sequels, *The Bride Of Frankenstein* (1935) and *Son Of Frankenstein* (1939) maintained his reputation.

During the Forties and Fifties, Karloff expanded his horizons, returning to the stage in critically acclaimed Broadway productions such as *Arsenic And Old Lace* (1941), and appearing in three horrors produced by **Val Lewton**: in Robert Wise's *The Body Snatcher* (1945), based on the story by Robert Louis Stevenson, he played a "resurrectionist" in nineteenth-century Edinburgh supplying doctors with cadavers; in Mark Robson's *Isle Of The Dead* (1945) he was a Greek freedom fighter convinced that a plague is being caused by vampire demons; and in Robson's *Bedlam* (1946), he was the sadistic head jailer of the infamous asylum. He also started editing horror anthologies, including *Tales Of Terror* (1943) and then *And The Darkness Falls* (1946).

His role of Dr Gustav Niemann, who was the brother of a former assistant to the original Dr Frankenstein, in *House Of Frankenstein* (1944), was his last in the Universal series, though he did play Baron von Frankenstein in *Frankenstein 1970* (1958) for Allied Artists. And the horror potboilers continued: they included *Abbott And Costello Meet The Killer, Boris Karloff* (1949), *The Strange Door* (1951), *The Black Castle* (1952), *Abbott And Costello Meet Dr Jekyll And Mr Hyde* (1953) and *The Haunted Strangler* (1958).

In the early Sixties, incapacitated by arthritis and pneumonia that meant he had to appear on screen in a wheelchair, Karloff got a second wind when he hosted the NBC *Thriller* series and director **Roger Corman** cast him in *The Raven*

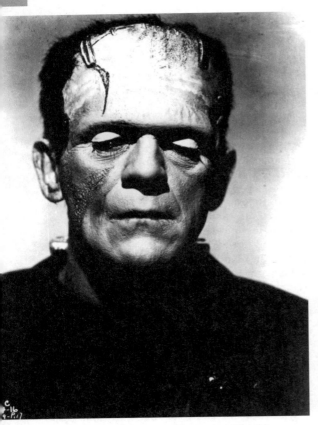

Karloff in the part for which he was billed "?"

Targets
dir Peter Bogdanovich, 1968, US, 90m

The horrors of the real world and "the reel world" are combined in former film critic Bogdanovich's shrewd, insightful and stunning directorial debut. Cast as veteran horror star Byron Orlok, appalled at a sniper's senseless shootings during a drive-in screening of the icon's own quickie *The Terror* (1962), Karloff gives a tremendously moving and personal portrayal of being an anachronism in a world of war, crime and murder. It's a skilful combination of nostalgia, exploitation and sincerity.

Monkeys

King Kong (1933) aside, blame Edgar Allan Poe for introducing the killer gorilla into genre cinema: his oft-filmed story *Murders In The Rue Morgue* (1841) was the first to connect simians with slaughter. Related comical scares proliferated in the silent era thanks to repeated filming of the Ralph Spence's hit play *The Gorilla*, the animals almost always men in suits. The cheaper the budget the rattier the costume and the more fun there was spotting the zip on the back. *The Ape* (1940) had killer **Boris Karloff** dressed in animal skin and *Gorilla At Large* (1954) featured murderer Anne Bancroft in similar disguise in 3-D. Elsewhere monkey glands or gorilla parts were often used in mad doctor experiments, like those in the dotty *Captive Wild Woman* (1943), and different species of deadly monkeys appear in *Link*, *Phenomena* (both 1985), *Monkey Shines* (1988), *Shakma* (1990) and *Congo* (1995).

(1963), another Edgar Allan Poe remake. A horror institution who changed with the times, during this period his output was variable, the most interesting films being *Corridors Of Blood* (1958), *Black Sabbath* (1964), *Die, Monster, Die* (1965) and *The Sorcerers* (1967), but in 1968, a year before he died in his sleep, came one of the best films of his career, **Peter Bogdanovich**'s *Targets*.

Freddy Krueger

Sporting a sickly green and blood-red jersey, a ratty brown fedora on his furnace-burnt head and a razor-fingered glove on his right hand, Freddy Krueger is the wisecracking dream demon whose weapon of choice is the nightmare. "He's the Wicked Witch of the West for a new generation," said **Robert Englund**, who brought "the bastard son of a thousand maniacs", as the film put it, to life, thanks to **David Miller**'s make-up artistry in *A Nightmare On Elm Street* (1984, see Canon) and six sequels, including the fiend grudge match *Freddy Vs Jason* (2003).

In the first of the franchise, **Wes Craven** positioned Krueger as an enchanting antihero. Capable of the most vicious acts, he was still someone the audience could identify with, even though he was a child murderer who had plagued the neighbourhood while his teen victims were still infants. Within any villain there is still potential for vulnerability and love, and although a nasty piece of work, Freddy has humanity and a sense of humour. And it was all evident thanks to a powerhouse portrayal by former bit-player Englund, who saw the possibility of horror fame and extended his larger-than-life performance into moneymaking merchandising and a multi-media crossover phenomenon that saw him host the spin-off TV series *Freddy's Nightmares* (1989-90).

Krueger's popularity with audiences in the original and the sequels – Jack Sholder's *Part 2: Freddy's Revenge* (1985), Chuck Russell's *3: Dream Warriors* (1987), Renny Harlin's *4: The Dream Master* (1988), Stephen Hopkins's *5: The Dream Child* (1989) and Rachel Talalay's *Freddy's Dead: The Final Nightmare* (1991) in 3-D – is the result of several factors. He has, unlike Frankenstein's lumbering creation, an educated voice, unlike Dracula, a wicked sense of fun, and a personality that can move from buffoon to butcher in an instant. "Freddy's not just a one-dimensional splatter film killer," explained Englund. "He's your classic bogeyman and a Freudian kind of nightmare. He's the physical incarnation of some of our deepest fears." Englund added shading to

Freddy Krueger, the demon played by Robert Englund

the unspeakably monstrous character throughout the series, and in the final "official" episode, *Wes Craven's New Nightmare* (1994), in which he played himself playing Freddy in a mature exploration of Hollywood myth-making and the need for dark villains in audiences' lives.

Other films quickly made reference to Freddy's growing cover-boy status: Tom Hanks impersonated him in *Dragnet* (1987), kidnapped Carla Headlee (Amy Madigan) sported a Freddy mask in *The Prince Of Pennsylvania* (1988) and *Critters 2: The Main Course* (1988) had Freddy's image adopted by a shape-shifting alien. The attention proved too much for Craven – the reason that between the first film and 1994 he contributed only the script for the third instalment and story ideas – but Englund happily rose to the occasion and spun off an entire career from his tongue-in-scarred-cheek routine. "The series was a hit," he remarked philosophically, "And I'd be a fool not to go where I'm wanted." That now includes the new *Freddy Vs Jason* franchise, set to extend the lives of both monster maniacs.

Freddy Vs Jason
dir Ronny Yu, 2003, US/It, 97m

In this face-off too many maniacs spoil the blood-stained broth. It's gory, with head-twisting, body severing and an instant nose-job with Freddy's razor fingers, but the poor quality of the story (Freddy entering Jason's dead body to cause dream panic) and the dialogue ("Freddy died by fire, Jason by water, surely there's something we can use there") mean that the result is complete chill-free claptrap.

Christopher Lee

Actor, 1922-

Tall, Dark And Gruesome was the title of his 1977 autobiography, but add aristocratic, commanding and authoritative, and Christopher Frank Carandini Lee is all summed up. Lee is the last king of horror, but this role is one that he inherited reluctantly: his disdain for being identified with the Count Dracula part he played in five Hammer movies is well known. For years he moaned about typecasting. Yet he starred in prestigious blockbuster productions such as *The Private Life Of Sherlock Holmes* (1970), as the detective's brother Mycroft, *The Man With The Golden Gun* (1974), for he was a cousin of 007 creator Ian Fleming, and *Gremlins 2: The New Batch*

Lee in *Dracula* (1958), in his most famous role

(1990), while still accepting roles in terror trash like *Hollywood Meatcleaver Massacre* (1977), *Curse II: Blood Sacrifice* (1991) and *The Funny Man* (1994).

In what he rightfully considered his due, Lee moved from horror has-been to living legend in his later years, appearing in *Sleepy Hollow* (1999), the *Lord Of The Rings* trilogy (2001, 2002, 2003), *Star Wars: Episode II – Attack of the Clones* (2002), *Episode III: Revenge Of The Sith* (2005) and *Charlie And The Chocolate Factory* (2005).

Born in 1922, to a mother whose Carandini family is one of Italy's oldest, after spending World War II in intelligence, Lee chanced upon an acting career when the Rank Organisation signed him to a seven-year contract in 1946 based on his foreign looks. *Corridor Of Mirrors* (1948) was his debut feature, but nothing of note came his way until he was chosen over Bernard Bresslaw to play the man-made Creature in Hammer's breakthrough hit *The Curse Of Frankenstein* (1957, see

Canon). Refusing to play the Creature again because of limited character scope, rather than fear at this stage of being typecast, Lee was cast in *Dracula* (1958, see Canon), the landmark horror that established him as a star. The films launched a personal and professional relationship with fellow icon **Peter Cushing** that would endure during the following decades.

Monster mash

As well as horror musicals, like *The Rocky Horror Picture Show* (1975), *The Little Shop Of Horrors* (1986), and *The Phantom Of The Opera* (2004), there have been some memorable terror tunes. Who could ever forget Burt Bacharach and Mack David's theme song for *The Blob* (1958) – "It creeps and leaps and glides and slides across the floor, right through the door and all around the wall ... Be careful of The Blob!" Here are ten of the strangest:

• "Alligator Man" by Stoneground – *Dracula AD 1972*

• "Attack Of The Killer Tomatoes" by John De Bello – *Attack Of The Killer Tomatoes* (1978)

• "Ben" by Michael Jackson – *Ben* (1978)

• "Daybreak" by Harry Nilsson – *Son Of Dracula* (1974)

• "Eeny Meeny Miney Moe" by Paul Dunlap – *I Was A Teenage Werewolf* (1958)

• "Geronimo" by Nancy Sinatra – *Ghost In The Invisible Bikini* (1966)

• "Love Is Just A Heartbeat Away" by Gloria Gaynor – *Nocturna* (1978)

• "Spider Baby" by Lon Chaney Jr – *Spider Baby, Or The Maddest Story Ever Told* (1968)

• "Strange Love" by Harry Robinson – *Lust For A Vampire* (1971)

• "The Zombie Stomp" by The Del-Aires – *Horror Of Party Beach* (1964)

His best horrors include *The Whip And The Body* (1963), which was one of his nastiest roles, as a vengeful undead sadist, *The Face Of Fu Manchu*, *Rasputin, The Mad Monk* (both 1965), *The Devil Rides Out* (1968) and *The Wicker Man* (1973); and in 1972, for his short-lived Charlemagne production company, he served as producer for *Nothing But The Night*. He gave notable renditions of the famous Bram Stoker vampire in Jess Franco's *El Conde Drácula* (*Count Dracula*, 1970) and in Edouard Molinaro's *Dracula père et fils* (*Dracula And Son*, 1975) and was also the Count in twentieth-century London in *Dracula AD 1972*, but his oddest role came when he played a gay Hell's Angel in *Serial* (1980).

For all his martyrdom for the genre, Lee demonstrated a remarkable ability to get inside the skin of a vast array of characters. Adrian Conan Doyle, the author's son, saluted his performance in the title role of *Sherlock Holmes And The Deadly Necklace* (1962), his five portrayals of Fu Manchu were praised by Elizabeth Sax Rohmer, the wife of the character's creator, and Maria Rasputin told him that he looked just like her father. With one of the longest CVs in movie history, in 2001 Lee was appointed CBE for his contribution to the film industry.

The Wicker Man
dir Robin Hardy, 1973, UK, 102m

Devout Christian policeman Sergeant Neil Howie (Edward Woodward) finds his beliefs tested to the limit while investigating a young girl's disappearance on the pagan shores of Summerisle. Literate scripting (by Anthony Schaffer, author of *Sleuth*), a memorable Scottish folk score, a challenging religious subtext and lyrical eroticism make for a provocative combination. Lee thinks that this cult horror classic, nearly destroyed when the negatives at Shepperton Studios were almost thrown out by new owners, is the finest film he's ever made.

Lewton, a producer who brought subtlety to the genre, with a boat made by his son

Val Lewton

Producer, 1904-1951

Feeling that the Universal monsters were old-fashioned and their recycled shock theatrics passé, maverick producer Val Lewton steered the creak-ing genre an entirely different way with a series of films that changed the face of fear. He was convinced that by withholding certain amounts of visual information the audience would fill in the nasty details, and he was right. On this learning curve he built up a stable of directors, editors and writers – including Jacques Tourneur, Robert Wise and Mark Robson – who shared his vision and learnt to create and manipulate a sense of unease through mere hints.

Born in Russia in 1904, Vladimir Ivan Leventon was raised in New York, where his mother Nina lived with actress sister Alla Nazimova. Starting in the MGM publicity department, he became an experienced fiction writer (one of his stories appeared in the book *Weird Tales*), before moving to Hollywood to be editorial assistant to *Gone With The Wind* producer **David O. Selznick**. In 1942 he joined RKO to help challenge Universal. He was allowed complete creative control – as long as he agreed to use the studio's already-tested sensationalist titles, to avoid messages, to spend less than $150,000 per picture or per month on shooting and to limit the length to around 75 minutes. Working to those guidelines and his own professed terror formula – "A love story, three scenes of suggested horror and one of actual violence" – Lewton rethought and revitalized the genre, though a series of revered nightmares that rejected mad scientists and monster make-up.

Lewton, who feared the feline, wrote *Cat People* (1942, see Canon) after dumping the original plot source, Algernon Blackwood's story *Ancient Sorceries*, and its huge success saved RKO from bankruptcy after their overspending on *Citizen Kane* (1941). *I Walked With A Zombie* (1943, see Canon) followed, and flopped, so Lewton changed tack by producing **Jacques Tourneur**'s *The Leopard Man* (1943). Based on the thriller *Black Alibi* by Cornell Woolrich, its supernatural leopard overtones are red herrings, the inventions of a psychopath to mask his murders, one of which – behind a locked door, revealed by trickling blood – was frequently copied.

Editor **Mark Robson** turned director for another Lewton classic, *The Seventh Victim* (1943), about an orphaned schoolgirl in New York discovering that her sister is a devil worshipper. It captured perfectly the nocturnal menace of a large urban city and the evil lurking beneath the everyday. Next Robson directed *The Ghost Ship* (1943), which concerned a jinxed vessel whose captain turns homicidal. It was quickly withdrawn from release because of a plagiarism lawsuit that Lewton contested vehemently but lost.

The Curse Of The Cat People (1944) began life being directed by Gunther von Fritsch but was then taken over by second unit director and editor **Robert Wise**. In many ways improving on the original, it focused on Amy (Ann Carter), the daughter of Irena (Simone Simon) and Oliver's (Kent Smith), being haunted by her dead mother's neuroses. A poetic balance of the real and the imaginary that transcended the limitations of the genre, Lewton's most personal production recalled some of his earliest memories and his strained relationship with his daughter, Nina. His final eccentric trio for RKO, *The Body Snatcher*, *Isle Of The Dead* (both 1945) and *Bedlam* (1946), starred **Boris Karloff**; for the first and last Lewton used the pseudonym Carlos Keith for the screenplays he wrote.

Lewton never occupied the commanding horror heights again. When he returned to the RKO fold, his power had been wrested by his former protégés; they offered him a job as story editor and then reluctantly fired him for being too slow, and he died of a heart attack aged only

46. But through the subsequent work of Tourneur (*Night Of The Demon*, 1957, see Canon), Wise (*The Haunting*, 1963, see Canon) and Robson (*Daddy's Gone A-Hunting*, 1969), the subtlety of his sophisticated studies in psychology, more reliant on suggestion than shock, would live on.

 Bedlam
dir Mark Robson, 1946, US, 79m, b/w

While trying to reform the notorious British asylum, Nell Bowen (Anna Lee) is wrongly entrusted to George Sims (Boris Karloff), the warden, in producer Lewton's eccentric frightener that evokes both horror and pity. Karloff renders his callous character's sadistic confrontations expressively, and this overshadows the visions of lunacy in the artful direction, which was inspired by the work of William Hogarth, including plate eight of *A Rake's Progress*.

Bela Lugosi

Actor, 1882-1956

Béla Ferenc Dezsõ Blaskó, who took his stage surname from Lugos, the Hungarian town of his birth, became the first king of horror with *Dracula* (1931), and his embodiment of the consummate vampire helped to usher in an era of massive popularity for the genre. But his star quickly faded because of the bad roles he chose, money problems and the formaldehyde addiction that would see his career end in Hollywood's gutter.

Always fascinated by acting, Lugosi entered the professional theatre as an operetta chorus boy, before a stint at the Budapest Academy of Theatrical Arts. By 1901 he was a leading actor with Hungary's Royal National Theatre, and he appeared first under the pseudonyms Arisztid Olt or Olt Arisztid, beginning with *A Régiséggyüjtö* (1917).

After fleeing to Germany during the political turmoil in Hungary of 1918-19, Lugosi starred in

F. W. Murnau's *Der Januskopf* (*Dr Jekyll and Mr Hyde*, 1920). In 1921, he emigrated to America and made his debut there in *The Silent Command* (1923), but he struggled to find work because of his thick Eastern European accent. However, learning lines phonetically gave him a distinctive depth that proved perfect for the 1927 Broadway transfer production of Hamilton Deane's West End hit *Dracula*. Reviews were bad, but audiences flocked to see it, and Lugosi spent three years in the role. It was a part in **Tod Browning**'s

Lugosi in his most famous role, in 1931; he was buried in his Dracula cape

The Thirteenth Chair (1929) that put him on the director's radar when *Dracula* came to be made as a movie.

He was propelled to international fame, but his refusal to play the Monster in *Frankenstein* (1931) opened the door to **Boris Karloff** and lost him career momentum; he did, however, play the Monster in *Frankenstein Meets The Wolfman* (1943). Although he remained a prolific screen presence in such commendable chillers as *White Zombie, Murders In The Rue Morgue* (both 1932), *The Island of Lost Souls* (1933), *The Black Cat* (1934) – the first of many collaborations with Karloff – and *Dark Eyes Of London* (1940), most were forgettable. Lugosi's choice of projects was indiscriminate at best, and his reputation went into rapid decline when he played successively more desperate parodies of his Dracula role, as he did in *Abbott And Costello Meet Frankenstein* (1948) and *Bela Lugosi Meets A Brooklyn Gorilla* (1952).

Lugosi's last gasp of fame had a surprising source. By 1953, he was collaborating with the notorious **Ed Wood**, widely recognized as the worst director in history. After the hilarious cross-dressing exploiter *Glen Or Glenda* (1953) and the ludicrously cheap *Bride Of The Monster* (1955), the duo were about to embark on the infamously awful *Plan 9 From Outer Space* (1956), but after filming only a handful of scenes, Lugosi died of a heart attack. He was buried in his Dracula cape.

Ed Wood became a cult figure and his work with Lugosi was immortalized in Tim Burton's affectionate biopic *Ed Wood* (1994). **Martin Landau** won the best supporting actor Oscar for his wonderful performance as Lugosi – a posthumous ironic twist to a career that took the Hungarian from the peak of horror to the background disco ditty "Bela Lugosi's Dead" by Bauhaus that featured in *The Hunger* (1983).

Dark Eyes Of London (aka The Human Monster)

dir Walter Summers, 1940, UK, 76m, b/w

Based on a novel by Edgar Wallace, the first British film to receive the "H for Horror" certificate, introduced in January 1937, features Lugosi in the roles of a manager of a home for the blind, Professor Dearborn, and an insurance company head, Dr Orloff, who tortures its residents for their indemnity money. Lugosi rises to the occasion when electrocuting or drowning innocent victims and instructing his blind henchmen to dump their bodies in the Thames. It's atmospheric and full of evil.

The Mummy

In November 1922 archaeologist **Howard Carter** found the tomb of the boy pharaoh Tutankhamun in the Valley of the Kings, near Luxor in Egypt. Global interest in the discovery was fuelled further when his sponsor, **Lord Carnarvon**, who was present when the tomb was opened, died of blood poisoning the following year. Soon other alleged happenings – a power failure in Cairo and the demise of Carnarvon's favourite dog at the precise moment of his death – led to growing talk of a curse that had been dormant since 1323 BC.

Although Egyptian exotica featured in silent movies such as *The Vengeance of Egypt* (1912) and *Eyes Of The Mummy* (1918), the curse legend first reached Hollywood in **Karl Freund**'s *The Mummy* (1932), which starred **Boris Karloff** as the ancient Egyptian prince Im-ho-tep. *The Mummy's Hand* (1940), *The Mummy's Tomb* and *The Mummy's Ghost* (both 1942) transformed Im-ho-tep into Kharis, who was portrayed by Tom Tyler in the first and **Lon Chaney Jr** in the following two. After the inevitable *Abbott And Costello Meet The Mummy* (1955), the many Universal story threads, such as curses and

reincarnation, went into the Hammer blender for *The Mummy* (1959), starring **Christopher Lee** in an athletic and eloquently mimed performance; the sequels were *The Curse Of The Mummy's Tomb* (1964), *The Mummy's Shroud* (1967), with frequent Christopher Lee stunt double Eddie Powell in the main role, and *Blood From The Mummy's Tomb* (1971), which, like *The Awakening* (1980), was based on Bram Stoker's *The Jewel Of Seven Stars*.

When the story was transplanted to Mexico, the curse of Xochitl brought her warrior lover Popoca back to life in *La momia Azteca* (*Attack Of The Mayan Mummy*, 1957) and director Rafael Portillo resurrected the character for *La maledicion de la momia Azteca* (*Curse Of The Aztec Mummy*, 1957); another Mexican mummy cycle began in *Las momias de Guanajuato* (*The Mummies Of Guanajuato*, 1972), with wrestler **Alejandro Cruz** as the Blue Demon. Amen-ho-tep was played by **Paul Naschy** in the Spanish *La venganza de la momia* (*The Mummy's Vengeance*, 1971), while flesh-eating zombie mummies came from Italy in *Dawn Of The Mummy* (1981). Universal revived their franchise as a pure adventure blockbuster with **Stephen Sommers**' *The Mummy* (1999) and *The Mummy Returns* (2001).

 The Mummy

dir Karl Freund, 1932, US, 72m, b/w

Boris Karloff (billed as "Karloff the Uncanny") stars as 3700-year-old priest Ardath Bey, formerly the ancient Egyptian prince Im-ho-tep, who after removing his own bandages in the British Museum offers eternal life to the reincarnation of the woman he loves (Zita Johann). Freund's directorial debut, after working as a cinematographer on films including *Metropolis*, is imbued with an eerie hallucinatory quality that makes it a moody horror classic.

Michael Myers

"This force, this thing that lives inside of him came from a source too violent, too deadly for you to imagine. It grew inside him, contaminating his soul, it was pure evil." So says Dr Sam Loomis (Donald Pleasence), the psychiatric Captain Ahab obsessed with tracking down his silent nemesis in *Halloween: The Curse Of Michael Myers* (1995). With the introduction of Michael Myers, the unstoppable masked maniac, **John Carpenter**'s *Halloween* (1978, see Canon) created the stalk-and-slash sub-genre and invented a new aspect of movie horror: the boundaries between the real and supernatural worlds were no longer clearly defined after Myers, despite being stabbed, blinded and shot, kept returning from apparent death and killing again.

In Carpenter's last-minute addition to his script, originally titled "The Babysitter Murders", Myers transcended death because he was literally Death incarnate. This left-field supernatural explanation is anticipated by Tommy (Brian Andrews), whom Laurie Strode (**Jamie Lee Curtis**), revealed in later movies to be Michael's younger sister, looks after on the fateful night "he came home" to Haddonfield after escaping from Smith's Grove mental institution. Seeing Myers lurking, Tommy tells Laurie he saw "the boogeyman". She tells him that there's no such thing, but his childish interpretation of events turns out to be closer to the truth than her reasoning. Indeed, it was the most terrifying "boogeyman" of all coming to get them – a human divested of all notions of right, wrong, guilt and reasoning.

Often referred to as The Shape, Michael Myers was named after the head of **Miracle Films**. The British distribution outfit entered Carpenter's *Assault On Precinct 13* (1976) into the London Film Festival and then released it, and Carpenter was so grateful for the critical acclaim and commercial success that kick-started his moribund career, he paid Myers what seemed at the time to be a campy tribute. It is now seen by his son Martin as a tremendous honour that will be a lasting memorial to his late father.

The menacing persona of Michael Myers expressed Carpenter's belief that "evil never dies", and six sequels later it still seems to be the case. Myers has been played by Carpenter's old friend Nick Castle, Dick Warlock, George Wilbur (twice), Don Shanks, Chris Durand and Brad Loree, and by Mikael Lindgren and Anders Ek in two unofficial Swedish shorts. Tommy Lee Wallace's *Halloween III: Season Of The Witch* (1983) was *sans* Myers; everyone thought that the psycho wave was over, so Nigel Kneale explored the roots of the Halloween myth, but this was a flop, and so Myers returned.

Halloween H20
dir Steve Miner, 1998, US, 87m

Jamie Lee Curtis's return to the fear franchise that made her famous sees her character Laurie Strode still haunted by the spectre of her homicidal brother Michael, who reappears so that she can "face her demon". Some inventive twists and moderate scares aside, stalk-and-slash director Miner approaches the unbelievable, even for this sub-genre. The appearance of Curtis's own mother, Janet Leigh, is one of the many *Psycho* riffs.

Roman Polanski

Director and actor, 1933-

The work of the Polish director, screenwriter and actor Roman Polanski is most notable for its recurring themes of violence, paranoia and loneliness. These issues are hard to divorce

Polanski, whose work has been influenced heavily by personal tragedies

from his experience of being sent at the age of eight to a German concentration camp, where his mother died, and from his moving between countries during a life punctuated by tragedies.

Born in Paris in 1933, Polanski moved to Poland in 1936 and was educated in Krakow and at the country's film school in Lodz. His first feature, *Knife In The Water* (1962), found a couple acting out a series of dangerous emotional games with a stranger, and its claustrophobia would be echoed in his later work. It was denounced by his country's communists but was nominated for the Oscar for best foreign language film.

After leaving for Paris, Polanski moved to Britain, where he made his first English-language films. In the psychological horror *Repulsion*

(1965, see Canon) the mutating apartment of a young Belgian woman represents stunningly her inner torment, and *Cul-de-Sac* (1966) portrays the sinister breakdown of family order on a remote island.

Then came a change of tack, when Polanski directed and starred in the Hammer parody *Dance Of The Vampires* (1967). It had awesome sets, sumptuous colour photography, a stunning title scene and two firsts: a Jewish vampire immune to crucifixes and a camp gay bloodsucker. The US version was cut and marketed with the title *The Fearless Vampire Killers, Or Pardon Me But Your Teeth Are In My Neck,* and Polanski asked for his name to be removed from the credits.

After moving to America, he helmed the blockbuster *Rosemary's Baby* (1968, see Canon). Based on the novel by Ira Levin and produced by William Castle, like *Repulsion* it concerned a lonely, frightened female, but this time the result was a credible atmosphere of witchcraft in everyday Manhattan. The film, for which Polanski won an Oscar nomination for best screenplay, played a crucial part in making horror respectable at the end of the Sixties.

In 1969 his life was shattered after his pregnant wife **Sharon Tate**, star of *Dance Of The Vampires*, who he had married in 1968, was murdered by members of the Charles Manson cult. This tragedy, one of the most notorious events of the late Sixties, was behind his graphic and bloody version of *Macbeth* (1971). Three years later, after playing a peasant in Andy Warhol's *Blood For Dracula* (1974), he directed the crime classic *Chinatown*, and then he took the tormented lead role in *The Tenant* (1976), which was an apartment horror like *Repulsion*, but also had elements of black comedy.

Facing charges in the late 1970s of raping a 13-year-old girl, Polanski fled to France, where he has remained, working at a slower pace. He directed the Hitchcock parody *Frantic* (1988), about a man whose wife vanishes, and after a break from horror to make the drama *Bitter Moon* (1992) he returned to form with the satanic horror *The Ninth Gate* (1999). He finally won the best director Oscar for his Holocaust film *The Pianist* (2002), which had similar themes to his horror classics.

 The Ninth Gate
dir Roman Polanski, 1999, Fr/Sp, 133m

Based on the bestseller *El club Dumas* by Arturo Pérez-Reverte, Polanski's triumphant return to horror has antiques book expert Dean Corso (Johnny Depp) hired to find an ancient tome that has the power to open the Ninth Gate of Hades and free the Prince of Darkness. A rich satanic spectacular of razor-sharp irony, sinister unease and subtle gothic chills, it satisfies the intellect and haunts the memory, and the burnished hallucinatory climax can be placed on a par with the spine-tingling finale to *Rosemary's Baby*.

Vincent Price
Actor, 1911-1993

Lean, effete and haughtily sinister, Vincent Price had a staggering and distinguished career as the master of the arched eyebrow, the hair-raising sneer and the menacing double take – but he was also an art collector and a celebrated lecturer on art history, a gourmand and a cookbook writer, a poet and a nationally syndicated columnist. In the year before his death, the aristocratic Renaissance man said: "I would like to be remembered by something I strongly believe in – that there is a great difference between earning a living and knowing how to live. An awful lot of people earn a living to put it in their bellies. It should be put in your head."

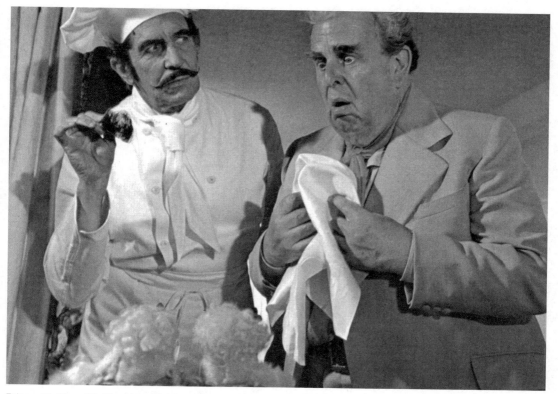

Price with Meredith Merridew (Robert Morley) in *Theatre Of Blood* (1973)

Born in St Louis (and eventually sharing his birthday with Christopher Lee), after taking a masters degree at the University of London, Price auditioned for a part in the off-West End play *Chicago* for a dare. Bitten by the acting bug, he starred as Prince Albert in the same company's next production, *Victoria Regina* (1935), and when it moved to Broadway as a smash-hit vehicle for diva Helen Hayes, Price went with it. After being signed up by Universal, Price's screen debut was in *Service Deluxe* (1938), and his first brush with

costume gothic horror came when he starred opposite **Boris Karloff** in *Tower Of London* (1939). The first of his highly acclaimed movies was the film noir classic *Laura* (1944); another was the biblical epic *The Ten Commandments* (1956).

But it was starring as crazed sculptor Henry Jarrod in *House Of Wax* (1953), the 3-D update from Warner Bros of their *Mystery Of The Wax Museum* (1933), that changed the course of his career. It made him a horror icon, which

Trust me, I'm a doctor

The only doctor you can really trust in horror movies is Dr Abraham Van Helsing, vampire hunter and Dracula defeater; otherwise they tend to bring dishonour to the medical profession. Here are the ten worst doctors to be seeing for an appointment:

• Dr Peter Blood (Kieron Moore) in *Dr Blood's Coffin* (1961), who exhumes corpses and puts living hearts in them to bring them back from the dead

• Dr Warren Chapin (**Vincent Price**) in *The Tingler* (1959), who suspects that fear causes a lobster-like organism to grow in the body if it is not released by a scream

• Dr Giggles (the nickname of Dr Rendell), played by Larry Drake in *Dr Giggles* (1992), who escapes from an asylum and then murders with surgical implements

• Dr Leon Kravaal (Boris Karloff) in *The Man With Nine Lives* (1940), who places his research victims in an underground ice chamber

• Dr Mallinger (Robert Flemyng) in *The Blood Beast Terror* (1967), who through genetic mutation turns his own daughter into a blood-sucking giant death's head moth

• Dr Richard Marlowe (Bela Lugosi) in *Voodoo Man* (1944), who uses black magic rites and the souls of kidnapped girls to revivify his long-dead wife

• Dr Rossiter (Anton Diffring) in *Circus Of Horrors* (1960), who uses revolutionary plastic surgery methods to turn scarred women into gorgeous big-top performers

• Sir John Rowan (Peter Cushing) in *Corruption* (1967), who kills prostitutes and uses their pituitary gland fluid to restore the beauty of his disfigured fiancée

• Dr Christian Storm (Michael Gough) in *Horror Hospital* (1973), who lobotomizes teenagers to make them his zombie puppets

• Dr Wells, played by Preston Foster in *Doctor X* (1932), who adds a murderous arm to his disfigured body with synthetic flesh

would be a blessing and a curse for the rest of his life.

After *The Mad Magician* (1954), again in 3-D, and *The Fly* (1958), Price joined producer/director **William Castle** for two popular horrors, *House On Haunted Hill* (1958) and *The Tingler* (1959). He then embarked on the eight Edgar Allan Poe adaptations directed by **Roger Corman** that would establish his horror persona: in *The Fall Of The House Of Usher* (1960) Price gave what is regarded as his best performance, as the hypersensitive Roderick Usher, who has a fear of premature burial, and other notable titles include *Twice Told Tales* (1963), *Witchfinder General* (1968, see Canon) and *Scream And Scream Again* (1970), the first film in which he featured along-side fellow maestros of malevolence Christopher Lee and Peter Cushing.

Price starred in three classics in the Seventies – the camp art-deco delight *The Abominable Dr Phibes* (1971), its imaginatively macabre follow-up *Dr Phibes Rises Again* (1972), and his personal favourite, *Theatre Of Blood* (1973) – and he joined forces with **Christopher Lee** and **Peter Cushing** again, plus **John Carradine**, for *House Of The Long Shadows* (1983), the only film in which all four feature together. **Tim Burton**, who had made the short film *Vincent* (1982), about a boy who dreams about being just like Price, because he was the horror actor Burton most admired, directed his last screen appearance, in the poignant *Edward Scissorhands* (1990).

Theatre Of Blood
dir Douglas Hickox, 1973, UK, 102m

In his mirthfully macabre magnum opus, Price plays the supposedly deceased ham actor Edward Lionheart, who dishes out Shakespearean deaths to the theatre critics who denied him a prestigious award. The inspired murders range from immolation at a hairdresser's to a gay Meredith Merridew (Robert Morley) being force-fed his twin poodles. Price, disguised as all the best Bard characters, is clearly having a ball. He loved Shakespeare and during the production he met his third and final wife, Coral Browne.

Sam Raimi
Director, 1959-

From director of a cheap, controversial horror exploiter to one of the most powerful figures in the movie business: Sam Raimi's career trajectory has been the ultimate Hollywood dream come true. But it's perhaps not surprising given the people with whom he shared a Hollywood apartment in his early days: *The Evil Dead* actor **Bruce Campbell**, *Evil Dead 2* writer Scott Spiegel, the Coen brothers, and Oscar-winning

Raimi filming the comedy horror *Army Of Darkness* (1993), and wearing a shirt on set, as always

actresses Holly Hunter, Frances McDormand and Kathy Bates.

Prior to turning his 1978 short *Within The Woods* into the *cause célèbre* shocker *The Evil Dead* (1982, see Canon), Raimi wasn't a horror fan at all. His favourite genre was comedy – as is visible in the references throughout his body of work to **The Three Stooges**, in re-created sequences and in the way he credits stand-ins and body doubles as "Fake Shemp", nods to the Stooges shorts where an extra was used after Shemp Howard died.

Realizing that his entry into the industry would be best served by a horror debut, which had a chance of making money fast, Raimi steeped himself in the lexicon of James Whale, Roman Polanski, EC Comics and Universal monsters. Like most horror directors, he had no film-school training, and his amateur bravura led him to fuse genres, which has given his movies broad appeal while also making him a distinctive auteur. He deftly mixed *The Phantom Of The Opera* with *The Hunchback Of Notre Dame* to concoct the engaging horror superhero crossover *Darkman* (1990); and he later moved further into the mainstream with *The Gift* (2000), culminating in his massive success with *Spider-Man* (2002) and *Spider-Man 2* (2004).

Raimi has also acted in various movies, including *Intruder* (1998), the two *Maniac Cop* movies (1988, 1992) and the mini-series *The Shining* (1997). "I wanted to learn what it would be like so I could give my actors the support they needed," he said. "The lesson I learnt is to keep it simple." Having produced various movies apart from his own – including *Lunatics: A Love Story* (1991), starring his brother Ted, and *Timecop* (1993) – he had success in the same job for TV, and, with *Evil Dead* partner **Robert Tapert**, was behind *Hercules: The Legendary Journeys* (1995-99) and *Xena: Warrior Princess* (1995-2001).

After producing the hit remake of *The Grudge* (2004), Raimi and Tapert's Ghost House Pictures is now a major force in horror, boasting a raft of enviable titles – *Scarecrow*, *Boogeyman* (2005), *Rise*, *The Grudge 2* and *Evil Dead Regeneration* (all scheduled for 2006), a remake of the film that began it all. Raimi, who always wears a shirt and tie when directing, in deference to his idol, Alfred Hitchcock, summed up his philosophy when he said: "I prefer making people laugh rather than scream, but both are similar unconscious outbursts when audiences get caught up in a story."

Darkman
Dir Sam Raimi, 1990, US, 91m

Raimi's first studio movie is an expressionistic amalgam of *The Phantom Of The Opera*, Grand Guignol pulp fiction and exaggerated psychedelic visuals. As scientist Peyton Westlake and Darkman, Liam Neeson expertly portrays the pathos and tragedy of the scientist donning synthetic skin masks to take revenge on the crooks responsible for his disfigurement.

George A. Romero
Director, 1940-

Born in the Bronx, long before making Pittsburgh his home and film location base, George Andrew Romero showed strains of non-conformism even at an early age: as a 14-year-old he was arrested by police for throwing a burning dummy from a rooftop for his first 8mm short, *The Man From The Meteor*. He continued to flout conventions when masterminding not one but two of the greatest films that have changed the course of horror, *Night Of The Living Dead* (1968, see Canon) and its sequel *Dawn Of The Dead* (1978, see Canon). They made him the definitive master of the zombie flick, which he still influences today.

In 1962 Romero established a successful commercial production company, and it was the grind of TV adverts, industrial films, political campaign shorts and documentaries that led him to transform the genre. After *Night Of The Living Dead*, because he did not want to get trapped, he chose to direct films that would not carry the horror tag; nevertheless, *There's Always Vanilla (1971)*, *Jack's Wife* (aka *Season Of The Witch*, 1972) and *The Crazies* (1973) still contained acute insights into the darker side of human nature that characterized all his work. Both feet were back firmly in the horror camp when he provided a new twist on Transylvanian terror in *Martin* (1977).

After *Dawn*, Romero directed the modern-day Camelot fable *Knightriders* (1981), the five-part EC Comics anthology *Creepshow* (1982), which began his association with novelist Stephen King, and the third part of his zombie trilogy, *Day Of The Dead* (1985), in which zombies are trained to be obedient by the military for integration back into society. In between his two *Dr Jekyll And Mr Hyde* variants, *Monkey Shines* (1988), where a paraplegic's pet simian acts out his subconscious wishes, and King's *The Dark Half* (1993), Romero made *The Facts In The Case Of Mr Valdemar* for the two-part tribute to Edgar Allan Poe, *Two Evil Eyes* (1990); the other director was *Dawn Of The Dead* collaborator **Dario Argento**.

Romero produced and wrote episodes for the TV series *Tales From The Darkside* (1984–86), wrote the *Cat From Hell* segment based on the Stephen King story in *Tales From The Darkside: The Movie* (1990), and produced and rewrote his earlier screenplay for **Tom Savini**'s 1990 *Night Of The Living Dead* remake. As an actor he had un-credited cameos in his own movies and played an FBI agent in *The Silence Of The Lambs* (1990, see Canon).

After a decade in the doldrums making critical remarks about the artistic value and splatter legacy of his watershed *Dawn Of The Dead* – he said that having children made his values change regarding shocking horror – Romero barely made a ripple when he came back with the total dud *Bruiser* (2000). But while he was unsuccessfully trying to get the vampire virus movie *The Ill* and the zombie musical *Diamond Dead* off the ground, the smash hit *Dawn Of The Dead* remake in 2004 revitalized interest in his illustrious career and led to the "fourth" in his zombie trilogy, *Land Of The Dead* (2005).

Zombie king Romero during a publicity stunt for *Day Of The Dead* (1985)

Martin
dir George A. Romero, 1977, US, 95m

In an impressive, offbeat and adult-strength update of the vampire myth, Martin (John Amplas), a dysfunctional teen living in a depressed steel industry town, is so traumatized by the religious persecution of his European family that he takes to violent blood-sucking for rebellion and relief. Romero's scarily bittersweet tragedy uses the garlic-and-crucifix sub-genre to comment on the collapse of religion and on fractured moral values in a brilliantly believable way.

Jacques Tourneur

Director, 1904-1977

Jacques Tourneur was crucial to producer **Val Lewton**'s quest to provide horror movies that contained "the reality of terror". An excellent in-house director who was part of the "little horror unit", as Lewton put it, that popularized B-movies during World War II, he was blessed with an eye that could develop spookiness and suspense from any narrative.

Born in Paris in 1904, Jacques Tourneur was the son of the director **Maurice Tourneur**, and in 1913 moved with his father to America, where he went to school in Hollywood and then worked on scripts for his father. They returned to Paris at the end of the Twenties, but after breaking away from his paternal ties Jacques went back to America and began to work as a second unit director. From 1939 he directed shorts and MGM B-movies, in which the visual quality disguised the lack of finance.

While he was arranging sequences on *A Tale Of Two Cities* (1935) Tourneur met Val Lewton, and the pair formed one of horror's key partnerships when, in 1942, Tourneur was the first director Lewton hired for his RKO production unit. He directed its most enduring and popular

success, *Cat People* (1942, see Canon), and the famous sequence of the woman in a basement swimming pool was based on an experience that Tourneur had one night when he almost drowned.

The next two films that Tourneur made for RKO showed, as *Cat People* had, expert composition and how fear can be created from shadows; and although *The Leopard Man* (1943) is underrated, *I Walked With A Zombie* (1943, see Canon) is an acknowledged masterpiece of darkness and light. Tourneur demonstrated similar directorial skills when working for RKO on the film noir *Out Of The Past* (1947), the war drama *Days Of Glory* (1944) and the thriller *Berlin Express* (1948).

After RKO unwisely decided to end their relationship, Tourneur moved to bigger budget pictures and tried his hand as a television director. But he returned to suggestive horror with *Night Of The Demon* (1958, see Canon), which was another psychological chiller dealing with rationality being eroded by encounters with the supernatural. Although a monster was inserted by the film's producers, just as a panther found its way into *Cat People*, it again showed the power of understatement.

After co-directing the sword-and-sandal spectacle *The Giant Of Marathon* (1960) with Italian maestro of the macabre Mario Bava – who along with Riccardo Freda and other Italian directors was influenced by Tourneur's scenes of hidden menace – he ended his sublime horror career ignominiously, with *The Comedy Of Terrors* (1964) and *The City Under the Sea* (aka *War-Gods Of The Deep*, 1965). He retired in 1966 and returned to France.

In his declining years Tourneur, who died in 1977, was frank about his short but successful period making horrors with Lewton. He said that they had a perfect collaboration, and that "Val was the dreamer, the idealist, and I was the materialist, the realist." But he continued: "We should have gone right on doing bigger, more ambitious pictures." He will always be remembered, however, for a stylish collaboration that after the Universal era of the Thirties broke new ground.

The Leopard Man
dir Jacques Tourneur, 1943, US, 66m, b/w

This moody chiller creepily stages a series of savage killings that occur in a small Mexican town after a leopard escapes from a nightclub act. Is the leopard responsible, or an insane maniac? Tourneur fills his blood-pumping story with classic examples of horror artistry, including the justly famous blood-under-locked-door punishment and the trapped-in-cemetery ordeal, and, unusually for a film produced by Lewton, good triumphs over evil.

Tourneur, a master of creating fear from shadows

Jason Voorhees

"Kill, kill, kill," whispers the barely audible chorus in Harry Manfredini's music scores for the *Friday The 13th* films. And that is exactly what the machete-wielding maniac Jason Voorhees has done in ever more inventive ways during most of the reviled, graphic and controversial body count series, masterminded by director/producer **Sean S. Cunningham**. "Jason grew out of basic things that would scare me as a little kid. I was sure there was somebody lurking under the bed, and I was afraid to move," he said.

In *Friday The 13th* (1980), which launched one of the most successful franchises in horror history, Jason wasn't a murderer; it was his mother Pamela Voorhees (Betsy Palmer). Because her son drowned at a summer camp while incompetent assistants were fooling around, she takes revenge on another sex-starved bunch when it reopens. Mrs Voorhees is beheaded at the climax, but it turns out in **Steve Miner**'s *Friday The 13th Part II* (1981), in the usual twisted logic of sequels, that Jason survived and is lurking in the nearby woods, waiting to mete out phallic machete vengeance on any sexually active co-ed student.

It wasn't until Miner's *Friday The 13th Part 3: 3-D* (1982) that Jason was transformed from a scrawny psychopath sporting a burlap bag with eye-holes into a brawny goon wearing the hockey mask that audiences have come to know and love. Despite its title, Joseph Zito's *Friday The 13th: The Final Chapter* (1984) wasn't, of course: respectable Paramount, who shocked the industry by picking up the first cheap and nasty film, were making far too much money from the series. In this episode Jason's body is taken to the morgue where a couple's petting session aggravates him back to life for another slaughter spree.

Danny Steinmann's *Friday The 13th: A New Beginning* (1985) had the troubled teenager (Corey Feldman) who "killed" Jason in the prior film seemingly take on his murderous persona. Tom McLoughlin's *Friday The 13th Part VI: Jason Lives* (1986) resurrected the mass murderer as a lightning-powered killer zombie, John Carl Buechler's *Friday The 13th Part VII: The New Blood* (1988) has a telekinetic psychic girl releasing Jason's soul from his Camp Crystal Lake watery grave and Rob Hedden's *Friday The 13th Part VIII: Jason Takes Manhattan* (1989) had Jason end up as toxic waste after stalking high-school graduates on a cruise ship to New York.

Jason entered an exciting new phase in Adam Marcus's *Jason Goes To Hell: The Final Friday* (1993). New Line Cinema had taken over the franchise and this, the goriest of them all, featured a parasite, which has kept Jason's corpse animated, passing between other bodies in its quest to find one of the surviving members of the Voorhees family for a new skin. The coda featured the steel-clawed hand of Freddy Krueger, from New Line's other profitable *Nightmare On Elm Street* skein, popping up to snatch away Jason's dropped hockey mask.

This hinted at the long-awaited face-off which, after Jim Isaac's *Jason X* (2001), became a reality in **Ronny Yu**'s *Freddy Vs Jason* (2003), the start of a new franchise. It was such a blockbuster hit that Jason Voorhees' true demise may have to wait until Sean S. Cunningham decides on his preferred cut-off point. "I had no idea the first film would be as big as it was, even less of an idea it would turn into a series with such longevity," he said. Jason has been played by the actors and stuntmen Ari Lehman, Warrington Gillette, Richard Brooker, Ted White, C. J. Graham, Ken Kirzinger and, four times, **Kane Hodder**.

Star debuts in shockers

Many, many movie stars have made their film debuts in horror movies they would rather forget. Here are ten of the worst.

• **Jennifer Aniston** appeared in *Leprechaun* (1993) as Tory Reding, the main target of the murdering Irish elf

• **Kevin Bacon** was in *Friday The 13th* (1980) as one of **Jason**'s victims, Jack Burrell

• **George Clooney** appeared in *Return Of The Killer Tomatoes* (1988) as pizza man Matt Stevens

• **David Copperfield** featured in *Terror Train* (1980) as Ken, the magician

• **Johnny Depp** made his film debut in *A Nightmare On Elm Street* (1984) – he was sucked into his mattress and spat out as a blood geyser

• **Tom Hanks** appeared in *He Knows You're Alone* (1980) as Elliott, whose first words are "I'm too tired to scream from the pain you've just caused me"

• **Philip Seymour Hoffman** featured in the zombie comedy *My Boyfriend's Back* (1993) as slow-witted, high school jock Chuck Bronski

• Schoolgirl Jenny was played by **Renée Zellweger** in *The Return Of The Texas Chainsaw Massacre* (1993); in the same movie **Matthew McConaughey**

Aniston (left) in *Leprechaun* (1993), before cutting it as Rachel in *Friends*

played smirking hillbilly Vilmer.

• **Donald Sutherland** had roles in *Castle Of The Living Dead* (1964) as Sergeant Paul, an old man and a witch in drag

• **Naomi Watts** was the top-billed star of the cheesy fright franchise episode *Children Of The Corn IV: The Gathering*

Jason X
dir James Isaac, 2001, US, 93m

Super-scary, and side-splitting without tarnishing Jason's iconic charisma, the best sequel has the cryogenically frozen killer, being transported to "New Earth" for a museum exhibition 400 years in the future, thawing out on board a spaceship and systematically murdering the crew. Reconstituted into *Terminator* gear for a brilliantly conceived virtual reality return to Crystal Lake, where he tries hilariously to kill holographic babes, this ingenious self-aware shocker is fantastic fun and provides gory interstellar chills.

The Werewolf

Wolves have shape-shifted into men since the dawn of time, in every ancient culture. With a history in literature that dates back to the thirteenth century (Marie de France's *Lay Of The Were-wolf*), the werewolf novel's most famous incarnation remains Guy Endore's *The Werewolf Of Paris* (1933), adapted extremely loosely by **Terence Fisher** for Hammer as *The Curse Of The Werewolf* (1960).

The first movie werewolf was female: Henry McRae's silent *The Werewolf* (1913) featured a Navajo witch raising her werewolf daughter. But although **Bela Lugosi** turned into a wolf off-screen in *Dracula* (1931) and was surgically made a wolf-man in *Island Of Lost Souls* (1932), the monster's proper debut was in Universal's *Werewolf Of London* (1935). Henry Hull played a botanist in Tibet, bitten by werewolf Warner Oland, fighting for possession of the rare moon flower "Marifasa Lupina", the only known anti-dote to lycanthrophy.

The cinematic myths invented for *Werewolf Of London* were rewritten by **Curt Siodmak** for *The Wolf Man* (1941). A horror classic, it made **Lon Chaney Jr**, the tormented Larry Talbot, a star, and established the folklore of gypsy curses, full moons, silver bullets and wolf-bane: "Even a man who is pure of heart/And says his prayers by night/May become a wolf when the wolfbane blooms/And the moon is full and bright." Chaney Jr also played the part of Talbot in *Frankenstein Meets The Wolf Man* (1943), *House Of Frankenstein* and *House Of Dracula* (both 1945) and put in an appearance in *Abbott And Costello Meet Frankenstein* (1948).

After the appearance of mad scientists in *The Werewolf* (1956) and *I Was A Teenage Werewolf* (1957), the beast within went back to its super-natural roots in the Italian *Werewolf In A Girl's Dormitory* (1961) and the Spanish *La marca del hombre lobo* (*Frankenstein's Bloody Terror*, 1967). The latter began a series featuring **Paul Naschy** as the werewolf Count Waldemar Daninsky, a role he would play more than a dozen times.

As the wannabe Hammer company Tyburn attempted the old-school *Legend Of The Werewolf* (1974) and Americans added Hell's Angels, hippies and politics respectively into the mix with *Werewolves On Wheels* (1971), *The Werewolf Of Woodstock* (1975) and *The Werewolf Of Washington* (1973), the next leap was taken by *The Howling*, *Wolfen* (both 1981) and *An American Werewolf In London* (1981, see Canon), thanks to advances in make-up and animatronic techniques.

Since that high watermark, werewolves have crept into horror movies at a regular pace, adding new elements to the oft-told stories: Red Riding Hood in *The Company Of Wolves* (1984), comedy in *Teen Wolf* (1985), gay camp in *Curse Of The Queerwolf* (1987), museum exhibition figures in *Waxwork* (1988), superstar **Jack Nicholson** in *Wolf* (1994), menstrual curses in *Ginger Snaps* (2000), war manoeuvres in *Dog Soldiers* (2002) and *Scream*-style parodies in *Cursed* (2004). *Wild Country* (2005) didn't stick to the established folklore at all.

Ginger Snaps
dir John Fawcett, 2000, Can, 104m

Lycanthropy is transmitted sexually as a menstrual curse in this intellectually potent, brutal shocker. The legendary Beast of Bailey Downs attacks death-obsessed sisters, played by Emily Perkins and Katherine Isabelle, and the latter, Ginger, turns aggressive dominatrix complete with tail. With the silver bullet melted down into a pierced navel ring and the wolfbane of Lon Chaney Jr's day changed to a drug called Monkshood, Fawcett provocatively places the lycanthrope myth in the cauldron of tortured adolescence.

James Whale

Director, 1889-1957

One of the few directors from the first golden age of Hollywood horror to view filmmaking as an art form, James Whale laid down many ground rules that determined the development of the genre, through his bizarre angles, sets with high ceilings, imaginative production design, meticulous editing and new sound techniques.

Born in Dudley, England, Whale trained as an art student and after drawing cartoons for newspapers he took up acting in a German prison-of-war camp during World War I. Returning to Britain to act and direct and to design for the stage, it was his peerless direction of R. C. Sheriff's critically acclaimed war drama *Journey's End*, both in the West End and on Broadway, that led him to Hollywood, where he helmed the film version of 1930.

Remaining in California with British actor **Colin Clive**, who was the lead in all versions of the piece, Whale quickly established his reputation thanks to two other war movies. He directed the dialogue inserts for Howard Hughes's *Hell's Angels* (1930), and then in *Waterloo Bridge* (1931)

demonstrated his mastery of sound and spectacle, so Universal asked him to direct *Frankenstein* (1931, see Canon). Whale, an out-of-the-closet homosexual, was urged by his long-term lover **David Lewis**, producer of Greta Garbo's *Camille* (1936) and Bette Davis's *Dark Victory* (1939), to consider **Boris Karloff** as the Monster.

Ironically, Whale took on the Mary Shelley adaptation simply to avoid being pigeonholed as a war movie director. Thanks to his sheer artistry he took screen fright to new levels. Every frame of *Frankenstein*, starring his bisexual buddy Clive, exhibited Whale's attention to detail in an attempt to create an aura of creepiness. This use of visuals to unnerve audiences was an innovation that every horror director was influenced by.

Whale spent the next four years desperate to avoid directing the *Frankenstein* sequel that he

Whale with Boris Karloff while shooting *The Bride Of Frankenstein* (1935)

knew Universal wanted. Meanwhile the studio turned a blind eye to what was a flagrant lifestyle for the era. To assuage them, and to ensure that the ex-pat British acting community continued working, he cast Karloff in *The Old Dark House* (1932, see Canon), **Claude Rains** in *The Invisible Man* (1933), a masterful special effects extravaganza, and **Elsa Lanchester** in the inevitable sequel to his classic, *The Bride Of Frankenstein* (1935, see Canon). All were notable for the impish strain of humour coursing through their horror veins.

For *The Bride Of Frankenstein*, which replaced the scrapped Karloff assignment *A Trip to Mars*, bitterness made Whale add over-the-top sexual, religious and camp whimsy. But his "anything goes" approach made for an accidental masterpiece and one of his most highly regarded horrors. Although he was tied briefly to *Dracula's Daughter* (1936), Whale never returned to the genre in which he made the reputation that he scorned, and his last hit was the musical *Show Boat* (1936). Two of his last four pictures found him passing on the torch to the new horror wave – **Peter Cushing**, who featured in *The Man In The Iron Mask* (1939), and **Vincent Price**, who featured in *Green Hell* (1940).

Whale then retired to a more private and hedonistic life that included painting and gay pool parties. After suffering several debilitating strokes, he drowned in his pool in Pacific Palisades, California, probably committing suicide. As is seen in the loose biopic *Gods And Monsters* (1998), in which Ian McKellen gives a superb, Oscar-nominated performance as Whale, the suicide note read: "The future is just old age and illness and pain.... I must have peace and this is the only way."

 Gods And Monsters
dir Bill Condon, 1998, UK/US,105m

This study of the twilight years of the "Father of *Frankenstein*" (the original title), mixing fact and fiction, focuses on Whale's infatuation with his hunky but heterosexual gardener, who he wants to seduce. The powerful examination of media immortality and the eccentric creative process, which won an Oscar for its screenplay, marvellously and poignantly combines half-forgotten images from Whale's shadowy war years, the Mary Shelley myth, his Hollywood experiences making *Bride* and drug-induced sexual hallucinations.

The Zombie

They've had nights, dawns and days, returns, revolts and nightmares, and children, kings and plagues, in cities, lakes and lands from Broadway to Mora Tau. And yet zombies are one of the few horror cinema staples invented for the medium without any genesis in literature. The word zombie was first mentioned in **William B. Seabrook**'s study of voodoo *The Magic Island* (1929), in which he reported his experiences on Haiti and his supposed encounters with the walking dead; the unique belief in them was part of the ritualistic religion carried over by African slaves in the eighteenth century.

Using a Creole word apparently derived from Nzambi, a West African deity, Seabrook described the zombie in detail. "The eyes were the worst. It was not my imagination. They were in truth like the eyes of a dead man, not blind, but staring, unfocused, unseeing. The whole face, for that matter, was bad enough. It was vacant, as if there was nothing behind it. It seemed not only expressionless, but incapable of expression."

Seabrook's lurid account led to the first walking dead movie, *White Zombie* (1932), which starred **Bela Lugosi** as Murder Legendre, the operator of a Haitian sugar mill run by legions of human automatons. Shot by the Halperin brothers on borrowed sets from *The Hunchback Of Notre Dame* (1923), *King Of Kings* (1927), *Frankenstein* and *Dracula* (both 1931), using the make-up talents of Universal's **Jack Pierce**, its unearthly Caribbean atmosphere set a tone for the living dead genre, as could be seen in films including *Revolt Of The Zombies (*1936), *I Walked With A Zombie* (1943, see Canon), the comedy *The Ghost Breakers* (1940) and *I Eat Your Skin* (1964).

Normal people were zombified by a "bokor" (voodoo sorcerer) who casts a spell or brews a potion until Hammer's *The Plague Of The Zombies* (1966, see Canon), which visualized the living dead as rotting reanimated cadavers. Further socio-political radicalization by **George A. Romero** in *Night Of The Living Dead* (1968, see Canon) ushered in the modern zombie (or "ghoul", as they were referred to within the narrative) – a ferocious flesh-eater on the attack constantly and indiscriminately. Death became even more of a lottery than usual, with no rational explanation, in Romero's apocalyptic vision, which pushed graphic screen violence to the extreme. Not voodoo rites but future social ills would cause the dead to walk the earth, when there was no more room in hell.

While the juju voodoo explanation didn't die out altogether (*Sugar Hill*, 1974, *Zombie Flesh-Eaters*, 1979, *The Serpent And The Rainbow*, 1987), Romero's slow-moving, brain-eating legacies loom large over the contemporary living dead sub-genre. His influence is evident in films including *Zombi Holocaust* (1981), *Braindead* (1992, see Canon) and *28 Days Later* (2002), and in the two *Resident Evil* films (2002, 2004) and the *Return of the Living Dead* series (1985, 1988, 1993, 2005, 2005).

 Shaun Of The Dead
dir Edgar Wright, 2004, UK, 99m

London becomes Zombieville. This rom-zom-com starring Simon Pegg, who co-wrote the script, gleefully plunders Italian zombie flicks – there's a restaurant called Fulci's – and George A. Romero's trilogy for inspiration (and he loved it). Humour straight from the student union, sitcom banality and extreme morgue mayhem play out against a perfectly captured video nasty feel, and Penelope Wilton and Bill Nighy make the gory horror farce moving as well as comic.

The Global Picture:
horror movies around the world

A Chinese Ghost Story (1987), the first horror
from Hong Kong to make an impact in the West

The global picture:

horror movies around the world

Horror's icons are mainly from America and Britain, and as the story of the genre shows, countries such as Italy and Japan have also been important in its development. But other nations and regions have developed their own cinematic styles, which have often influenced (while being influenced by) mainstream horror.

Horror fans had truly international taste long before "world cinema" came into its own, and still watch more foreign films than devotees of any other genre. Why should horror fans care if a movie is dubbed from Italian, German or Spanish, or subtitled with dialogue in Mandarin, French or Russian, if it delivers fright on the night?

Argentina

Argentina is the most European of Latin American countries, in cultural terms, and in the Forties and Fifties had a huge film industry that exported all over the Spanish-speaking world. But because movies were government-funded, horrors were impossible to finance.

Una mujer sin cabeza (*Headless Woman*, 1947) from director Luis César Amadori got made only because it was a parody of *The Old Dark House* genre. Things began changing with Mario Soffici's *El extrano caso del hombre y la bestia* (*The Man And The Beast*, 1951), featuring an imaginative transformation by make-up artist Neron Kesselman, achieved in the shadows of a passing train, and with Román Viñoly Barreto's *El vampiro negro* (*Black Vampire*, 1953) and Enrique Carreras's *Obras maestras del terror* (*Master Of Horror*, 1960), an anthology of three stories by Edgar Allan Poe.

Then actor-turned-director **Emilio Vieyra** came on the scene in the mid-Sixties and practically invented the Argentinian horror film, during a brief golden age around the world of sexed-up shock, laced with drugs, rock and romance, that has never been repeated. Nothing like *La venganza del sexo* (*The Curious Dr Humpp*, 1966) has been seen since. *Placer sangriento* (*Feast Of Flesh/ The Deadly Organ*, 1967) was made for $16,000 in ten days and centres on a monster-masked sex maniac who injects heroin into beach babes and then lures them back to his place by playing ethereal organ music. Vieyra's next film, *La bestia desnuda* (*The Naked Beast*, 1967), was a *Phantom Of The Opera* clone modelled on his favourite American *film noir* thrillers in which none of the actors involved knew who the masked maniac was until the shooting of the reveal scene.

What followed for Vieyra was the only vampire film ever made in Argentina, and one of the first to combine sex with horror. *Sangre de virgenes* (*Blood Of The Virgins*, 1968) has swingers on a ski holiday in the Patagonian mountains seeking shelter in a deserted lodge, the domain of resurrected buxom blonde vampire Ofelia (Susana Beltrán). With its copious nudity and bloodletting for an era stuck in the moribund Hammer milieu, and its unusual special effects (red-tinted shots of seagulls were used for images resembling vampires), Vieyra's sleazy tone and eagerness to push boundaries could not be more striking, especially given that he was working within the confines of a repressive police state. It's not surprising that it was banned for seven years in its home country – or that no filmmaker has attempted to make anything similar.

 ### La venganza del sexo (The Curious Dr Humpp)
dir Emilio Vieyra, 1966, Arg, 85m

In one of the most bizarre horror movies ever made, mad scientist Dr Humpp (Aldo Barbero) follows the orders of a talking brain and force-feeds aphrodisiacs to copulating couples so that he can extract sexually potent blood to use as a flesh-preserving elixir. Seventeen minutes of (boring) simulated lovemaking was inserted into the American version of this exploitation extravaganza that already featured strippers, lesbianism and burning bodies.

A poster for Argentina's only vampire film, which hints at the reasons why it was banned for several years there after being made in 1968

Australia

Until the introduction of substantial government funding in 1970 generated a major horror movie wave, Australia had almost none to its name, apart from John Cosgrove's *The Guyra Ghost Mystery* (1921), an account of a famous "true" haunting, and Raymond Longford's *Fisher's Ghost* (1924), about Australia's most famous apparition.

Ted Kotcheff's *Wake In Fright* (aka *Outback*, 1971) was the first borderline horror to use the recurring Australian themes of the moral collapse of civilization and man's alienation from nature, and it was then **Peter Weir** who successfully translated national motifs into both local and international success; *The Cars That Ate Paris*, *Picnic At Hanging Rock* (both 1974) and *The Last Wave* (1977) all conveyed the surreal, Aboriginal mystic edge of the indigenous horror genre.

The first director to go explicitly after the American market was **Terry Bourke**, with the survival horror *Night Of Fear* (1973), the pseudo-historical psycho chiller *Inn Of The Damned* (1975) and the sordid slasher *Lady, Stay Dead* (1982). **Jim Sharman** used well-heeled universal motifs to explore themes of suburban social paralysis – in films including *Shirley Thompson Versus The Aliens* (1972) and *The Night The Prowler* (1978) – but his main claim to fame will always be that he directed the cult spectacular *The Rocky Horror Picture Show* (1975) and its less successful sequel, *Shock Treatment* (1981).

It was Hitchcock-influenced director **Richard Franklin** who minted an effective and distinctly recognizable Australian mood, in *Patrick* (1978) and *Roadgames* (1981), the latter starring Jamie Lee Curtis. Both were written by Everett de Roche, an ex-pat American responsible for the best Aussie horrors of the next decade, including Colin Eggleston's *Long Weekend* (1979), Simon Wincer's *Snapshot* (1979), renamed *The Day Before Halloween* in America, and rock video wunderkind Russell Mulcahy's debut, *Razorback* (1984).

One vampire variant was Rod Hardy's *Thirst* (1979), produced by the country's most prolific horror figure, **Antony I. Ginnane**, who was a producer or executive producer, often in association with actor David Hemmings, on dozens of Antipodean films during the following decades. These included *Patrick*, *Snapshot* and Hemmings's *The Survivor* (1981), based on the book by James Herbert. Meanwhile the teen psycho horror *Dangerous Game* (1987) was director Stephen Hopkins's calling card (*A Nightmare On Elm Street 5: The Dream Child* followed in 1989), and *Dead Calm* (1989) made the same impact for director **Phillip Noyce**, and Nicole Kidman. That ocean-set horror was for a long time the last great Australian horror film, despite *Dead Sleep* (1990) and Kimble Rendall's *Cut* (2000); but then came Greg McLean's wilderness worst-case scenario thriller *Wolf Creek* (2005).

Patrick
dir Richard Franklin, 1978, Aust, 110m

From the depths of a three-year coma, hospitalized Patrick (Robert Thompson) wreaks telekinetic revenge on his enemies. Kathy (Susan Penhaligon) is the nurse who "talks" to him through blinks of the eye and suspects that he's not as benign as everyone thinks. Stylishly directed, several scenes produce calculated jolts: the bathtub electrocution, the malfunction of an elevator door and the moment Kathy's typing is mentally taken over by Patrick. It's the best *Carrie* clone there is.

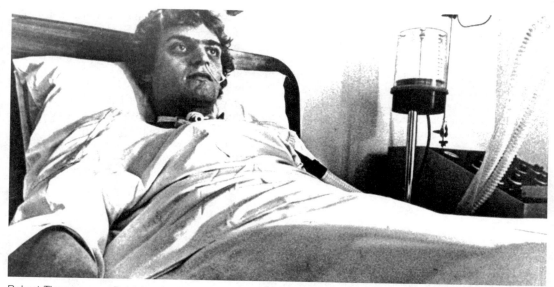

Robert Thompson as Patrick, who in Richard Franklin's film of 1978 does not take things lying down

Belgium

When Belgium has contributed to the horror genre, it has usually been with a film of note.

Harry Kümel made an early Seventies splash with the chic, decadent and very elegant *Daughters Of Darkness* (1971), based on the Countess Báthory myth, and the stunningly designed *Malpertuis* (1971), in which Orson Welles corrals the Greek Gods and sews them into human skins. The comic *Mama Dracula* (1980) and the necro-psychological horror *Lucker*

(1986) barely caused a blip on the international stage, unlike *Man Bites Dog* (1992), even though it had many characteristics that were typical of Belgian cinema: surrealism, documentary realism, reflexivity and a meaningful use of violence.

Co-directed by Rémy Belvaux, André Bonzel and Benoît Poelvoorde, *Man Bites Dog* stars the latter as a freelance hit man going about his daily business, with Belvaux and Bonzel as characters in the fly-on-the-wall documentary crew recording his every move. Though detached at first from the sudden slaughter that their camera captures, before long they help his thrill-killing spree. A sick satire on the media seeking to provide the goriest pictures that the public seem to want, the shocker mixes dark philosophy with trenchant wit. But then there's the infamous gang-rape scene, the moment when audiences stop laughing and start looking away uncomfortably. That's the point of this cleverly constructed slice of chilling irony.

After another fallow period, in 2004 came a further significant contribution to the genre,

Fabrice Du Welz's international collaboration *Calvaire* (*The Ordeal*). Looking like the result of putting *Deliverance*, *Delicatessen* and *Wrong Turn* through a Belgian blender, this hipster horror concerned an amateur cabaret singer who is forced to stay in a remote guest house after breaking down en route to his next gig; the full terror dawns when the innkeeper embarks on his demented agenda. Graced with superb photography, *Calvaire* (meaning "martyrdom" in French) reverberated with the freshness of classic horror that had been distorted though an offbeat European lens.

Brazil

Brazilian horror *is* José Mojica Marins, a legend in his native country for inventing an "aesthetics of garbage" sub-genre, in which his evil alter ego Zé do Caixão (literally "Joseph of the Grave", but known outside Brazil as "Coffin Joe") features in movies, TV shows and comics and has even stood as a political candidate. Marins's cheaply made offbeat movies twist together gothic horror, disturbing Expressionism, disgusting surrealism, Sadeian sex and barbarism, and emerge uniquely weird and disorientating.

At the same time that Herschell Gordon Lewis was getting gore flicks going in America with *Blood Feast* (1963), Marins became disillusioned with the Catholic Church and expressed his frustrations through film, using horrific and sexual imagery to explore deeply personal and political issues and entering the field precisely because it was socially unacceptable. Marins's most extreme

film is *O ritual dos sadicos* (*Awakening Of The Beast*, 1970), a depraved nightmare about drug experiments, which was banned by the Brazilian government for almost twenty years.

Marins's life had been transformed when, while living in the back of a cinema in Vila Anastacio, São Paulo, he saw a dead man rise in the middle of his own wake. The local grocer had actually suffered a cataleptic fit, but what the future samba composer and funeral parlour owner saw put him on the road to fame as Zé do Caixão, the dandy undertaker and libertine with long nails whose contempt for the world leads him to inflict torture and suffering on lesser mortals. (Separating Marins from his human art counterpart is extremely difficult – though the equivalent would be Alfred Hitchcock being fused with Norman Bates.)

Marins began his horror career with the

violent and blasphemous *À meia-noite levarei sua alma* (*At Midnight I'll Take Your Soul*, 1963), about a gravedigger searching for a woman to bear him a son; and although no one in Brazil had produced a horror film before, he had a huge hit. The film made Zé do Caixão a bogeyman who was used by parents to frighten their children, and spawned the sequel *Esta noite encarnarei no teu cadáver* (*Tonight I Will Eat Your Corpse*, 1967). Also notable was *Delírios de um anormal* (*Hallucinations Of A Deranged Mind*, 1978), a collage of disturbing, bizarre and perverse scenes censored from his earlier films.

Dogged by Draconian censorship and financial problems that compromised his artistic control, in recent times Marins has worked mainly as a director, hired by producers to helm their scripts. The documentary *Maldito – O estranho mundo de José Mojica Marins* (*Coffin Joe: The Strange World Of José Mojica Marins*, 2001) features re-creations of his misfortunes and his run-ins with authority.

The Strange World Of Coffin Joe
dir José Mojica Marins, 1968, Br, 80m, b/w

Coffin Joe introduces three tales of terror already adapted for his TV show. In *The Doll Maker* the main character uses human eyes in his handiwork. The wordless *Obsession* is a display of necrophilia. And *Ideology* features Marins as a human behaviour specialist staging horrific re-creations to test out his theories. Using real circus freaks and vile documentary footage, and ending with a cannibal banquet, the final part of this moody trilogy is brutal and shocking.

Coffin Joe in *Esta noite encarnarei no teu cadáver* (1967)

The Czech Republic

The dark fairy tales of the Czech writer and director Jan Svankmajer, often based on the works of Edgar Allan Poe and the Marquis de Sade, have received much critical attention and have been widely celebrated. And in recent times Marek Dobes's *Choking Hazard* (2004) had the distinction of being the Czech Republic's first zombie movie; like *Shaun Of The Dead*, released in Britain that same year, it was also a romantic comedy.

But the small crown of Czech gothic horror cinema belongs to director **Juraj Herz**. Primarily known in the West for his nauseous black comedy *Spalovac mrtvol* (*The Cremator*, 1968), his two horrors are *Upír z Feratu* (*The Vampire Of Ferat*, 1981) and *Morgiana* (1971); the former has a vampire car running on blood for fuel and the latter is based on the story *Jessie And Morgiana* by Aleksandr Grin, Russia's Edgar Allan Poe, and is a more elaborate version of Poe's *The Black Cat*.

France

The French might have had the best horror film magazine, *Midi-Minuit Fantastique*, but they certainly haven't had the industry to match.

Although notable titles did appear from time to time – such as Henri-Georges Clouzot's *Diabolique* (1954, see Canon), Georges Franju's *Eyes Without A Face* (1959, see Canon), Roger Vadim's *Blood And Roses* (1960), Alain Jessua's *Traitement de choc* (*Shock Treatment*, 1973) and Jean Rollin's sex-vampire output – horror movies were rarely made in France. The director of *Switchblade Romance* (2003, see Canon), **Alexandre Aja**, explained: "The problem with the French is they don't trust their own language [when it comes to horror]. American horror movies do well, but in their own language, the French just aren't interested."

All that changed during spring 2000 when, against all the odds, a locally produced horror became a runaway hit and confounded the watchdogs of French cinema. Lionel Delplanque's *Promenons-nous dans les bois* (*Deep In The Woods*) was an adult version of *Little Red Riding Hood*, shot through with the stage-managed style of Tim Burton and the outré goriness of Dario Argento (see Icons). It put chic chills back into the nation's consciousness and single-handedly kicked off Gallic horror production, for in rapid succession came Christophe Gans' elegant blockbuster *Brotherhood Of The Wolf*, Pitof's *Vidocq* (both 2001), Julien Magnat's *Bloody Mallory* (2002), Eric Valette's *Maléfique* (2003) and Pascal Laugier's *Saint-Ange* (2004).

Germany

Since some of the pioneers of American horror were veterans of Germany's film industry, such as Peter Lorre and Karl Freund, and thanks to such seminal early offerings as *The Cabinet Of Dr Caligari* (1919, see Canon) and *Nosferatu* (1922, see Canon), the country is commonly acknowledged as the birthplace of the horror film.

So it is extraordinary that it was the novels, plays and short stories of British crime writer Edgar Wallace that dominated German horror in the late Fifties. Nicknamed *krimis*, derived from *taschenkrimi*, the term for pocket crime novel, the Wallace horror movies began in 1959 with *Der Frosche mit der Maske* (*The Fellowship Of The Frog*), which was directed by **Harald Reinl**, who went on to specialize in the form. The best recreations of Wallace's fictional universe, complete with colourful masterminds, dapper detectives and lurking femme fatales, were *Die toten Augen von London* (*Dead Eyes Of London*, 1961) and *Die blaue Hand* (*Creature With The Blue Hand*, 1967), both of which were directed by Alfred Vohrer, starred **Klaus Kinski** and were promoted in other countries as all-out horrors.

Christopher Lee (see Icons) often popped over the water to appear in Wallace adaptations, such as *Das Geheimnis der delben Narzissen* (*The Devil's Daffodil*, 1961); and in Reinl's *Die Schlangengrube und das Pendel* (*Blood Demon*, 1967), based on a story by Edgar Allan Poe, Lee played the vampire Count Regula. Other costume horrors, however, were few and far between until *Hexen bis aufs Blut gequaelt* (*Mark Of The Devil*, 1970) stomped all competition into the ground, becoming a number one box-office

hit in Germany, having cleverly been given the made-up rating "V for Violence". (In Britain the film was banned and in America those who might have needed them were issued with vomit bags that were marked with a tongue logo in vivid red.)

The next significant horror movie emerged when **Ulli Lommel** directed *Zärtlichkeit der Wölfe* (*Tenderness Of The Wolves*, 1973), produced by **Rainer Werner Fassbinder**, about a homosexual mass murderer. Like Fritz Lang's *M* (1931), it was based on the true story of Fritz Haarmann, who was executed in 1925 for the dismemberment and cannibalism of at least forty boys. By never trying to exploit its character or situations, Lommel allowed terror to seep through slowly and quietly, and therefore more effectively. It was the director's calling card for fame in America, which he first found with *The Boogeyman* (1980).

The complete opposite of the slow-burning *Tenderness Of The Wolves* was Jörg Buttgereit's in-your-face outrage *Nekromantik* (1987). Daktari Lorenz and Beatrice Manowski (credited on this film as Beatrice M) play the death-obsessed duo whose house is adorned with body parts collected from road accidents and who find sexual fulfilment with the acquisition of a male cadaver. Buttgereit's raw 8mm taboo terror came complete with a warning that "Some of this film may be seen as offensive and shouldn't be shown to minors", and for once the caution was spot-on. A sequel followed in 1991, after the original, banned by the German government, proved popular on the festival circuit.

Matching Buttgereit for bad taste was **Christoph Schlingensief** with his *Das Deutsche*

Kettensägen Massaker (*The German Chainsaw Massacre*, 1991), a heavy-handed gore-fest that embroidered scary fact. As the film relates, four percent of the citizens who left their East German homes on October 3, 1989, high on reunification promises, never appeared beyond the crumbling Berlin Wall. So what happened to them? According to this account they were turned into wurst by crazed cannibals eager for new sources of meat. Schlingensief went for another reunification shocker with the neo-Nazi nightmare *Terror 2000* (1992).

Meanwhile Michael Bergmann's campy *My Lovely Monster* (1990) was a vain attempt to marry Germany's past and slapstick shock, with a silent horror film character stuck in a Hamburg cinema wanting to turn himself into a piece of cellu-

loid. But ten years later, **Stefan Ruzowitzky's** *Anatomie* (2000), the tale of an ancient secret society renowned for its ruthless research on humans, starring superstar **Franka Potente**, became the biggest box-office sensation in German horror history. *Anatomie 2* followed in 2003.

Hexen bis aufs Blut gequaelt (Mark Of The Devil)
Michael Armstrong, 1969, Ger, 97m

For a cheap horror exploiter this unbelievably gory voyage into witch-hunting in nineteenth-century Mitteleuropa is well made and well performed. The spectacular scenery, like the lush Eurovision score, adds contrast to the carnage, which serves as a vitriolic attack on the Church. The British-born director defended his sex-obsessed mutilations by saying "The worst sort of violence is the sort you don't look away from."

M (1931), which was based on the same true story as *Zärtlichkeit der Wölfe* (1973)

Hong Kong

Flying ghosts, hopping vampires, living skeletons, tree demons, killer tongues and other possessed body parts: all these and more can be found in horror from Hong Kong.

Drawn from spiritual beliefs about bad luck, fate and respect for the ancestral dead, all of which are present in Confucianism, Buddhism and Taoism, the region's horror films began with Li Beihai's *Yanzhi* (1925). Five decades on Hammer tried fusing their own gothic sensibility with the martial arts movie craze popularized by the Shaw Brothers, in **Roy Ward Baker**'s *The Legend Of The Seven Golden Vampires* (1974), in which Professor Van Helsing (Peter Cushing) lifts an undead curse from the village of Ping Kuei, but after "the first kung-fu horror spectacular", a co-production trend did not develop and there was a return to Hong Kong's traditional terrors, where hell is a fog-shrouded limbo stuffed with desperate souls waiting for an opportunity for reincarnation.

The country's horror cycle really began with **Sammo Hung**'s comedy *Gui da gui* (*Spooky Encounters*, 1980), which featured a zombie-vampire hybrid as a *kyonsi* (hopping ghost) of Chinese folklore – and was an enormous but surprise hit. Hung reworked the formula of ghoulishness, action and low comedy in *The Dead And The Deadly* (1982), *Hocus Pocus* (1984) and the inevitable *Spooky Encounters 2* (1989), and cash-ins on his success include **John Woo**'s satanic pact farce *To Hell With The Devil* (1981) and Lau Kai-Wing's *Till Death Do We Scare* (1982), which featured the work of make-up genius **Tom Savini**. But Hung followed up best on his success, by producing and working as a director on the *kyonsi* series that started with *Mr Vampire* (1985). One of the more outrageous

Mr Vampire rip-offs was Billy Chan's *Crazy Safari* (1991), which took the horror hopper to Africa to fight a tribal head possessed by the spirit of Bruce Lee. John Woo's favourite actor, **Chow Yun-Fat**, appeared in two similar productions.

The country's horrors took a more serious turn when **Hark Tsui**, after directing the cannibal comedy *Diyu wu men* (*We Are Going To Eat You*, 1981), made the epic ghost story *Zu: Warriors From The Magic Mountain* (1983). Then, in 1987 he was the producer behind *A Chinese Ghost Story* – the first Hong Kong horror to make any proper impression in the West. It told of an impoverished monk in love with a spirit enslaved by a demon; to please her he faces decapitated heads, screaming skulls and a life-sucking giant tongue. Beautifully shot, with visual flair and dynamism, it reinvigorated the genre with its poetic approach to the supernatural. Two official sequels followed in 1990 and 1991, but by then the market had been glutted with imitations, including *Rouge* (1987), produced by **Jackie Chan**; the best of the bunch is **King Hu**'s *Painted Skin* (1992).

As the Chinese repossession of Hong Kong loomed in 1997, many of the biggest names in horror there went to America. Before **Ronny Yu** emigrated, however, he directed two elegant *The Bride With The White Hair* horrors (both 1993), featuring lashings of blood and lethal hair tendrils. Hark Tsui's *Green Snake* (1993) told of love between a human and a serpent. By far the biggest box-office success in this period, however, was the anthology *Troublesome Night* (1997), with eighteen sequels to date, generally warning callow youth about the dire supernatural consequences of disrespecting the dead.

A Chinese Ghost Story (1987), which showed a poetic approach to the supernatural

Yin yang lu (Troublesome Night)
dir Wai-Man Cheng, Long-Cheung Tam & Herman Yau, 1997, HK, 98m

This comedy horror consists of a raconteur telling four strange tales. In the first, six campers narrate spooky stories with help from actual ghosts. The second has a driver who loses her way while she is trying to contact her unfaithful husband via telephone. The third features a supernatural seduction and the fourth is based on a haunted cinema. With the same characters turning up in each different twilight zone, the accent is more on comic cleverness than gory fright, but it remains good creepy fun throughout.

India and Pakistan

Popular with the urban poor and in rural areas, Bollywood horror movies feature higher rations of sex, blood and guts than most chaste mainstream releases, but in order to cover as many bases as possible, they also, of course, have singing and dancing.

The earliest Indian horrors were intended not to scare but to give love stories strange new dimensions, and revolved around themes of reincarnation and rebirth; the most famous is Kamal Amrohi's *Mahal* (1949), which features **Ashok Kumar** moving into a haunted mansion, and this was the first major movie to feature the concept of lost souls.

Bollywood horror entered a mini boom in the mid-Seventies, led by **Raj Kumar Kohli**'s *Nagin* (*The Female Snake*, 1976), about the bloody revenge of a shape-shifting serpent after her mate is killed. A big success, it was followed by Kohli's werewolf shocker *Jaani dushman* (*Beloved Enemy*, 1979) – but this time the cursed creature preys on young brides dressed in the traditional red wedding ceremony outfit. Then Padmini Kolhapure played the possessed child in the best of the films inspired by *The Exorcist*, *Gehrayee* (*Depth*, 1980), and the American slasher trend inspired superstar Rajesh Khanna to play a serial killer in **Bharathi Rajaa**'s *Red Rose* (1980). Seen as highly misogynistic, it triggered protests by Indian feminists, at the same time that *Dressed To Kill* did in the West, but it did not prevent Khanna from returning to the horror genre.

But the Bollywood B-movie horror was defined by **the Ramsay Brothers**, the most notable among them being the director Tulsi Ramsay. After their initial success, *Do gaz zameen ke neeche* (*Two Yards Under the Ground*, 1972), which concerned a murdered man who is chemically revived, the family operation concentrated exclusively on horror during the next two decades. *Darwaza* (*The Door*, 1978) opened the way for them to become the most prolific purveyors of Hindi horror, and their *Purana mandir* (*The Old Temple*, 1984), which told of a curse placed on the female members of a rich middle-class family, was a massive success that characterized Eighties Bollywood horror. Hit after hit followed, including *Saamri* (*Satan*, 1985) in 3-D and the Dracula-inspired *Bandh darwaza* (*The Closed Door*, 1990).

The Ramsays had a successful formula: plots that revolved around evil spirits and deformed creatures terrorizing villages, and as much sex and nudity as the censors would allow. They rarely used other recipes, until turning their attention to television with *The Zee Horror Show* (1993), which in theory left an opportunity for other directors. Despite a proliferation of low-grade horror from India since the start of the decade, it's less ambitious, and it's doubtful that the country's horror output will reach the heights of the Ramsay era again.

Zinda laash (The Living Corpse)
dir Khwaja Sarfraz, 1967, Pakistan, 103m, b/w

The only Pakistani horror of note, this obscure "Lollywood" oddity – *Dracula In Pakistan*, as it was called in America – put local censors in such a tizzy that virtually no more Pakistani-based horror has been made. Set in contemporary times, and inspired by the atmosphere of Hammer – the main actor, Rehan, even looks a bit like Christopher Lee – the narrative features well-placed pieces of Urdu music.

Indonesia

Movie production in the world's largest archipelago was initially aimed at the working classes who lived in the small villages. Intended only for local consumption, all Indonesian movies produced through the mid-century decades of conflict, chaos and corruption were indigestible mixtures of violence, sentimentality, knockabout comedy and music. This changed in the Seventies when imports from America swamped the movie houses; distributors were forced into home-grown production because for every movie they made they were given a license to release five American ones. And what were the cheapest movies to produce? Horrors.

It is considered that the first Western-style horror film to be produced in Indonesia was *Beranak dalam kubur* (*Birth In The Tomb*, 1972); it starred **Suzzanna**, "the Queen of Indonesian Horror", who made her name specializing in roles of Indian-derived terror deities such as the Snake Queen and the White Crocodile Queen. Suzzanna's most famous horrors include *Ratu ilmu hitam* (*Queen Of Black Magic*, 1979), *Sundelbolong* (*Ghost With Hole*, 1982) and *Nyi blorong* (*The Hungry Snake Woman*, 1982).

These featured weird witchcraft and mystical martial arts rooted in deep cultural traditions, with cheapjack special effects and geysers of ludicrously staged gore courtesy of **El Badrun**, the local Tom Savini. Heads float off bodies with entrails attached, based on the myth of the *penanggalan*, a woman murdered in prayer who spreads disease via her exposed innards; flying torsos are chopped up in mid-air; and villains are transformed into everything from snakes to wild boars. Indonesian horror was a clutter of everything trashy.

One of its most adept practitioners was **H. Tjut Djalil**, who directed the few Indonesian horrors that were released internationally. But *Leák* (*Mystics In Bali*, 1981) and *Jaka Sembung & Bergola Ijo* (*Warrior 2*, 1985), the latter starring Barry Prima as the popular comic-based Robin Hood hero Jaka Sembung, were considered too narrow in appeal, so in his next movie Djalil took the unprecedented step of casting an American lead and filming in the concrete jungle of downtown Jakarta.

The outcome was *Lady Terminator* (1988), which was hugely controversial (because of the plentiful nudity) and massively successful, faring extremely well overseas while the video industry blossomed. It features the most feared queen of them all, the sexually rapacious Queen of the South Seas, who lives in a palace on the ocean floor and summons drowned studs to service her wanton needs: "She mates … then she terminates," read the memorable poster tagline. Djalil followed it with *Dangerous Seductress* (1992), which had almost the same story; this time the Queen of Darkness possesses an American tourist.

Other popular horrors to make it abroad were El Badrun's *The Devil's Sword* (1984) and, by **Sisworo Gautama Putra**, the cannibal flick *Primitif* (*Savage Terror*, 1978) and *Pengabdi Setan* (*Satan's Slave*, 1982), which was inspired by the American movie *Phantasm* (1979). By the mid-Nineties, however, the boom was over, because the flailing dictatorship of General Suharto saw horrors as politically threatening; the Devil was a thinly veiled allegory for the rule of the Government. More recently the rise in digital video movies has had an impact on Indonesia, with the $30,000 *Ouija Board* (2004) a reasonable success.

Italy

Italy's pivotal importance to horror is covered extensively in the History, Canon and Icons chapters.

Italy has periodically revived horror around the world via films such as Riccardo Freda's *I Vampiri* (*Lust Of The Vampire*, 1956). **Mario Bava** (see Icons), who helped to direct it, also made the first *giallo* thriller, *The Evil Eye* (1962), a format developed by the legendary **Dario Argento** (see Icons), in his debut *The Bird With The Crystal Plumage* (1970). Argento's *Suspiria* (1976, see Canon) inspired many directors to move towards his style.

Italy is of course also responsible for the *mondo* films, the famous "shockumentaries" which featured depraved archive footage; most notable was **Ruggero Deodato**'s *Cannibal Holocaust* (1979, see Canon). And Italy kick-started the Eighties exploitation revival, with *Zombie Flesh-Eaters* (1979), directed by **Lucio Fulci**. These are but a few of the many influential Italian directors and classic movies covered elsewhere in this book.

Japan

As is clear from the History chapter, Japanese horror has relied heavily on ghost stories, often seen in kabuki theatre.

These *kaidan eiga* arrived on the postwar global film scene when Keisuke Kinoshita turned an 1825 kabuki play into *Shinshaku Yotsuya kaidan* (*The Ghost of Yotsuya – New Version*, 1949); the most renowned adaptation, however, was Nobuo Nakagawa's in 1959. In between came Kenji Mizoguchi's *Ugetsu Monogatari* (*Tale of the Pale And Mysterious Moon After The Rain*, 1953), based on domestic ghost stories, which reached a wide audience at the Venice Film Festival in 1953.

In the Fifties and Sixties international themes began to affect the domestic film industry: in 1957 Nakagawa made *Kaidan Kasanegafuchi* (*The Kasane Swamp*), based on a nineteenth-century vampire tale, and similarly, two years later came his vampire film *Onna Kyuketsuki* (*The Lady Vampire*) and Morihei Magatani's *The Blood Sword Of The 99th Virgin*. But national themes were still influential, as was evident in the the Sixties through the classics *Onibaba* (*The Hole*, 1964, see Canon), which told of destitute peasants, *Kwaidan* (*Ghost Story*, 1964), which was based on domestic ghost stories, and *Kuroneko* (*The Black Cat*, 1968), which featured the Japanese female cat vampire.

Eventually the *kaidan eiga* became less popular and the influence of Western horrors rose, as could be seen in the increase in films like Yoshiyuki Kuroda's *Yokai daisenso* (*Great Monster War*. 1968) and Michio Yamamoto's Seventies vampire trilogy, including *Chi o suu me* (*Lake Of Dracula*, 1971). From the Sixties onwards there was more fusing of genres, too, which often meant that ghosts were combined with gore.

Also influential have been *manga* (comics), and this was particularly so in the Eighties, as was clear in films such as *Vampire Hunter D* (1985). But during the Eighties and Nineties, when animation also became more popular, the country's various sub-genres were still made predominantly for the home market. It was only when Hideo Nakata's *Ringu* (*The Ring*, 1998) and Takashi Miike's *Audition* (1999), both of which combined strains of Western horror with an oriental feel, reached foreign shores that Japanese horror broke out again. The American remake of *Ringu* in 2002 was a huge hit and inspired many similar adaptations while also making it easier for Japanese directors such as Kinji Fukasuku (*Battle Royale*, 2000) to reach an international audience.

Malaysia and Singapore

It wasn't just Universal and Hammer who struck box-office gold with the vampire formula: so did the film industry of Malaysia and Singapore. The Malay culture has many supernatural creatures, and the studios made a money-spinning series out of the revenant *pontianak*, a mythological female vampire, taking the form of a night owl, who is the stillborn child of a *langsuyar* and sucks infant babies' blood; the *langsuyar* is the ghost of a woman who died in childbirth.

The golden age for these movies, produced by arms of the Hong Kong studios of the Shaw Brothers and Cathay, was from 1957 to 1965, and **Balkrishna Narayan Rao**'s *Pontianak* (*The Vampire*, 1957) began the trend. Shot in black and white, it concerned a hunchback village outcast, played by beauty queen Maria Menado, who is transformed by magic into a gorgeous sex bomb. Marrying the local catch, when she sucks venom from his snakebite, she becomes the vampire; she is later dispatched by a nail through her head. It was a box-office phenomenon, and Rao quickly followed it with sequels. (Meanwhile Filipino director **Ramon Estella** hopped aboard the bandwagon with further *pontianak* films, each containing violent horror suspense along with humorous song and dance routines.)

Such moneymaking led to a new Malay monster, the "oily man", a slippery spirit who hypnotizes women into submission, rapes them while they are transfixed by his bewitching stare and then leaps through the air to vanish into the night; the character appeared in various films during this period, including L. Krishnan's *Orang minyak* (*Oily Man*, 1958). Attempts to revive the *pontianak* genre, such as *Pontianak* (1975), by director/producer Roger Sutton, and the modern-day *Return To Pontianak* (aka *Voodoo Nightmare*, 2000), by Ong Lay Jinn (aka Djinn), have not been successful.

Mexico

In the 1930s only the United States produced more horror movies than Mexico.

The main spur was the Spanish-language *Drácula* (1931), though it was a cacophony to Mexican ears because of the international cast, with **Carlos Villarías**, the nearest Mexico had at the time to a star like Bela Lugosi, as Conde Drácula. Immediately after this classic, films such as *La llorona* (*The Crying Woman*, 1933) and *El fantasma del convento* (*Phantom Of The Convent*, 1934) hit home with a different formula by mixing supernatural twists with indigenous cultural experiences – mainly breakdowns of trust.

In the middle of the decade, the popular theme, in films including *El misterio del rostro pálido* (*The Mystery Of The Ghastly Face*, 1935), starring Villarías, *El superloco* (*The Crazy Nut*, 1936), and *Herencia Macabra* (*The Macabre Legacy*, 1939) was of normality being corrupted by outside forces. By 1939, when *El signo de la muerte* (*Sign Of Death*) was made, comedy had began to dominate the horror film – as it did in its US counterpart – with funnyman **Cantinflas** taking centre stage, and the first age of Mexican horror came to a close.

Just like everywhere else in the mid-Fifties, film audiences declined because of television and cheaper movies became the order of the day. The producer and former matinee idol **Abel Salazar** saw the writing on the wall. He looked for inspiration towards Hammer and back at the Universal monster factory and put into production a canny series of hybrid shockers that were permeated with European Catholic traditions but also steeped in macabre Mexican folklore. Salazar's first genre offering was the no-brainer *El vampiro* (*The Vampire*, 1957), essentially

Dracula in Mexico City, which featured wonderful sets, a great atmosphere and marvellous direction by **Fernando Méndez**, who like everyone involved in the *nuevo horror* had a wealth of film experience behind him. Salazar himself played the Van Helsing figure Dr Enrique, and there was a terrific performance from **Germán Robles**, the Mexican Christopher Lee, as Count Karol de Lavud, who seduces the sexy owner of a hacienda to reach his undead brother buried below; and everyone returned for the sequel, *El ataúd del vampiro* (*The Vampire's Coffin*, 1958). Robles then found himself another vampire franchise with *La maldición de Nostradamus* (*The Curse Of Nostradamus*, 1960), which was cut down from a ten-part TV series, and its sequels.

Torture, the Inquisition, comets, astronomers, and a brain-sucking 300-year-old demon featured in another Robles/Salazar cult favourite, *El barón del terror* (*The Brainiac*, 1962). Famous for its deliberately artificial special effects and interiors on the insistence of director Chano Urueta, who hated being reduced to horror films to make a living, it was precisely that outré atmosphere that made it work. Rafael Baledón's *La maldición de la llorona* (*The Curse Of The Crying Woman*, 1961) was Salazar's swansong, and masterpiece: the legendary tale of the woman cursed to eternally search for her dead children contained a montage of sequences culled from his entire horror catalogue.

The horror craze continued with films such as *Échenme al vampiro* (*Bring Me A Vampire*, 1959) and *Muñecos infernales* (*Curse Of The Doll People*, 1961), and running alongside in popularity were movies starring the comic-book superhero and

Axel Jodorowksy (right) in *Santa Sangre* (1989), the last great Mexican horror movie

silver-masked wrestler **Santo** (born Rodolfo Guzman Huerta). When both genres began to show signs of fatigue they were combined into one, the supernatural Santo series beginning with *Atacan las brujas* (*Santo Attacks The Witches*, 1965). Santo also appeared with the famous wrestler Blue Demon (Alejandro Cruz) in *Santo y Blue Demon contra los monstruos* (*Santo And Blue Demon Vs The Monsters*, 1969).

A veteran of the Santo movies was actor and director **René Cardona**, whose variable horror career encompassed making two of the sleaziest shockers of all time – the notorious video nasty *La horripilante bestia humana* (*Night Of The Bloody Apes*, 1968), and the most widely released of his films, *Supervivientes de los Andes* (*Survive!*, 1976), the true story of plane-crash survivors forced to eat their dead compatriots. Cardona later turned the genre over to his son René Cardona Jr, who carried on in the same dubious tradition with the *Jaws* rip-off *Tintorera* (1977) and the *Birds* rip-off *El ataque de los pájaros* (*Evil Birds*, 1987). The dynasty continues with René Cardona III, who made *Vacaciones de terror* (*Vacations Of Terror*, 1988) and its sequel in 1990.

While the Cardonas were barely raising the genre above the bargain basement, the surrealist Panic Theatre group, including **Juan López Moctezuma** and **Alejandro Jodorowsky**, thought differently: their aim was to "create a whirlpool of emotion to break down rigid structures of perception". Jodorowsky certainly did that with his mega (and the first) "midnight movie", which played in New York and then around the United States, the cult epic *El Topo* (*The Mole*, 1970); and Moctezuma tried to duplicate it with *La mansión de la locura* (*Dr Tarr's Torture Dungeon*, 1972), which was set in an asylum run by the lunatics who have locked up their keepers and was loosely based on the

Edgar Allan Poe story *The System Of Dr Tarr And Professor Feather*. Moctezuma's convent-set vampire tale *Alucarda* (1978) later went all out for sex and gore.

It was Jodorowsky who directed the last great Mexican horror movie, *Santa Sangre* (1989), which was produced by Dario Argento's brother Claudio. It tells the story of deranged circus performer Fenix (Axel Jodorowsky, the director's son), and his armless mother, with a shocking message that murder leads to a state of graceful redemption. A sublime tapestry of challenging emotions, *Santa Sangre* is a signature Mexican arthouse horror. "I will shoot you with celluloid," said Jodorowsky. "Wound you with images you

will never forget. My psyche is full of graves and I merged them with an actual murderer's reality to direct it. But God really made *Santa Sangre*; I was just a pawn in the accident."

 La horripilante bestia humana (Night Of The Bloody Apes)
dir René Cardona, 1968, Mex, 83m

One of the film's alternative titles, *Horror And Sex*, sums up this cheap, madcap remake of the director's own *Las luchadoras contra el médico asesino* (*Doctor Of Doom*, 1962), which is spiced up by nudity, women wrestlers and actual heart-transplant footage. Dr Martinez (Armando Silvestre) puts a gorilla's heart into his dying son's body and says "I was prepared for everything but this" as he's reanimated into a hairy deformed killer. Chiller con carne.

The Netherlands

"From the short story of the same name in *Flemish Tales* by Pieter Van Weigen", boast the opening credits for the Euro-horror *Il mulino delle donne di pietra* (*Mill Of The Stone Women*, 1960). The windmill-turned-wax museum has a fairy-tale atmosphere, but no such volume ever existed, and even though the Dutch have a rich fairy-tale tradition – *The Entangled Mermaid*, *The Princess With Twenty Petticoats*, *Why The Stork Loves Holland* – their few horror films resemble thrillers, layered with standard chiller conventions like Italian *gialli*.

With the exceptions of *The Fourth Man* (1983), a mysterious and macabre tale full of symbolism from **Paul Verhoeven** before he joined the Hollywood mainstream, and **George Sluizer**'s *Spoorloos* (*The Vanishing*, 1988), the best-

known Dutch horrors are directed by rock video whiz kid **Dick Maas**. His debut feature, *De lift* (*The Lift*, 1983), dealt with an evil elevator that raised the hackles with scenes of claustrophobia and decapitation; and he remade it as *Down* (aka *The Shaft*, 2001). Both *Amsterdamned* (1988) and *Do Not Disturb* (1999) swapped the slasher playground of summer camps for the Dutch canal system, the former famously opening with the suspended body of a mutilated prostitute trailing blood over a glass-topped boat.

The quirkiest of all the country's horrors is Rudolf van den Berg's *The Johnsons* (1992); only in liberal Holland could shivers be contrived from merging underage sex and surreal horror. The plot concerns the legend from an Indian tribe of a girl giving birth to a monster that will destroy mankind, and supernatural mumbo-jumbo never looked so good nor carried its Freudian psychology into such hauntingly weird areas.

Spoorloos (The Vanishing)
dir George Sluizer, 1988, Neth/Fr, 106m

Three years after his girlfriend suddenly vanishes,

obsessed Rex is finally given the chance to learn the horrifying truth by meek sociopath Raymond. Devoid of flashiness or stylish pretension, *Spoorloos* takes time to develop its characters, but is unusual for being a psychological shocker that delivers a climactic sucker punch. The director's misconceived Hollywood remake in 1993 trampled over everything that made his original so potent and tacked on a gory and ridiculous happy ending.

New Zealand

New Zealand has given the horror world Peter Jackson (see Icons), but before he broke the mould with *Bad Taste* (1988), the high point of the country's terror was Michael Laughlin's *Strange Behaviour* (aka *Dead Kids*, 1981), about a mad doctor's mind experiments. It was followed by Sam Pillsbury's *The Scarecrow* (1982), which was based on a novel by Ronald Hugh Morrieson, the nearest that New Zealand has to a horror writer.

The New Zealand horror tradition really began with **David Blyth**'s *Death Warmed Up* (1984), the first film in the genre to be financed by the country's Film Commission. Inspiring Peter Jackson's later gore frenzies, Blyth's punk chiller, full of burning torsos, exploding heads and brain surgery, charts the revenge taken on a genetic surgeon who has turned patients at his island hospital into mutant zombie killing machines. Blyth said, "I wanted an outrageous and grotty approach. I didn't care that the special effects looked tacky – they captured the underlying spirit of the film. I wanted it to be the New Zealand equivalent of *The Evil Dead*." Blyth's vampire follow-ups, *Red Blooded American*

Girl (1990) and *Moonrise* (1991), did nothing to promote his career.

Other notable New Zealand productions include Gaylene Preston's *Dark Of The Night* (aka *Mr Wrong*, 1985), John Day's *The Returning* (1990), Garth Maxwell's clairvoyant slasher *Jack Be Nimble* (1993), starring Alexis Arquette, and Greg Page's *The Locals* (2003). In the wake of Peter Jackson's defection to Hollywood, **Scott Reynolds**' *The Ugly* (1997), about a mental patient incited to kill by supernatural entities, shook up the moribund industry again.

Reynolds's psychic thriller *Heaven* (1998) and his tension-filled twister *When Strangers Appear* (2001) are just as bizarre and interesting. **Glenn Standring** followed in Reynolds's footsteps with *The Irrefutable Truth About Demons* (2000), in which an anthropologist becomes the target of a satanic sect. It was the first horror film in the country's history to make a profit through global pre-sales alone, before it was released anywhere, and this allowed Standring to helm the postmodern vampire myth *Perfect Creature* (2005).

The Ugly
dir Scott Reynolds, 1997, NZ, 91m

Can a celebrity lawyer get inside the head of a serial killer to see if he's still insane? *The Ugly* – the name comes from a torn page of *The Ugly Duckling* – goes on a horrific journey into past crimes that has repercussions on the present when the perpetrator says he's coerced by supernatural "visitors". A uniquely designed, stylish chiller with imaginative metaphors, which shows the killer's perspective – all the deaths are drenched in black blood – it's a tension-filled original.

The Philippines

The most notable of the many horror films made in the Philippines in the Fifties, Sixties and Seventies by director/producer Eddie Romero and Gerardo de Leon were the *Blood* trilogy of joint US/Filipino productions, *Mad Doctor Of Blood Island*, *Brides Of Blood* (both 1968) and *Beast Of Blood* (1971). Foreign audiences also became familiar with Filipino backdrops after Roger Corman (see Icons) got in on the act by co-producing and distributing in America many of the exploitation films of Filipino producer Cirio H. Santiago, such as the Charles B. Griffith creature feature *Up From The Depths* (1979). But despite the familiarity with these shockers, virtually nothing was known about the homeland horror industry.

It had begun in the silent era with *Ang manananggal* (*The Viscera Sucking Witch*, 1927) and variations on the *aswang* (witch) theme appeared throughout the following decades, in films such as *Mang Tano, nuno ng mga aswang* (*Mr Tano, Elder Of The Witches*, 1932). And there are two further sub-genres of Filipino horror: the occult ghost story and the slasher thriller. The latter appeared after the American vanguard in the Seventies, and when they did they were mainly gory, sexed-up versions of true stories, in which a poor tortured female was the victim of a rich privileged abuser. Carlo Caparas's *The Myrna Diones Story, Lord Have Mercy* (1993) starred **Kris Aquino**, daughter of the former President, Cory Aquino, who soon became known as "the Massacre Queen", and in 2004 she starred in one of the biggest Filipino successes of all time, the *Ringu*-inspired *Feng Shui*.

Mysterious islands

Placing action on uncharted islands, usually with tropical jungles, is the easiest way to establish a strange eco-system, either human or animal, that will face the unwary castaway. The classic situation of being trapped on an island, and having no option but to fight the unknown, features in *Island Of Lost Souls*, *The Most Dangerous Game* (both 1932), *King Kong* (1933), *Isle Of The Dead* (1945), *The Flesh Eaters* (1961), *Tower Of Evil* (1971), *Zombie Flesh-Eaters* (1979) and *It's Alive III: Island Of The Alive* (1986). Islands are very rarely used as actual locations because of shooting difficulties, but usually an establishing shot does the trick.

Mad Doctor Of Blood Island (1968), the first in a famous trilogy of US/Filipino productions

That hit forms part of the trajectory of the occult ghost story, which always features unresolved issues haunting the present. **Antonio José Perez**'s *Haplos* (*Caress*, 1982) is representative of the cycle, with its poltergeist plot concerning friends reunited. The country's colourful Spanish past lent costume flair to Armando Garces's *Maruja* (1967), a spectre romance in the style of *Romeo And Juliet*; based on a nineteenth-century novel by national hero José Rizal, *Maruja* was remade in 1978 and 1995, but the best entry in the occult ghost story sub-genre is Mike de Leon's directo-

rial debut, *Itim* (*Black*, 1976), which features the vengeful spirit of a failed abortion and contains masterful imagery and an atmosphere that is flamboyantly creepy.

But the most prevalent Filipino genre is the *aswang* movie, which was particularly popular in the Nineties, with productions including *Aswang* (1992), directed by **Peque Gallaga** and **Lore Reyes**, and Don Escudero's *Impakto* (*The Devil*, 1996), which has a doctor's wife bearing a child who turns out to be a bloodsucking devil. That *aswang* variation bears the name *tiyanak*; others are the *mandurugo* (vampire), the *manananggal* (the man-eating were-beast), the *mangkukulam* (evil-eyed witch), the *kapre* (tree giant) and the *nuno sa punso* (anthill dwarf). The folkloric myths have all featured in horrors, including *Sa piling ng aswang* (*With The Witch*, 1999), also by Gallaga and Reyes, who have been the key figures behind the longest running horror franchise in Filipino history, the *Shake, Rattle And Roll* series, which began in 1984 and includes five sequels; each consists of horror and comedy revolving around *aswangs*, curses and ghosts.

Recently, the success of *Feng Shui* has encouraged local filmmakers to come up with more ghost tales, such as *Pasiyam* (*Nine Days*, 2004), the title referring to the traditional period of prayer for the deceased, to prevent the soul from wandering on earth and disturb the living. In Jose Javier Reyes's *Spirit Of The Glass* (2004) a beach trip goes awry when holidaymakers inadvertently summon a gang of malevolent spirits via a Ouija board, and in **Yam Laranas**'s *Sigaw* (*Scream*, 2004) apartment block residents are as trapped by their own frailty as they are by the confined space and the ghosts that haunt the place. "I want the audience to bring home their fear," said Laranas. "To be afraid of being left alone in their house or in their room, to feel a chill when they walk in empty dark corridors."

Aswang (The Unearthing)
dir Wrye Martin & Barry Poltermann, 1994, US, 82m

Directors from Wisconsin adapt Filipino folklore in this mean and moody Lynchian *Evil Dead/Texas Chainsaw* hybrid about unwed pregnant Kat (Tina Ona Paukstelis) agreeing to give up her offspring to Peter (Norman Moses) and pose as his wife to fulfil the conditions of his inheritance. But, as she learns too late, it's all set up so that her unborn baby can be sacrificed to a foetus-eating vampire. Gritty and grimy.

Poland

The international praise won by Roman Polanski, born in France but raised in Poland, for *Repulsion* (1965) and *Rosemary's Baby* (1968) meant that during the late Sixties Polish horror was in the spotlight for the first time.

The film that received the most attention was **Wojciech Has**'s *Rekopis znaleziony w Saragossie* (*The Saragossa Manuscript*, 1965), which was based on a story of a military captain's descent into hell, and later came *Sanatorium pod klepsydra* (*The Sandglass*, 1973), in which doctors conquer death by slowing down time, allowing past events to be revisited, and in particular Jewish experiences of the Holocaust.

Better known outside Poland than the work of Has were the films of **Walerian Borowczyk**, and in particular *Contes immoraux* (*Immoral Tales*, 1974), a quartet of stories that included two historically based tales of evil. *Erzsebet Báthory* featured **Paloma Picasso**, daughter of Pablo, as the infamous Countess Dracula, who bathed in virgins' blood to keep young, and *Lucrezia Borgia* starred Florence Bellamy enjoying heretic sex and torture. Borowczyk's *Beauty And The Beast* fable *The Beast* (1975) garnered a horror following more for being an erotic nightmare than anything else, and *Docteur Jekyll et les femmes* (*Dr Jekyll And His Women*, 1981) starred **Udo Kier** as a crueller version of Robert Louis Stevenson's Victorian villain, terrorizing women with a phallus-shaped knife. Blood-soaked and highly graphic, it was, like *The Beast*, censored heavily by the authorities.

Censors around the world were also given headaches by **Andrzej Zulawski**. When *Possession* (1981) was launched at the Cannes Film Festival, many critics were stunned during the sequence where Isabelle Adjani gives birth to a full-grown man after making love to a slimy monster (created by **H. R. Giger** of *Alien* fame), and for some the whole film, an allegory about doomed relationships and metaphysical evil, was repulsive. Zulawski returned to the theme of a monstrous entity encroaching upon human relationships in the supernatural *Szamanka* (*The Shaman*, 1996).

Rekopis znaleziony w Saragossie (The Saragossa Manuscript)
dir Wojciech Has, 1965, Pol, 124m, b/w

Count Jan Potocki's sprawling early-nineteenth-century novel about a military captain's descent into hell was adapted by Has into an ambitious and intellectually demanding exploration of the occult. With an experimental score by Krzysztof Penderecki, who features on the soundtracks for *The Exorcist* and *The Shining*, it contains moments of true horror, including the scene where the captain wakes up in a satanic landscape filled with skeletons and hanging bodies.

Russia

Russian cinema has always seen horror as an unacceptable genre, preferring instead to use moments of horror in other kinds of films, including adaptations of works by Aleksandr Grin, and of Nikolai Gogol's *Viy*, the vampire tale that Mario Bava turned into *Black Sunday* (1960, see Canon).

The movie advertised as "the first Russian horror film" was **Oleg Teptsov**'s *Gospodin oformitel* (*Mister Designer*, 1988), which starred Viktor Avilov as an artist daring to challenge God by bringing a doll to life, and being punished for his sins. More a philosophical tone poem than full-blooded horror, the film drew a cult following.

It was followed by **Yevgeny Yufit**'s *Papa, umer ded moroz* (*Daddy, Father Frost Is Dead*, 1992) which concerned a psychic biologist who witnesses bizarre events, from his son's suicide to suburban sado-masochism and during the mid-Nineties the Gorky studio embarked on a series of low-budget horrors, but they all failed to find an audience. However, Nikolai Lebedev's *Zmeinyi istochnik* (*The Snake Spring*, 1997) and Aleksei Balabanov's *Pro urodov i lyudey* (*Of Freaks And Men*, 1998) led to a watershed moment for Russian horror in 2004.

Timur Bekmambetov's *Night Watch*, the first part of a trilogy based on Sergei Lukyanenko's novel about a battle between the forces controlling night-time and daytime, out-stripped *Spider-Man 2* at the Russian box office and became the biggest success that the country's film industry has ever produced. Various elements of the smash hit show the impact of Westernization – its CGI enhancement and rock video style of direction make it similar to Hollywood blockbusters – and it is set to be followed by *Day Watch* and then *Dusk Watch*.

Scandinavia

The Norse myths of Sweden, Finland, Norway and Denmark come mainly from the Icelandic Eddas, which were written down a few centuries before Christianity reached these territories. But while the creatures of J. R. R. Tolkien's *The Lord Of the Rings* owe themselves to these sagas, the few Scandinavian horror films that exist rarely invoke similar images.

Ingmar Bergman's *Jungfrukällan* (*The Virgin Spring*, 1960) is a case in point. It's more a revenge story, with a father reverting from Christian faith to paganism, to slaughter the brothers who raped and murdered his naïve daughter. Wes Craven (see Icons) stole the motors of Bergman's masterpiece for his powerful shocker *The Last House On The Left* (1972).

The tension between paganism and Christianity, revealing a deep-rooted Scandinavian cultural fear usually evident in depictions of witchcraft, is also evident in Bergman's *The Seventh Seal* (1957), in which a man plays chess with the Grim Reaper during the Black Plague, and *The Devil's Eye* (1960), in which the Devil summons Don Juan from Hell to seduce a virgin. And similar satanic themes have been made clear in

Stellan Skarsgård in *Insomnia* (1997), which was eventually remade in Hollywood

243

films from the region that range from **Benjamin Christensen**'s *Witchcraft Through The Ages* (1922) and **Carl Theodor Dreyer**'s *Vredens dag* (*Day Of Wrath*, 1942) to Anders Rønnow-Klarlund's *Besat* (*Possessed*, 1999) and Mikael Håfström's *Strandvaskaren* (*Drowning Ghost*, 2004).

The other Scandinavian strand of horror is the serial killer chiller with a quirky twist. Ole Bornedal's *Nattevagten* (*Nightwatch*, 1994), concerning a mortuary attendant, Erik Skjoldbjærg's *Insomnia* (1997), a mystery focusing on the detective, and Johannes Runeborg's *Sleepwalker* (2000), about an architect whose family goes missing, all contain gimmicks and gore – the reason why each was snapped up by the Hollywood remake industry.

South Africa

If you haven't heard of South African horror, you won't be alone. The country's sweeping vistas might be recognizable in the many films that use the landscape as an atmospheric backdrop, but the country's horror films of note, with their imported has-been stars, shoddy technique and cliché scares, can be counted on the fingers of one hand.

Ray Austin's *House Of The Living Dead* (1973) deals with a mad scientist conducting occult soul transference experiments. **Darrell Roodt**'s *City Of Blood* (1983) concerns a medical examiner discovering that a prostitute murderer is in fact a zombie witch doctor; and Roodt has another shaman curse a platoon of soldiers after they wipe out a village in *The Stick* (1987). In V. V. Dachin Hsu's *Pale Blood* (1990) George Chakiris and Wings Hauser are modern-day vampires, and Neal Sundstrom's *Slash* (2002) features a rock band getting stuck on a haunted farm.

Spain

Spain does not have a tradition of horror literature, though strains can be found in the work of Francisco de Quevedo and Miguel de Cervantes, and therefore lacks the gothic vein that provided rich source material for other national film industries. (Some films, such as Jaume Balagueró's *Los sin nombre* (*The Nameless*, 1999), inspired by Ramsey Campbell, took cues from Great Britain.) Because of the power of the Catholic Church, too, and the lack of an industrial revolution to spawn technological fear, virtually no horror movies appeared before the boom of 1968 to 1975.

Edgar Neville's *La torre de los siete jorobados* (*Tower Of The Seven Hunchbacks*, 1944) was the exception before the Sixties, when Julio Coll's *Fuego* (*Pyro*, 1964), featuring a maniac disfigured by fire, also came along. And in 1961 **Jess Franco** – often known as one of a catalogue of pseudonyms – embarked on the first of his horrors in a career that took in more than 150. *Gritos en la noche* (*The Awful Dr Orloff*, 1961) starred Howard Vernon as the titular mad doctor in a cheesy variation on *Eyes Without A Face*. Over the years, Franco's movies have ranged from the absolutely terrible to the weirdly remarkable, and he's given fans his unique take on the works of J. Sheridan Le Fanu, Oscar Wilde, Victor Hugo and the Marquis de Sade. But the jury is still out on Franco: some think he's an audaciously crazed surrealist, others a rank amateur with little command of proper cinema technique. *The Sadist Of Notre Dame* (1979), which took five years to make, can support either side of the argument.

But the true saviour of Hispanic panic was *La marca del hombre loco* (*Hell's Creatures*, 1968), which proved the right film at the right time and brought about the horror boom. **Paul Naschy** was just a stocky weightlifter until bit parts in sand-and-sandals B-movies led to his signature role here of wolf-man Waldemar Daninsky, and he made his iconic alter ego a top box-office draw in his home country. He eventually turned director, using the name Jacinto Molina, with *Inquisición* (*Inquisition*, 1976), but before that he bit the men and bedded the women in a variety of fun frighteners. A beloved national institution, he continues to make films today, recent efforts including *Rojo Sangre* and *Countess Dracula's Orgy Of Blood* (both 2004).

Meanwhile, after directing *Malenka* (*Fangs Of The Living Dead*, 1969) **Amando de Ossorio** created truly unique and frightening monsters in the zombie Knights Templar series that began with *La noche del terror ciego* (*Tombs Of The Blind Dead*, 1971). Sequels soon followed, with more nightmare imagery of the crusty Knights' withered hands protruding from coffins to mount their ghostly steeds. There were also moments of horror glory during this period for **Narciso Ibáñez Serrador**, for his extraordinary twosome, *La residencia* (*The House That Screamed*, 1969) and *¿Quien puede matar a un nino?* (*Would You Kill a Child?*, aka *Island Of The Damned*, 1976), a harrowing film in which a couple go to a fictitious Balearic island and find nothing but rebellious children who have murdered all the adults. Among the films that were sexually explicit and gory for the Franco era was Jorge Grau's *No profanar el sueño de los muertos* (*The Living Dead At The Manchester Morgue*, 1974, the city being chosen because Grau always wanted to go there).

The most notable horror to emerge from Spain in the Eighties was one of the genre's most virulently disturbing movies, *Tras el cristal* (*In A Glass Cage*, 1987). **Agustin Villaronga**'s controversial portrait of pure evil explores a circle of abuse by focusing on a paedophile who used his post as a Nazi concentration camp doctor to torture and sexually abuse boys, and who is later kept alive on an iron lung by a young home carer, Angelo. Villaronga uses traditional suspense mechanics in places, but the film remains firmly outside simple genre boundaries and achieves a nightmarish intensity that divides audiences into those who admire it for its quality of craftsmanship and those who despise it for being taboo.

In the Nineties, having been banished to the backwaters of television in the wake of Pedro Almodóvar's camp successes, Spanish horror became a more significant player on the international scene thanks to two key directors. It was Almodóvar himself who recognized the talents of Bilbao-born **Álex de la Iglesia** and produced his debut feature, *Acción mutante* (*Mutant Action*, 1993). That sci-fi horror comedy led to the amazing lampoon of doom prophecy horrors, *El día de la bestia* (*Day Of The Beast*, 1995), about a priest who deciphers an ancient sacred text and deduces that the Antichrist will be born in Madrid on Christmas Day. "I wanted to explode the seriousness of such movies as *The Exorcist* and *The Omen*," said Iglesia, who has since moved into more mainstream fare. "My priest isn't aware of his 'big' responsibility to save the world and that's why it's funny and frightening at the same time."

The second Spanish director to find international fame in the Nineties had an even greater impact. **Alejandro Amenábar** made his astonishing debut with *Tesis* (*Thesis*, 1996), about a Madrid film student realizing that her school is being used as a snuff movie base; and then he had his major break with the unique fantasy *Abre los ojos* (*Open Your Eyes*, 1997), which was remade with Tom Cruise as

Vanilla Sky (2001). Then Nicole Kidman agreed to star in the stylish and spooky ghost story *The Others* (2001). "I wanted to play with the supernatural in its simplest forms and craft a more classic adult horror than had been seen for a while," said Amenábar of one of Spain's greatest horror successes.

La campana del infierno (The Bell Of Hell)
dir Claudio Guerín Hill, 1973, Sp/Fr, 106m

Director Claudio Guerín Hill died on the last day of shooting his fascinating Spanish psycho-horror, falling from the bell tower featured in the macabre climax. Renaud Verley stars as the man taking revenge on the relatives who to gain his inheritance had declared him mentally unstable, and Hill keeps Verley's character ambiguous while he indulges in disturbing mind-games and physical torture. It's loaded with anti-Catholic satire, surreal images, perverse sex and bizarre plot twists.

Transylvania

Home to Vlad the Impaler, the bloodthirsty ruler who was the inspiration for Bram Stoker's *Dracula*, and Countess Báthory, who apparently bathed in blood, Transylvania has provided the setting for many folkloric horror movies. Historically part of Hungary and now a province of Romania, the area is a backdrop for virtually every vampire movie, a few with werewolves, such as *Howling II: Stirba Werewolf Bitch* (1986), and the comedies *Transylvania 6-5000* (1985) and *Transylvania Twist* (1990); and, of course, Tim Curry's sublime Frank. N. Furter was "just a sweet transvestite from transsexual Transylvania" in *The Rocky Horror Picture Show* (1975). The area has even been important in film production: at the start of the new millennium Romania became the location of choice in Eastern Europe for many cost-conscious horrors, including *Seed of Chucky* (2004), *Spirit Trap*, *Return Of The Living Dead: Necropolis*, *Return Of The Living Dead: Rave To The Grave* and *Bloodrayne* (all 2005).

Turkey

Although the first Turkish feature film appeared in 1917, no real movie industry existed until the Fifties, when producers began to experiment with the genre pool.

A vague chiller appeared in 1949 – *Ciglik* (*Scream*) – but the first identifiable horror was *Drakula Istanbul'da* (*Dracula In Istanbul*, 1953), based on an abridged version of the Bram Stoker novel translated by Ali Riza Seyfi; and **Atif Kaptan** was the first to play Dracula as Vlad the Impaler, the Romanian who had fought the Turks. The Vlad character appears in many Turkish costume epics, but the first film to depict him as an actual vampire in his own era was *Kara boga* (1974).

Female vampires turned up in another historical epic, *Malkoçoglu* (1966), which like many popular light Turkish horrors, was based on a comic strip. And a vampire witch named Gosha featured prominently in the *Tarkan* comic created by Sezgin Burak; played by Swedish dancer Eva Bender, Gosha appeared as the always nude, blood-bathing seducer in films including *Tarkan: Gümüs eger*

(*Tarkan: The Silver Saddle*, 1970). The fictional Italian anti-hero Killing and his arch-villain's signature skeleton costume were also paraded through a variety of movies, starting with *Kilink Istanbul'da* (*Killing In Istanbul*, 1967). One featured Frankenstein, as would Nejat Saydam's 1975 comedy *Sevimli Frankestayn* (*Cute Frankenstein*), an almost exact replica of Mel Brooks's *Young Frankenstein* (1974).

One of the few relatively straight Turkish horrors was *Oluler konusmaz* (*The Dead Don't Talk*, 1970), which is set in a ghostly hotel. Another was **Metin Erksan**'s *Seytan* (*Satan*, 1974), a straight remake of *The Exorcist* (1973) with an Islamic backdrop; the notorious stabbing

A poster for Metin Erksan's remake of *The Exorcist* in 1974

sequence had a knife rather than a crucifix (not that anyone knew, because the original wasn't released in Turkey until 1982). And before Gus Van Sant's dreadful remake of *Psycho* in 1998, **Mehmet Alemdar** had beaten him to it with *Kader diyelim* (*Let's Say It's Fate*, 1995), which includes jaunty musical numbers. Alemdar also directed one of the few Turkish serial killer horrors, *Suphenin bedeli* (*The Price Of Doubt*, 1995).

By popular critical census the best Turkish horror film is **E. Kutlug Ataman**'s arty *Karanlik sular* (*The Serpent's Tale*, 1993), in which a rich aristocrat is told that his son didn't drown in an accident but discovered an ancient text with the power to dispense eternal life. Incorporating the identity crisis of the Turkish nation, torn between

its European and Asian influences, *Karanlik sular* was rich in horror metaphor – and a dismal box-office flop. It prevented the possible progress of horror in a culture that had never fully embraced the genre.

Drakula Istanbul'da (Dracula In Istanbul)
dir Mehmet Muhtar, 1953, Tur, 85m, b/w

The first Turkish horror, this was also the first adaptation to show Dracula scaling down his castle's walls and to contain the contentious scene, completely absent in the Universal landmark, of him feeding a newborn baby to his female companion. The Turks axed most of the Christian symbolism, and Dracula is killed when his head is cut off and stuffed with garlic, all after having a stake through the heart.

The Information: where to turn next

An audience watching a 3-D film in the
early 1950s: a great deal of memorabilia
owes its availability to such gimmicks

The Information:
where to turn next

So you know the story of horror all around the world, have come across the classics and love the icons: where next? This chapter – inevitably by no means exhaustive – will give you the best starting points for buying horror merchandise and for finding out more about the genre.

Memorabilia and merchandise

The market for horror collectibles has grown to massive proportions over the past few years.

It's still only film critics and journalists who can get the most sought after tie-in merchandise (like the *Darkman* cigar-cutter, the *Torture Garden* packet of seeds and the *Legend Of The Seven Golden Vampires* box of vampire dust), but the range for the consumer to buy is growing far bigger, and you can find magazines, posters, autographs, masks, games, photographs, collector cards, fridge magnets and action figures in stores, at conventions and online.

DVDs are available through mainstream media retailers and through specialists, often with online facilities, and it is worth looking at labels, since all of them are now releasing horror movies with introductions and commentaries; even the magazine *Fangoria* has its own label. Criterion, which has released a few horrors, such as *Diabolique* and *Peeping Tom*, is the widely acknowledged Rolls Royce of the DVD, and for foreign horror the leaders include Dagored, Mondo Macabro, Nocturno and No Shame.

These are the best places to turn to, aside from general websites such as www.ebay.com, when searching and buying:

The Cinema Store
www.the-cinema-store.com

A wide range of film merchandise available for ordering online from this store based in the heart of London.

Cinestore
www.cinestore.com

An easy-to-navigate French website offering a wide range of DVDs and novelties to buy online.

Creepy Classics
www.creepyclassics.com

An American website offering online ordering of hard-to-find horror movies from around the world on DVD and video.

Forbidden Planet
www.forbiddenplanet.com

Goodies and DVDs galore from the British-based retailer, slanted at cult, fantasy and sci-fi film fans.

Hollywood Book and Poster Company
www.hollywoodbookandposter.com

The website of an American store that opened in 1977 and specializes in film, television and wrestling memorabilia.

Horror Movies
www.horrormovies.com

This American web-site sells posters, collectibles and DVDs, which are presented with reviews.

The rare "Illusion-O" glasses from William Castle's *Thirteen Ghosts* (1960)

Moviemarket
www.moviemarket.co.uk

Sophisticated website of a business specializing in film photographs and posters for purchase online.

ProfondoRosso
www.profondorossostore.com

A *bottega* in Rome that specializes in horror, fantasy and sci-fi, founded in 1989 by Dario Argento.

Events

Film festivals

In the beginning film festivals were tourist attractions to promote particular areas rather than the movies or the stars: Cannes, Venice, San Sebastian, Vienna, Montréal and Berlin all started life that way. To have an impact alongside such heavyweights, other towns and cities had to find a niche, and as the fantasy genre began to grow in popularity in the Fifties horror and science fiction film festivals became the ideal.

The first genre festival to gain any international profile was in Trieste, Italy, which in 1963 memorably gave the Golden Asteroid to Roger Corman's *The Man With The X-Ray Eyes*.

The main horror festival then became **Avoriaz**, in the French Alps, which started in 1973 and attracted international journalists for sixteen years, until the governing bodies pulled the event; the town of Gerardmer, further down the mountains, happily took over. Both Avoriaz and Trieste, now the SciencePlusFiction festival, awarded prizes decided by a jury of international film critics, but far fairer is what the **European Federation of Fantastic Film Festivals** now does: panels including stars and directors, selected by the Federation, attend each festival in the member cartel and choose a European film that is given a Méliès D'Argent award (named after Georges Méliès). Every selected film is then showcased in one big programme and the panels choose a Méliès D'Or winner.

There are many horror film festivals around the world nowadays, lasting from four days to three and a half weeks, and you could spend your whole life just going from one to the next, as the important ones follow each other with little overlap. The best way to see the world on the cheap is to make a short film or digital-video feature and to submit it to every venue: even if it's only above average you'll be invited, usually all-expenses paid, to introduce it on stage and to be interviewed about it by the local press.

Of the film festivals that either showcase horror exclusively or have it as a main strand, here are the top five, in order of importance:

Sitges: Festival Internacional de Cinema de Catlunya
www.cinemasitges.com

The nearly 40-year-old state-funded Sitges, at the gay-friendly beach resort just outside Barcelona usually every October, is the best festival in terms of selection, presentation and celebrity. The major films in competition are projected at the Gran Melia Sitges Hotel, and other cinemas in the picturesque town play host to film events or director retrospectives.

Fantasporto: Oporto International Film Festival
www.fantasporto.online.pt

Taking place every February/March in the hilly city of Oporto in north Portugal, Fantasporto has been going for more than 25 years. Venues have changed from single screen cinemas to multiplexes, but its importance as a cultural event for the host nation – the President is often in attendance – and for filmmakers from around the world remains the same.

Brussels International Festival Of Fantastic Film
www.bifff.org

First organized in 1983 by the Belgian PeyMey directors' group, the BIFFF takes place in Brussels every March. The two-week event has a reputation for noisy audiences but its programming is second to none and has established the reputations of many of the genre's filmmakers in French-speaking territories.

Puchon International Fantastic Film Festival
www.pifan.com

A relatively new festival location, the small town of Puchon, near Seoul in South Korea, hosts a vibrant nine-day event every July, and is responsible in no small part for focusing Western eyes on the burgeoning Eastern horror scene.

Fantasia International Film Festival
www.fantasiafestival.com

Since 1996 FanTasia has showcased contemporary horror movies for around four weeks every July/August

Ray Milland as Dr Xavier in *The Man With The X-Ray Eyes* (1963), which helped Trieste gain international status for its film festival

in Montréal, where it has become a hugely popular summer tradition.

Five of the best of the rest:

• Neuchâtel International Fantastic Film Festival, Switzerland, July (www.nifff.ch)
• FrightFest, London, August (www.frightfest.co.uk)
• Ravenna Nightmare Film Fest, September (www.ravennanightmare.com)
• Cinemuerte, Vancouver, October (www.cinemuerte.com)
• New York City Horror Film Festival, October (www.nychorrorfest.com)

Conventions

Horror conventions, which are often organized by stores that specialize in the genre, are more accessible to fans than festivals and are usually weekend events where attractions include merchandise, screenings and stars signing autographs.

While there are fewer conventions for horror than there are for sci-fi and fantasy, many have sprung up in the past few years, mainly in America; and there are also one-off events, for example to celebrate particular anniversaries, which are advertised through horror websites. Here's where to go for the best regular conventions:

Chiller Theatre
www.chillertheatre.com

An American event for videos, models and toys, with a useful and welcoming website.

Cinema Wasteland Movie And Memorabilia Expo
www.cinemawasteland.com

An American event with guests and events from a store specializing in drive-in era horror and exploitation.

Cinevent Classic Film Convention
www.cinevent.com

An annual convention held in Columbus, Ohio, specializing in silent and early sound films.

Fangoria's Weekend Of Horrors
www.creationent.com/cal/dod.htm

The website for the weekend organized by the American magazine *Fangoria*, with dealers, costume competitions and giveaways.

The Festival Of Fantastic Films
www.fantastic-films.com/festival/

This festival is organized by Britain's long-established Society of Fantastic Films, which also has regular meetings in Manchester.

Horrorfind Weekend
www.horrorfind.com

This useful website from America presents an event with celebrities, dealers, movies, writers and seminars.

Memorabilia
www.memorabilia.co.uk

This regular bash at the Birmingham NEC, particularly good for its celebrity signings, is billed as Europe's largest collectors' event.

Monster Bash
www.horror-wood.com/Bash.htm

The family-friendly American weekender has films, talks and Q&A sessions.

The World Horror Convention
www.worldhorrorsociety.org

The society organizes the well-established convention, which has a literary slant, at different venues in America.

Books and magazines

Books

When the genre took off during the Fifties and the number of horror films being made reached gigantic proportions, books were an offshoot of the burgeoning horror magazine market, and were often written by people responsible for magazine articles. While the earliest books were always overviews of the genre, the trend today is for a focus on a particular area or title, such as Lawrence McCallum's *Italian Horror Films Of The 1960s* (McFarland, 1998) or Mark Kermode's *The Exorcist* (British Film Institute, 1997).

Many of the following are out of print, but all are worth the effort to track down.

The BFI Companion To Horror
Kim Newman, ed. (Cassell and BFI, 1996)

Running from Abbott, Bud to Zucco, George, this detailed and wide-ranging companion covers horror from its pre-cinema beginnings to the modern day.

Bizarre Sinema: Horror all'Italiana 1957–1979
Stefano Piselli & Riccardo Morrocchi, ed. (Glittering Images, 1996)

A superbly illustrated guide to Italian horror with the focus on the sub-genre's earliest purveyors, Riccardo Freda and Mario Bava.

Danse Macabre
Stephen King (Macdonald, 1981)

The bestselling author writes informally on the entire phenomenon of horror movies.

Stephen King, who as well as writing fiction wrote a book on the phenomenon of horror movies that was typically broad for the era

Dark Carnival: The Secret World of Tod Browning, Hollywood's Master of the Macabre
David J. Skal & Elias Savada (Anchor Books, 1995)

An insightful and illuminating biography of how the pioneering creator of *Dracula* (1931) and *Freaks* (1932) is tied to the genre's invention. A classic volume.

English Gothic: A Century of Horror Cinema
Jonathan Rigby (Reynolds & Hearn, 2000)

The ups and downs of the horror genre from its nineteenth-century beginnings to the present day.

Eyeball Compendium
Stephen Thrower, ed. (FAB Press, 2003)

Horror cinema at its most obscure, excessive and marginalized put under the spotlight, with an emphasis on sex, art and exploitation.

Fear Without Frontiers
Steven Jay Schneider (FAB Press, 2003)

An exploration of horror cinema around the world, with hidden terror treasures from other cultures.

Gore: Autopsie d'un cinéma
Marc Godin (Editions du Collectionneur, 1994)

If it's gory, violent or nasty, it'll be featured in this stunningly illustrated book on splatter through the ages.

The Hammer Story
Marcus Hearn & Alan Barnes (Titan Books, 1997)

The definitive and authorized history of the British film studio.

A Heritage Of Horror: The English Gothic Cinema 1946-1972
David Pirie (Gordon Fraser, 1973)

The British horror movie evaluated with insightful precision. A classic volume.

Heroes Of The Horrors
Calvin Thomas Beck (Macmillan, 1975)

Biographical facts on all the vintage actors who created the immortal monsters, from Lon Chaney to Vincent Price, and plot synopses.

Horror: The Aurum Encyclopedia
Phil Hardy, ed. (Aurum, 1985; revised and updated, 1993)

A classic volume, with year by year reviews, that was the first reference book to cover far-flung global productions in depth.

Horror In The Cinema
Ivan Butler (Zwemmer, 1970)

A groundbreaking early horror primer.

Horror Movies: An Illustrated Survey
Carlos Clarens (Secker & Warburg, 1968)

The first level-headed and well-researched text of true merit to focus on the genre. A classic volume.

The Horror People
John Brosnan (St Martin's/Macdonald & Jane's, 1976)

All you could ever want to know on all the leading horror film personalities, with interviews.

Horror!
Drake Douglas (Macmillan, 1966)

Leaning towards literature, Douglas includes chapters on all the movie monsters.

Men, Women And Chainsaws: Gender In The Modern Horror Film
Carol J. Clover (Princeton University Press, 1992)

Low-life horror is feminist art, according to this landmark textbook.

The Modern Horror Film
John McCarty (Citadel, 1990)

A chronological homage to the horror film, beginning with Hammer's *The Curse Of Frankenstein* (1957).

Mondo Macabro: Weird & Wonderful Cinema Around The World
Pete Tombs (Titan, 1997)

Global horror sub-cultures explored by Tombs, who owns the tie-in DVD label of the same name.

The Monster Show: A Cultural History Of Horror
David J. Skal (Norton, 1993)

"The best book on horror movies I've ever read," said Robert Bloch, the author of *Psycho*.

Nightmare Movies: A Critical History Of The Horror Film 1968–88
Kim Newman (Bloomsbury, 1984; revised and updated 1988)

The definitive guide to twenty years of horror.

A Pictorial History Of Horror Movies
Denis Gifford (Hamlyn, 1973)

The popular compendium of horror, which sold widely in bookstores, is playful and informed.

Ten Years Of Terror: British Horror Films Of The 1970s
Harvey Fenton & David Flint, ed. (FAB Press, 2001)

An encyclopaedic account of independent horror's heyday.

The Vampire Cinema
David Pirie (Hamlyn/Crescent, 1977)

On the cult of the vampire as a source of inspiration to filmmakers, starting with silent cinema and including later Hammer incarnations.

Video Nasties!
Allan Bryce (Stray Cat, 1998)

Everything you wanted to know about the most horrifying films that have been banned, from *Absurd* to *Zombie Flesh-Eaters*.

Magazines

The horror magazine market really established itself in America in 1958, with *Famous Monsters Of Filmland*.

France got in on the act in 1962 with *Midi-Minuit Fantastique*, but the contrast between the two could not have been more marked. *Famous Monsters* was angled towards the juvenile while *Midi-Minuit* was intellectual and cine-literate, did not shy away from the erotic aspects of the genre and championed certain films (by Corman and Bava, and Hammer) long before they were fashionable; among its contributors were future horror scriptwriter Chris Wicking and cult director Jean Rollin. The American *Castle Of Frankenstein* (which began life as *The Journal Of Frankenstein* in 1959), which featured writing by future horror director Joe Dante, was a mixture of both and although it's no longer around it's still one of the world's best-loved horror magazines today.

The British *Supernatural*, featuring future horror author **Ramsey Campbell**, lasted only two issues in 1969, but paved the way for British magazines such as *The House Of Hammer*, *Shivers* and *The Dark Side*. Meanwhile America's defunct *The Monster Times* and *Photon*, and the sporadic *Little Shoppe Of Horrors*, were supplanted in 1970 by the groundbreaking *Cinefantastique*, now shortened to *CFQ*; in its wake followed *Fangoria*, *Psychotronic*, *Filmfax*, *Rue Morgue*, *Scarlet Street* and *Video Watchdog*. Italy's short-lived *Horror*, published in 1970, was followed by *Amarcord* and *Nocturno*.

In terms of content, while *Famous Monsters Of Filmland* focused mainly on the golden era of **Universal**, most magazines that followed it were broader in outlook, juxtaposing reviews and news with retrospective features on the entire canon. In recent times there has been a movement back

The director Joe Dante, an early writer for the magazine *Castle Of Frankenstein*

towards specialization. This, and the brief lives typical in magazine markets, means that many of the magazines listed below have shown remarkable longevity.

The Dark Side
www.ebony.co.uk/darkside

How many angles on zombie and cannibal movies can there be? Find out in this unapologetically retro British publication that mixes sleaze with bad puns and has a bent towards the video nasty era. It publishes many book tie-ins, which have included *Zombie*, *Fantasy Females* and *Video Nasties*.

Fangoria
www.fangoria.com

For more than 25 years this American publication has ruled the horror market with its up-to-date set reports, informed reviews and coverage of all things gory and gruesome. The magazine hosts its own conventions and has a DVD label and an invaluable website. The editor, Anthony Timpone, says that the magazine has gone from strength to strength because it covers all horror's bases. He also says: "The magazine is more popular than ever because horror is bigger than ever … horror films open almost every weekend, and DVD sales have made the industry more profitable than ever."

Femme Fatales
www.femmefatales.com

Scream queens and glamour pin-ups are accented by *Femme Fatales*, which uses its subjects in exclusive photo-shoots.

Filmfax
www.filmfax.com

The editorial staff of the American magazine *Filmfax* pride themselves on documenting gaps in the history of horror. It deals with radio, television and film produced between the late Twenties and the mid-Seventies.

Little Shoppe Of Horrors
www.littleshoppeofhorrors.com

Every issue of this magazine is devoted to some aspect of Hammer or British horror. It often resembles a book more than a journal.

Mad Movies
www.madmovies.com

With an accent on gloss, gore and girls, this French magazine covers all aspects of the horror genre.

Midnight Marquee
www.midmar.com

Every aspect of the horror movie genre is covered in this Baltimore-based journal, from the arcane and barely remembered to more popular fare.

Nocturno
www.nocturno.it/index.php

This Italian magazine, unusually, gives more space to its past and present home horrors than new American releases.

Psychotronic
www.psychotronicvideo.com

If it's weird, wild and wonderful, it's somewhere in Michael J. Weldon's magazine, or in his indispensable book *The Psychotronic Video Guide*.

Quatermass
quatermass@hotmail.com

This Spanish magazine with a horror nostalgia base is published sporadically – there have been six issues since 1993 – but is beautifully laid out and lavishly presented.

Rue Morgue
www.rue-morgue.com

This Canadian magazine is devoted to all aspects of horror in entertainment and culture.

Scarlet Street
www.scarletstreet.com

The magazine of mystery and horror from New Jersey celebrates classics old and new.

Shivers
www.visimag.com/shivers/

The more refined British equivalent of *Fangoria*, Visual Imagination's sister publication to their sci-fi *Starburst* goes easier on the gore shots and heavier on the European coverage.

Uncut
www.midnight-media.demon.co.uk

Uncut concentrates on gore and censored movies with near-the-knuckle illustrations to match.

Video Watchdog
www.videowatchdog.com

"The perfectionist's guide to fantastic video" is how tireless editor Tim Lucas describes his indispensable Cincinnati-based magazine. Most directors subscribe to find out about their own DVD transfers! Serious but not humourless, academic or overly technical, it's the crucial magazine for delving into matters of letterboxing, missing or restored footage and alternative versions. In fourteen years of publishing, it has amassed a larger body of wide-reaching horror interviews and criticism than any other monthly.

Fanzines

Wannabe horror film journalists who couldn't get published in the prominent magazines of the day, like *Fangoria* and *Cinefantastique*, simply did it themselves. When **Mark P** (aka Mark Perry) photocopied a few sheets of paper that had his thoughts on punk rock and sold them as *Sniffin' Glue* in 1976, he had no idea how his cheapskate style and semi-literate typewritten enthusiasm would translate to the world of horror movies.

The first equivalent was projectionist **Bill Landis**'s *Sleazoid Express*, published fortnightly in New York from 1980 and costing 50 cents. It was available at movie-related shops and at the newly emerging video stores, and photocopies on coloured paper progressed to white foldouts with lurid ad-blocks. It was packed with pithy reviews of grind-house exploiters as well as mainstream horrors, and Landis and future co-editor **Jimmy McDonough** also interviewed personalities in the genre's underbelly, with precision. Landis compiled the book *Sleazoid Express* from the groundbreaking fanzine while McDonough also wrote *The Ghastly One: The Sex-Gore Netherworld Of Filmmaker Andy Milligan*, one of the finest examinations ever of the life of a cult horror director.

As a riposte to *Sleazoid Express* **Rick and Rosemary Sullivan** started up the free *Gore Gazette*, because "Landis's reviews were becoming increasingly critical and unfairly analytical of a genre that just don't hold up to that style of criticism and were never made to". Hence the lionization in the *Gore Gazette* of such directors as Herschell Gordon Lewis (*Blood Feast*, 1963), Jean Rollin (*Rape Of The Vampire*, 1967) and Jess Franco (*The Sadist Of Notre Dame*, 1979), who had been considered uninteresting hacks. Britain offered *Pretty Poison* and *Crimson Celluloid* before the influential *Shock Xpress* made its debut in 1985; it lasted three years and then, as offshoots of the magazine, books were produced that were full of new material. Also emerging from *Shock Xpress* was the London's popular "Shock Around the Clock" 24-hour horror festival, which later turned into FrightFest.

Fanzines were the voice of the street, read by the video generation who could access all the titles their elders had either travelled miles to see or waited years to view. The influence that they enjoyed as a result was a precursor to the significance of the internet, which has killed them off.

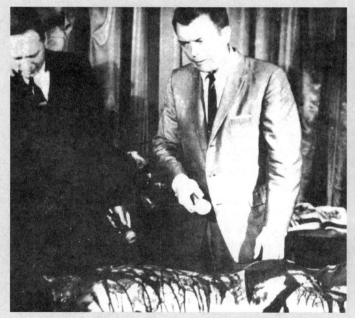

A key scene from *Blood Feast* (1963) by Herschell Gordon Lewis, who was a fanzine favourite

Websites

Among the best websites for further information on horror movies are general film websites. These include:

The Internet Movie Database
www.imdb.com

This database contains more than 200,000 film entries, each of which lists details such as cast and crew members, awards and trivia; and these are cross-referenced so that individuals can also be looked up, for lists of their films and biographies and further facts. There is separate information on the horror movies that are highest rated and most requested through the website.

All Movie Guide
www.allmovie.com

This is a less sophisticated website than the IMDB but the material that it offers, on a wide variety of movies, is at times more thorough.

Silent Era
www.silentera.com

This site for all things before the talkie era is particularly strong on events and recent re-releases.

Premiere
www.premiere.com

Empire
www.empireonline.co.uk

Variety
www.variety.com

These are just three of the film magazines and trade journals that have their own websites.

Ain't It Cool News
www.aintitcoolnews.com

Dark Horizons
www.darkhorizons.com

These are two websites that provide the latest news on the film industry. Also useful are those that are part of larger portals, such as http://movies.yahoo.com/ and www.virgin.net/movies, which also offer showtimes for the US and UK respectively.

The following websites specialize in horror, though it should be noted that for the smaller outfits, web addresses frequently change:

Arrow In The Head
joblo.com/arrow/

News, reviews and interviews, all in actor/scriptwriter John Fallon's singular informed style.

The Astounding B-Monster
www.bmonster.com

The coolest cult movie chronicle. Tap in any title and get the lowdown.

Bride Of House Of Universal

movies.groups.yahoo.com/group/brideofhouseofuniversal/

For fans of classic Universal movies and monsters.

Dread Central

www.horrorchannel.com/dread/index.php

Up-to-date news and reviews from the online offshoot of the Horror Channel on American cable.

DVD Drive-In

www.dvddrive-in.com

If it's a horror film and is on DVD or video, you'll find information on it here.

Eccentric Cinema

www.eccentric-cinema.com

DVD reviews with handy symbols designating "action-packed", "bare flesh", "blood 'n' guts", "extra cheese" and so on.

HammerWeb

www.hammerfilms.com

The official website for Hammer Films.

Horrorview

www.horrorview.com

Features an excellent section on Asian horror movies.

Latarnia: Fantastique International

www.latarnia.com

This is the place to go for Spanish horror, Italian gothic classics, Mexican wrestlers and more.

Monster Kid

www.monsterkid.com

A fun salute to the horror movie magazines of the Sixties, inspired by the magazine *Famous Monsters Of Filmland*.

The Wonder World Of K Gordon Murray

www.kgordonmurray.com

This website is dedicated to the distributor/producer who took countless Mexican horrors to America.

Picture credits

The Publishers have made every effort to identify correctly the rights holders and/or production companies in respect of images featured in this book. If despite these efforts any attribution is incorrect the Publishers will correct this error once it has been brought to its attention on a subsequent reprint.

Cover Credits

Anchor Bay, UK/Boulevard Entertainment

Illustrations

Alan Jones Collection (30) William Castle Productions Columbia Pictures Columbia Tristar Home Video (41) (196) (211) Trimark Pictures Trimark Pictures Vidmark/Trimark (223) Australian Film Commission Australian International Film Corp Patrick Productions Victorian Film Corporation Filmways Australasian Distributors Australian International Film Corporation Pty Ltd Elite Entertainment (252) William Castle Productions Columbia Pictures Columbia Pictures Boum (168) (221) Ventura Distribution (225) Ibérica Filmes Image Entertainment (247) Saner Film Corbis (174) (257) Getty Images (9) (18) Famous Players-Lasky Corporation MediaInternational Republic Pictures Home Video Kino Video/Madacy Entertainment/Image Entertainment Kobal (83) Filmsonor S.A. Vera Films Criterion Pictures Corp Criterion Collection (157) Vortex Blue Dolphin Film Distribution Ltd. Bryanston Films Ltd. New Line Cinema Vortex, Inc. Pioneer Video (166) (169) Metro-Goldwyn-Mayer (MGM) Metro-Goldwyn-Mayer (MGM) (209) (262) Box Office Spectaculars Box Office Spectaculars Image Entertainment (207) Kobal /Meliés (14) George Albert Smith Films Kobal/Monarchia (153) Emmepi Cinematografica Films Georges de Beauregard Monarchia Top Film Allied Artists Pictures Corporation Vci Home Video Kobal/Toho (124) Kindai Eiga Kyokai Tokyo Eiga Company Toho Company Ltd. Criterion Collection

Kobal/United (73) Redbank Films United Artists Metro-Goldwyn-Mayer Studios Inc. Mgm/Ua Studios Kobal/Universal (19) Universal Pictures Universal Pictures Universal Pictures Corp. Image Entertainment (76) Universal Pictures Universal Pictures Universal Pictures Corp. Image Entertainment (213) Mary Evans Picture Library (1) (4) Moviestore (7) Paramount Pictures Mandalay Pictures American Zoetrope Paramount Pictures Pathé Distribution Ltd. Karol Film Productions GmbH & Co. Paramount Home Video (11) Dimension Films Woods Entertainment Dimension Films Miramax Film Corporation Dimension Home Video (16) Decla-Bioscop AG Goldwyn Distributing Company Video Yesteryear Image Entertainment (21) Universal Pictures Universal Pictures Realart Pictures Inc. Universal Pictures Corp Universal Studios (22) Nero-Film AG Foremco Pictures Corp Goodwill Pictures Inc Paramount Pictures Criterion Collection (24) Metro-Goldwyn-Mayer (MGM) Metro-Goldwyn-Mayer (MGM) (32) American International Pictures (AIP) Sunset Productions Inc. Academy Pictures Corp American International Pictures (AIP) Columbia Tristar Home Video (35) Aldrich Seven Arts Pictures Warner Bros. Warner Bros. The Associates & Aldrich Company, Inc. Warner Studios (36) Metro-Goldwyn-Mayer (MGM) Metro-Goldwyn-Mayer (MGM) Warner Home Video (39) 20th Century Fox Twentieth Century Fox Twentieth Century-Fox Film Corporation Twentieth Century Fox Home Video (43) Cinema 77 Films Filmways Pictures Warwick Associates Filmways Pictures Orion Pictures Corporation Warwick Associates Mgm/Ua Studios (46) Filmcat Fourth World Media MPI Maljack Greycat Films Maljack Productions Mpi Home Video 2 (47) CNCAIMC Grupo Del Toro October Films Lions Gate Home Entertainment (48) Dimension Films Woods Entertainment Dimension Films Miramax Film Corporation Dimension Home Video (49) Kadokawa Shoten Publishing Co. Ltd Omega Project Universal Studios/ MGM/UA (52) 13 Ghosts Productions Canada Inc. Dark Castle Entertainment Warner Bros. (2001) Columbia TriStar Film Distributors International Warner Bros./Columbia Pictures Industries, Inc. Warner Home Video (53) Carpathian Pictures Universal Pictures Universal Pictures Universal Studios Universal Studios (55) Hard Eight Pictures New Line Cinema Zide-Perry Productions New Line Cinema New Line Home Entertainment (57) Hoya Productions Warner Bros. Warner Bros. Warner Studios (60) American Werewolf, Inc Guber-Peters Company Lyncanthrope Films PolyGram Filmed Entertainment Universal Pictures PolyGram Video American Werewolf, Inc. Artisan Entertainment (65) WingNut Films Avalon/NFU Studios New Zealand Film Commission Trimark Pictures PolyGram Filmed Entertainment WingNut Films Limited Vidmark/Trimark (67) Universal Pictures Universal Pictures Universal Pictures Corp. Universal Studios (69) Decla-Bioscop AG Goldwyn Distributing Company Image Entertainment (85) Universal Pictures Universal

Pictures Universal Pictures Corp. Universal Studios (90) Renaissance Pictures New Line Cinema Renaissance Pictures Ltd. Anchor Bay Entertainment (93) Hoya Productions Warner Bros. Warner Bros. Warner Studios (97) Universal Pictures Universal Pictures Universal Pictures Corp. Universal Studios (99) Metro-Goldwyn-Mayer (MGM) MGM (103) Argyle Enterprises Metro-Goldwyn-Mayer (MGM) Warner Home Video (105) 20th Century Fox Achilles Twentieth Century Fox Film Corp. Twentieth Century Fox Corporation Twentieth Century Fox (107) RKO Radio Pictures Inc. RKO Radio Pictures Inc. Turner Home Entertainment (108) Universal Pictures Zanuck/Brown Productions Universal Pictures Universal Pictures Universal Studios (116) Columbia Pictures Corporation Sabre Film Production Columbia Pictures Columbia Tristar Hom (120) Jofa-Atelier Berlin-Johannisthal Prana-Film GmbH BijouFlix Kino International (126) Anglo-Amalgamated Productions Michael Powell Rialto Pictures LLC Warner Home Video Criterion Collection (128) Universal Pictures Universal Pictures Universal Pictures Image Entertainment (134) Shamley Productions Paramount Pictures Universal Pictures Universal Pictures Universal City Studios, Inc. (137) Compton Films Tekli British Productions Compton Films Royal Films International Compton Tekli Film Productions Ltd. Koch Vision Entertainment (141) Paramount Pictures Paramount Pictures Paramount Pictures Corp./William Castle Enterprises, Inc. Paramount Home Video (145) Hawk Films Ltd Peregrine Producers Circle Warner Bros. Warner Bros. Warner Studios (149) Orion Pictures Corporation Orion Pictures Corporation Orion Pictures Corporation Image Entertainment (155) Alexandre Films Europa Corp. EuropaCorp. Distribution Lions Gate Films Inc. Optimum Releasing Alexandre Films EuropaCorp (160) Paramount Pictures Paramount Pictures Universal Studios (162) American International Productions Tigon Pictures American International Pictures (AIP) (163) Gaumont British Picture Corporation Ltd. Gaumont British Picture Corporation of America Janus Films Woolf & Freedman Film Service Metro-Goldwyn-Mayer (171) (176) (179) Hammer Film Productions Limited Warner Home Video (187) (190) (192) Gaumont British Picture Corporation Ltd. Gaumont British Picture Corporation of America Janus Films Woolf & Freedman Film Service Metro-Goldwyn-Mayer (193) Heron Media Home Entertainment New Line Cinema Media Home Entertainment New Line Cinema Warner Communications Company (U.K.) New Line Home Entertainment (198) Universal Pictures Universal Pictures Realart Pictures Inc. Universal Pictures Corp Universal Studios (201) (203) United Artists United Artists Alpha Video Distributors (205) (228) Nero-Film AG Foremco Pictures Corp. Goodwill Pictures Inc. Paramount Pictures Criterion Collection (236) Productora Fílmica Real Produzioni Intersound Expanded Entertainment Haxan Films Mainline Pictures Republic Pictures Corporation (243) Nordic Screen Production AS Norsk Film A/S Norsk Filminstitutt First Run Features Norsk Filmdistribusjon Criterion Collection (254) Alta Vista Productions American International Pictures (AIP) American International Pictures (AIP) World Beyond Video MGM/UA Video (260) Ronald Grant Archive (27) Universal International Pictures MCA Universal Pictures Universal International Pictures Universal Pictures Co. Inc. Universial Studios (29) Warner Bros. Warner Bros. Warner Home Video (33) Champs-Élysées Productions Lux Film S.p.a. Lopert Pictures Corporation Rialto Pictures LLC Criterion Collection (40) American International Pictures (AIP) Power Productions American International Pictures (AIP) , Columbia-Warner Distributors Metro-Goldwyn-Mayer (79) Hammer Film Productions Limited Goldstone Film Enterprises Regal Films International Warner Bros. Warner Home Video (88) Hammer Film Productions Limited Goldstone Film Enterprises Rank Film Organization Universal International Pictures Hammer Film Productions Warner Home Video (147) Canadian Film Development Corporation Cinépix DAL Productions Trans American Films Image Entertainment (173) Eminent Authors Pictures, Inc. Goldwyn Pictures Corporation Goldwyn Distributing Company Gouverneur Morris Kino Video (178) (182) (184) (188) Scary Movies LLC Toolbox Murders Inc. Lions Gate Films Inc. Toolbox Murders Inc. Lionsgate (194) Hammer Film Productions Limited Rank Film Organization Universal International Pictures Hammer Film Productions Warner Home Video (217) Cinema City Film Productions Film Workshop Ltd Manga Films S.L. Tai Seng Video (230) Cinema City Film Productions Film Workshop Ltd Manga Films S.L. Tai Seng Video (240) Hemisphere Pictures Inc. Hemisphere Pictures Inc. Motion Picture Marketing Inc. Image Entertainment (249)

Index

Page references to films discussed in the Canon chapter, people or things described in the Icons chapter, and specific feature boxes are indicated in **bold**.

ROUGH GUIDES GOES TO THE MOVIES

THE ROUGH GUIDE TO
comedy
1843534649

THE ROUGH GUIDE TO
gangster
1843534231

THE ROUGH GUIDE TO
horror m
1843535211

1843535203

The Rough Guide to
sci-fi movies
John Scalzi

Available from all good bookstores, £9.99/$14.99